**GREAT NEGRO BASEBALL STARS and how they
made the major leagues**

First Published 1953

ACKNOWLEDGMENTS

In assembling material for this book, the author has perforce relied on the assistance of many courteous, cooperative persons. He is singularly indebted to four of them: J. G. Taylor Spink, editor of the Sporting News, who generously granted permission for use of certain facts meticulously assembled by his staff; Larry Taylor, script writer for The Jackie Robinson Story, which was filmed in Hollywood and released through Eagle-Lion Studios; Warren Gardner, Jr., a friend and magazine writer, whose research was invaluable; and William (Bill) Nunn, Sr., managing editor of the Pittsburgh Courier, one of the nation's most baseball-conscious newspapers.

The author also wishes to acknowledge important help by Joe Greene, an old-timer of Negro baseball fame; Chet Brewer, an all-time-great pitcher; Horace Stoneham, president of the New York Giants; Bill Veeck, president of the St. Louis Browns; George Sisler, an official of the Pittsburgh Pirates, formerly with the Brooklyn Dodgers; Cleveland Jackson, former sports editor of the Cleveland Call-Post; Ed McAuley and Frank Gibbons, Cleveland baseball writers who first made it possible for the author to enjoy privileges accorded members of the Baseball Writers Association, and Los Angeles writers like Bob Hunter and Al Wolf, who extended similar privileges; John J. Johnson, sports editor of the Kansas City Call; Tom Baird, current owner, and J. L. Wilkerson, a former co-owner, of the Kansas City Monarchs; Mrs. Effa Manley, former general manager of the Newark Eagles; Marsh Samuel, former publicist of the Cleveland Indians; Bill Starr, president of the San Diego Padres; Dan Burley, former sports editor of the New York Amsterdam News, currently an associate editor of Ebony and Jet magazines; press relations directors of the Boston Braves, Brooklyn Dodgers, Chicago White Sox, St. Louis Browns, and New York Giants; Ernie Wright and Wilbur Hayes, former officials of the Cleveland Buckeyes;

Raleigh (Bizz) Mackey, former manager of the Newark Eagles; Al Munro Elias Baseball Bureau, Inc.; Dave Grote, National League Service Bureau; Earl Hilligan, American League Service Bureau; and the dozens of Negro players whom the author has been privileged to know.

CONTENTS

1

ABE LINCOLN IN BROOKLYN

Shortly after the St. Louis Cardinals upset the New York Yankees in the 1942 World Series, Branch Rickey quit the new champions of baseball to assume presidency of Brooklyn's colorful Dodgers. His move, severing a business association that had lasted a quarter of a century, was destined to prove historic beyond all logical expectations and, perhaps, heroic beyond all conscious intentions.

Behind Rickey, especially at St. Louis, was a truly illustrious career. Ahead of him was one to become far more inspiring, more controversial and, for a man apparently born for success, more satisfying than the first.

Then edging into his sixty-second year, Rickey, an Ohioan by birth, had worked his way through enough "minor" careers to satisfy a small community of men. He had taught school, coached football and baseball teams, amateur and pro, played football and baseball, and practiced law. As a major league player, he was hardly journeyman. In eleven games with the New York Yankees in 1907, for example, he committed nine errors. In a single game, twelve base runners stole on his weak arm. Later, as a field manager, he was unsuccessful because, in his own words, "I was too tense." As an executive, however, it would be conservative to say that he was fabulous, or as Hollywood would say it, colossal.

That executive portion of his career began in earnest in 1917 when he moved across the hall, so to speak, from his job as vice-president and general manager of the St. Louis Browns to become president of the Cardinals. When he took over, the Cards were $175,000 in debt and approaching bankruptcy in players. To solve these problems, he wound up his futuristic brain and invented the farm system, which enabled a club poor in finances to become wealthy in performers. He also originated the Knothole Gang, and other gimmicks. Years after the Cards were solidly entrenched as a baseball power, a financially sound institution, it was said of Rickey, "He changed penury to pennants."

Rickey-assembled Cardinal teams won National League pennants in 1926, 1928, 1930, 1931, 1934 (when the Dean boys, Dizzy and Dally, were blowin' 'em past opposing batters), and the aforementioned 1942. Four times they won world championships and, over the years, contributed many great players and lively chapters to diamond history. They were at their noisiest and most colorful stage in the early thirties during the reign of the "Gashouse Gang," a hell-for-breakfast group led by Pepper Martin, the "Wild Horse of the Osage."

When he moved to the Brooklyn Dodgers, the National League's 1941 pennant winner and World Series victim of the Yankees under the field management of Leo Durocher and the executive direction of Larry MacPhail, Rickey took along a reputation that argued with itself. Friend and foe alike agreed that he was baseball's brainiest executive, a man who tended to his job more assiduously than anyone else in the game. Other club heads had complimented him by approving the farm system. Yet many considered him a cheapskate ("El Cheapo," New York sports writer Jimmy Powers called him) because, it was said, he paid small salaries. Although his acumen would have been admired had he been manufacturing watches, cars, or radios, there were some observers who deplored Rickey's ability to discover and sign a great prospect for little or no cash outlay, then sell him a few years later at a high-finance price. His habit of observing Sundays away from ball parks, in deference to his religious training and beliefs, was heaved up to prove that he was hypocritical. Some people couldn't understand how he could tally the fact that his clubs played Sunday ball with his personal abstinence.

And although the insides of baseball often reveal dog-eat-dog mores, Rickey was frequently attacked for unloading worn-out players on supposedly innocent club owners at exorbitant prices. There was, for instance, the famous deal between the Cards and Chicago Cubs in which Dizzy Dean was shipped off in return for a $185,000 check. When Ol' Dizzy's arm turned out to be dead, there were cries that Rickey had done it again—found himself a sucker, that is. Few bothered to uncover, or publicize, the fact that Rickey had told P. K. Wrigley, Cub owner, that Dizzy's arm was dead— before the deal was consummated.

But these defections could not hide Rickey's greatness. As much was admitted by Powers, author of the New York Daily News sports column, "Powerhouse," and a Rickey critic for almost thirty years. Writing in Sport Magazine in December, 1948, Powers said:

"Rickey, in our opinion, is the greatest judge of baseball players in the world. We know there are instances where he has overlooked a priceless piece of ivory, but these are isolated cases. The long-range picture is so overwhelmingly in his favor that no other candidate can be advanced to compete with him in this respect. He is No. 1, period and exclamation point.

". . . Rickey is his own worst enemy when it comes to seeing that his good deeds get as much publicity as his bad ones."

He concluded the article, which was entitled "Don't Get Me Wrong—I Love Branch Rickey," by saying "To sum up, he (Rickey) is a good businessman, a hard worker, game enough to lick a once dread disease (tuberculosis), a loving father of a fine family, a faithful husband, an inventor of new streamlined methods that have helped baseball. He has taken stands that have cost him money. He is a good Christian churchman, and while he has shaded some deals mighty close and has separated fans from many millions of ticket dollars, his record of winning clubs indicates they got their money's worth."

The New Yorker magazine phrased its account a bit differently in its May 27, 1950, issue. Rickey, it said in a Profile by Robert Rice, "has lavished on baseball as much erudition as many another man has on science or belles-lettres, and for subtlety his analyses of the factors that go into winning a game compare favorably with the work of many philosophers. In a standard lecture on base-running that Rickey likes to deliver to gatherings of apprentice players, he discusses, with the complexity and precision of a trained logician, the proper moment for bending the knee of the right leg during a slide into second base; when he informs a young pitcher about the effect upon an opposing batsman of a ball thrown so that it rotates in a certain direction at a certain speed, he finds himself paraphrasing the Einsteinian concept of space-time."

The New Yorker continued: "Rickey's insistence on bold and surprising tactics has led him to invent a number of extremely imaginative plays. One of his favorites is used only when there is a fleet runner on second base and a superlative actor at the plate—a right-handed actor, preferably. As the pitcher throws the ball, the batter gets into an exaggerated crouch, shortens his hold on his bat, clenches his teeth, and narrows his eyes, in the manner of a man with a wild determination to bunt. This is almost sure to bring the opposing third baseman charging in toward the plate. The batter lets the ball go by him, and the runner steals third base with ease, since the third baseman is in no position to prevent it."

To see the man Rickey "in person," as theatre habitués are wont to say, was not readily to recognize his greatness. He did not dress the part of a successful executive as characterized, say, in Esquire ads. Out of doors, he was typed by the way his hat drooped over his head and an expensive stogie protruded through his thin lips. A neat bow tie contrasted with the rest of his dress.

In seeing him in the office, however, especially where one was liable, perhaps forced, to concentrate on his face, one quickly concluded that he was in the presence of a Very Important Person. Rickey's alert, piercing eyes, looking out from behind rimmed spectacles, commanded attention—and heavy, wiry eyebrows fought to detract attention from the eyes. One, in retrospect, very easily became confused as to which was the more commanding feature, the eyes or the eyebrows. Unaccustomed to seeing such virility in eye adornments, one was very likely to vote for the eyebrows.

Little, if anything, in Rickey's baseball record during forty years as a player, coach, and top-level executive indicated deep interest in Negro players. Even had he sought a camouflage for his liberal views, he could not have found a better one than St. Louis, for Sportsman's Park, owned by the Browns and leased by the Cards, segregated Negro patrons in the Dixie habit. It was said that Sam Breadon, Cardinal owner during Rickey's regime, was dead-set against lowering the Jim Crow ban on Negro customers, for fear he would offend and lose white patrons.

When Rickey first requested permission from Brooklyn directors to scout Negro players, there was a general raising of eyebrows, in surprise, for this, to say the least, was a startling proposal. That they were surprised proves, of course, that those "inside baseball" had little reason to suspect his liberal views in regard to the game.

But Rickey's friends knew of these views, for they had heard the story of Charley Thomas. It happened in the early 1900's, when Rickey, coach of baseball at Michigan, took a team to South Bend, Indiana, for a game. Thomas, one of his players, was refused a hotel room because he was a Negro. In a final effort to find lodging for him, Rickey and the team captain persuaded a clerk to place a cot in their room for Thomas. Charley, as Rickey related many times to friends, was crushed by the incident.

"He sat on the cot, crying and staring at his hands," Rickey said. "He turned them over and over.

" 'It's these,' he kept saying. 'These hands. They're black. If it weren't for my skin, I wouldn't be any different from anybody. If only my hands were white!' And, the poor fellow would pull violently at one hand with the other. He seemed to be trying to wrench the black skin off his hands by main force."

Attempting to soothe Thomas's painful feelings, Rickey declared, "Tommy, the day will come when they won't have to be white."

Rickey was to say that he decided after the Thomas incident that he would contribute something to better racial understanding, if ever the opportunity were presented to him.

Wartime presented the opportunity. Uncle Sam constantly thinned the ranks of capable young ball players, replacing their bats and balls with rifles and hand grenades. Rickey, setting out to compensate for these war losses as well as build for the future, began seriously to consider the possibility of hiring Negro players. Indeed the time was ripe for such a move, for World War II had given Negroes a larger slice of fair employment than any previous development in American history, including the Emancipation Proclamation.

Almost simultaneously, the Brooklyn directors okayed Rickey's search for Negro talent and a wartime scouting program. Rickey was making hay while the sun shone, for the general trend in baseball was to decrease scouting activities during the national emergency. He realized, however, that many young players signed then would bud as stars when peace came.

Rickey launched his search for Negro players with customary foresight and thoroughness. In deference to baseball's "lily-white" practices, he needed a gimmick. He made it when, with the assistance of Gus Greenlee, a Negro businessman, owner of the Pittsburgh Crawfords ball club, and primary founder of Negro baseball's biggest classic, the annual East-West game at Chicago, he "formed" the United States League. It was, to all intents and purpose, another Negro circuit to compete with the existing Negro American and National leagues. Rickey was to sponsor a club, the "Brown Dodgers," which was to play at Ebbets Field when the Dodgers were absent.

Armed with the gimmick, he was free to send his scouts in search of Negro players. They were instructed to scrutinize these players both in the United States and Latin American countries. Among the scouts were Wid Matthews, now general manager of the Chicago Cubs; George Sisler, the all-time great first baseman; Clyde Sukeforth, and Tom Greenwade. All of them, with the exception of Greenwade, thought they were searching for Brown Dodger prospects. Greenwade later said that he knew all along Rickey planned to sign Negro players for the Dodgers of National League fame and fluctuating fortunes.

Among the players these scouts watched were such stars as Buck Leonard, hard-hitting, fancy-fielding first baseman of the Homestead Grays; James (Cool Papa) Bell, the Grays' fleet-footed, slash-hitting outfielder; Marvin Williams, the Philadelphia Stars' second baseman; Sam Jethroe, the Cleveland Buckeyes' swift, switch-hitting center fielder; Lorenzo (Piper) Davis, the Birmingham Black Barons' dependable second baseman; Roy Campanella, the Baltimore Elite Giants' young catcher; and Jackie Robinson, the Kansas City Monarchs' shortstop.

To many of their supporters it seemed that all of these, and other, Negro players were ready for the major leagues. But Rickey was looking for more than a talented performer. He was looking for A Man.

"I had to get a man," he was to explain, "who would carry the burden on the field. I needed a man to carry the badge of martyrdom. The press had to accept him. He had to stimulate a good reaction of the Negro race itself, for an unfortunate one might have solidified antagonism of people of other colors. And, I had to consider the attitude of the man's teammates."

That this man would have to carry a heavy load was a natural fact. No Negro, his race fully admitted, had performed in organized baseball in modern times. Many of the players and fans were Southerners. The tradition of the game was Jim Crow. And the reasons for it ranged from simple race prejudice to the-Devil-will-get-you bugaboos like the fear, expressed to Mrs. Effa Manley, general manager of the Newark Eagles, by a major league club head that the introduction of Negroes into the game would lead to serious trouble.

"I would like to sign Negro players," this club head said. "But, you know how fans idolize ball players. Many of our fans are white women. It might cause unpleasantness if these women became 'attached' to a Negro home run hitter. . . ."

Unlike white players, then, Negro players—especially the one elected to be a pioneer—had not only to hit and field, throw and run with éclat, they had to walk a straight path, narrower than for any previous performers, and live as strait-laced as religious servants dressed in the cloth.

As scouting reports were checked, one name was mentioned more frequently than any other. The name: Jackie Robinson. By coincidence, the same name had been mentioned to Rickey after he held a conference in the spring of 1945 to announce formation of the United States League.

One of the writers present was Wendell Smith of the Pittsburgh Courier, America's largest Negro newspaper. He was not made enthusiastic by Rickey's announcement, first because he represented a publication which had for a long time blasted baseball's Jim Crow tradition, second because he had just returned from an ill-fated trip to Boston, where the Red Sox had gone through the motions of trying out three Negro players. The tryout had been arranged by Isadore Muchnick, a Boston City Councilman, who had threatened to revoke the Sunday baseball permit of the Red Sox unless they gave Negro players "a chance."

As Smith afterward recalled, "The club in Boston agreed to 'look over' the three Negro players"—Robinson, Jethroe, and Williams. While they traveled from New York to Boston, according to the Courier writer, these players wondered if they honestly stood a chance of landing in major league ball, or if this were just another farce.

"This may just be a shot in the dark," Robinson observed, "but it could mean something for the future. If they don't select us, they may at least realize that there are Negro players around the country worthy of consideration. None of us may ever get a chance to play on a big league club, but we might be opening up something for the future."

They believed, Smith said, that they could play big league ball—if given the opportunity. As Smith continued the story:

"Upon our arrival in Boston, the first thing we did was contact Councilman Muchnick, who in turn notified the Red Sox that the three Negro players had arrived in town and were ready for a tryout.

"The representative of the Red Sox promised Muchnick he would set a time for the tryout after discussing the situation with Joe Cronin, the Red Sox manager.

"The discussion with Cronin must have been long and tedious because nothing happened for two days. Finally, Muchnick put some extra pressure on the management of the club and it was decided that the three players would be given a tryout at noon on April 16.

"Robinson, Williams and Jethroe reported at Fenway Park at the specified time, got their uniforms and went out onto the field.

"Approximately ten white hopefuls were already working out. They were high school prospects and being tutored by two Red Sox instructors.

"Hugh Duffy, an old coach, was in charge of the workout. After Robinson, Jethroe and Williams had fielded a few balls hit by the high school prospects, Duffy called them to hit.

"Williams was the first to step into the batter's box. . . .

"Then Robinson stepped into the batter's box. He . . . walloped the first pitch against the big sign on the fence. It was a line drive that whistled as it soared through the infield and continued to gain height.

"Robinson clouted a few more drives equally well and then stepped aside for Jethroe. . . .

"The workout lasted about 45 minutes. When it was all over, Duffy called the three 'recruits' aside and shook hands with them.

" 'You boys look like pretty good ball players,' he said. 'I hope you enjoyed the workout.' "

That was all. Nothing more was ever heard from the Red Sox.

After the conference announcing the United States League, Rickey called Smith aside, told him he had heard about the Boston trip, and asked if there were any Negro players good enough to make the major leagues.

"If you aren't serious about this, Mr. Rickey," Smith replied, "I'd rather not waste our time discussing it. But, if you are serious, I do know of a player who could make it. His name is Jackie Robinson."

"It seems to me," Rickey said thoughtfully, "I've heard of that fellow somewhere."

One of Rickey's scouts, after several looks at Robinson, reported that the player's arm was too weak for a shortstop. Greenwade, the Midwestern scout, was assigned to follow the Monarchs and concentrate on Robinson. His subsequent opinion was that Robinson was an excellent bunter and base runner, but that "he does not have a real good arm. It is good enough for second base—but, not for shortstop."

Shortstop was not his spot then, Rickey conceded. What about second base?

Sisler was sent to scout Robinson's possibilities as a second baseman. A conservative appraiser of diamond talent, Sisler's opinion carried weight with Rickey. Robinson, Sisler opined, could play second base.

Rickey decided that Jackie Robinson was his Man.

Late in the season of 1945, Sukeforth was detailed to fetch Robinson from the Monarchs and take him to Rickey's office. The job wasn't easy. Since Negro league schedules, unlike those in organized ball, were played all over the East, Midwest, South, and Southwest, finding the Monarchs was a problem. Once they were located, Sukeforth headed for Chicago, to intercept them on a date with the American Giants. He found Robinson on the field at Comiskey Park, home of the American League White Sox, by fingering a scorecard. Jackie was No. 8. Sukeforth sought out the player, introduced himself, and sketched his mission. Robinson, his experience at Boston still fresh in mind, was wary. But Sukeforth was earnest, convincing. Finally, Robinson—taking the "what-have-I-got-to-lose?" attitude—agreed to entrain for Brooklyn.

There Sukeforth introduced the club president and the Negro player. Rickey had a bold plan in mind, and Jackie was hardly able to believe what he heard, for Rickey soon got to the point.

"You are not here as a candidate for the Brooklyn Brown Dodgers," Rickey said, puffing deliberately on a big cigar, appraising Robinson. "I've sent for you because I'm interested in having you as a candidate for the Brooklyn National League club. I think you can play in the major leagues. How do you feel about it?"

Jackie was plainly startled.

"Me? Play for the Dodgers?" he asked incredulously.

Rickey explained that he wanted to win pennants and that to do it he needed ball players. He explained how the war had set his team back in quality and quantity of playing talent. He explained that for three years he had been scouting hitherto untapped sources, such as the Negro leagues.

Orientation over, Rickey leveled his gaze on Robinson and asked, "Do you think you can do it, Jackie? Make good in organized baseball?"

"If I got the chance," Jackie said, his furrowed brow evidence of deep thought.

Rickey then placed Jackie in a position no previous ball player, rookie or star, had ever been forced to fill. He explained the realities of the problem to be faced by a Negro pioneer in organized baseball. He portrayed scenes in which Jackie would be made a "different person," a target, or a goat, solely because of color and race, employing gimmicks of drama a stage director would have gladly paid for in big money. He dug into the pit of racial epithets, epithets that cut like a switch-blade, epithets that always fire a Negro's blood to the boiling point. A superb actor, he played the gamut of likely events, incidents, moments of embarrassment, and moments when any man would want to fight back.

Once or twice, as he heard and saw Rickey play perfectly the role of a bigot, Jackie's face flushed and his strong, brown hands tightened, agonizingly, into fists. But he held his peace. Eventually, Rickey explained the tremendousness of the job in different terms.

"We're tackling something big here, Jackie," Rickey said. "If we fail, no one will try it again for 20 years. But, if we succeed. . . ."

In prospect, Rickey insinuated, was a spot in Green Pastures. He went on: "We're dealing with the right of any American to play baseball—the American game."

Turning to Sukeforth, Rickey sought an appraisal of Robinson's abilities. Sukeforth itemized them. Then Rickey wanted to know if Jackie could take it. Sukeforth didn't know. Rickey asked Robinson what he thought. Jackie said he would try.

"You think you've got the guts to play the game?" Rickey asked heavily. "No matter what happens? They'll shout insults at you . . . they'll come in to you spikes first . . . they'll throw at your head."

Jackie calmly suggested that he could turn the other cheek. That satisfied Rickey. Rickey drew out an agreement. Robinson signed. Jackie was advised to marry his best girl in the near future. He was told that he would be assigned, first, to a minor league club, and was encouraged to tell his mother about the development by long distance telephone, at the club's expense.

Next, the pattern of Jackie's behavior in organized ball was set. "Jackie," Rickey emphasized, "remember one thing: no matter what happens on the ball field, you can't fight back."

The first composite step in Rickey's plan had been completed. He had scouted Robinson baseball-wise and investigated him character-wise. He had discovered his athletic strengths and weaknesses and had adjusted his program to fall in line with them. He had learned that Robinson was a good fellow, a clean liver, that the only noticeable mark against him was his West Coast reputation for "talking back" to white people. But Rickey recognized that had Robinson himself been white, his competitive spirit would have been lauded in bold type.

Rickey had met Robinson, met him and tested him in the crucible of surprise and hurled epithets. He had alternated the pace, talking to him with easy grace, with liquid fluidity, then, abruptly, had switched back to the attack, so to speak. Robinson had come through, so far, like a champ. Rickey was satisfied.

Now he was poised to make his bold move as the Abraham Lincoln of baseball. He was set to compose baseball's version of the Emancipation Proclamation.

2

EMANCIPATION PROCLAMATION

The Big Day was October 23, 1945. The tenor of the times was reflected, more or less accurately, by these news items: In Washington, a House of Representatives committee called for drastic reforms in the OPA to speed the nation's return to an unfettered price economy. In Detroit, General Motors was threatened with another strike by the United Automobile Workers union. In Warsaw, the American Embassy buzzed with speculations as to why Russian officers had halted an air attaché's car and demanded a lug wrench. The attaché had surrendered the wrench after he was told by the Russians, "We take what we want!" And, in Philadelphia, a jury listened to stories of frequent love-making as detailed in thirty-three torrid letters, then deliberated six hours, only to disagree over a middle-aged secretary's efforts to collect twenty-five thousand dollars she claimed was left to her by the "boss" who, she said, liked to call her "the cream in my coffee."

That October 23 was to become one of baseball's most remembered, most historic, days was not implied when Hector Racine, president of Montreal's International League team, the Royals, summoned press and radio representatives to a conference with the comment that he had an important announcement to make.

Mildly speculative, twenty-five writers and radio men assembled at his office. What's up? they wondered. Maybe Montreal had been admitted to the major leagues. Or, perhaps the Royals' manager had been fired. They were totally unprepared for Racine's announcement that the Royals had signed Jackie Robinson, a Negro player, Jackie the only Negro present, restrained his exuberance admirably.

The story, the sounding of baseball's Emancipation Proclamation, was that Robinson, former shortstop of the Kansas City Monarchs, had signed a contract calling for both salary and bonus; that he was the product of Rickey's three-year, twenty-five-thousand-dollar search for Negro talent; that he had signed the contract following a conference with Racine, Lt. Romeo Gauvreau, the Royals' vice-president, and Branch Rickey, Jr., head of the Brooklyn farm system; and, that he was the first Negro ever signed to a contract in organized baseball.

The last item was a bit of an error, as baseball writers discovered a few days later. In the fledgling days of organized ball, (1884), Moses Fleetwood Walker, a bare-handed catcher, and his brother, Welday, had played for Toledo of the old American Association, then regarded as a major league. (In 1872, a Negro named Bud Fowler had played with the New Castle, Pennsylvania, team, the first-known instance of an interracial club.) Other Negroes had performed in predominantly white circuits until the turn of the century. Then they fell victim to baseball's anti-Negro ban. Robinson, however, was organized baseball's first Negro of "modern time," and the fact was no less important because of a slight historical error.

Young Rickey spoke: "Mr. Racine and my father," he said, "will undoubtedly be severely criticized in some sections of the United States where racial prejudice is rampant. They are not inviting trouble, but they won't avoid it if it comes. Jackie Robinson is a fine type of young man, intelligent, and college-bred. And, I think he can take it, too."

Subsequently, Robinson was interviewed. Surprisingly well composed, he said, "I can't begin to tell you how happy I am that I am the first member of my race in organized ball. I realize how much it means to me, to my race, and to baseball. I can only say that I'll do my very best to come through in every manner."

A listener was Al Parsley, writer for the Montreal Herald. He detailed his impressions of Robinson for his newspaper's readers:

"There were many things about Jack Robinson which impressed you," he wrote. "He talked with that easy fluency of an educated man; then, you remembered that he was a senior at the University of California in Los Angeles before he enlisted.

"You felt that somehow Jack Robinson was most sincere in his views on a problem that baseball men, big and little, have found no way of solving over many years. He has a great realization of his responsibilities, and he said without bravado: 'Maybe I'm doing something for my race.' When he said that, it was felt by one or two of his auditors that it was a speech that maybe Joe Louis could have made.

"At that, though of darker hue, Robinson looks slightly like Louis in general appearance. He has the same serious, near-sombre mein and he is so forthright in his ideals."

Later, Rickey, Sr., commented on probable effects of the move by remarking, "It may cost the Brooklyn organization a number of ball players. Some of them, particularly if they come from certain sections of the South, will steer away from a club with colored players on its roster. Some players now with us may even quit. But, they'll be back after they work a year or two in a cotton mill!"

There was challenge in his words, perhaps even more than in Lincoln's most famous declaration, for, as is often forgotten, Lincoln made his move only because he felt compelled to do so. Rickey had broken, completely, emphatically, cleanly, with underwriters of baseball's unwritten ban on Negro players. He expected reactions, and he was not to be disappointed, for they were immediate.

The signing of Robinson naturally was appreciated most by the Negro press and Negro fans. They hailed the move with extreme joy, reflecting the race's great, burning desire for acceptance and approval, for admittance to their full rights as American citizens, including the right to play a game called baseball. The good news was batted across country in shouting type. The Courier detailed the story for national consumption. The Chicago Defender announced it to the Midwest, up and down the Mississippi River valley area, and elsewhere. The Los Angeles Sentinel told it to the West Coast, and the Afro-American to the Eastern seaboard. All of them said it in words that meant a great step forward had been made, hallelujah!

To all Negroes, big people and little people, Robinson became a symbol. His signing pointed to approaching realization of their dreams for a better democracy, for a fulfillment of the promises of the Constitution which would make obsolete their general lot of second-class citizenship. What happened in baseball, they figured, might eventually occur in discriminatory colleges, factories, churches, public eateries, railroad trains, businesses. And players in Negro baseball took hope. Robinson's success could mean escape from the physically and mentally wearying grind of four-team doubleheaders, long hops on buses, restless nights in fleabag hotels where hot water was as rare as gold coins. Every kid playing on a rubble-strewn sandlot with hickory stick and lopsided ball became a bit more serious about the way he swung his bat, stooped for a grounder, or slid into the block of stone that represented second base. Better days were ahead.

Robinson also became a symbol to others. To those of prejudiced minds, he represented the promise that brown-skinned players would soon freckle "white" baseball. They didn't like it. The Negro, they figured, was moving out of his place.

One of the all-time diamond greats said, for instance, that admission of Negroes to baseball was not practical because of the social angles involved. Baseball, he said, was more than a mere game. It was close personal contact, living in the same hotels, camaraderie, card playing, a tightly knit profession. A Negro, he said, would not fit into the scheme of things. The same man, Rogers Hornsby, a couple of years later had a Negro pupil enrolled at his Hot Springs,

Arkansas, baseball school and in 1952 managed a major league club whose roster included that fabulous hurler, Satchel Paige.

Major league players hedged, most of those interviewed insinuating, if not saying outright, that they opposed the move. Dixie Walker, Brooklyn's most popular player and a Southerner, said Robinson's signing was all right with him—as long as Jackie did not play on a team with him. There was only one major league player who spoke out heartily in favor of Robinson's appearance on the scene and he was Rudy York, home run slugger for the Detroit Tigers. York said he thought Robinson's signing was a grand idea and he wished Jackie good luck.

Clark Griffith, president of the Washington Senators, said organized baseball should not interfere with "organized" Negro baseball, which, at the time, paid fat rentals for the use of his park.

One of America's foremost sports writers professed friendship for Negroes, but commented that often they demanded "rights" far beyond their capabilities.

Many objecting persons bombarded the late W. G. Bramham, president of the National Association of Professional Baseball Players, with letters and telephone calls. Although his office was located in Durham, North Carolina, calls were received from as far away as California. Since there was nothing illegal, by the letter of written baseball law, about admission of Negroes, he was powerless to bar Robinson from the game. But, he had an opinion.

"Father Divine will have to look to his laurels," sports writer Jack Homer quoted Bramham in the Durham Herald, "for we can expect Rickey Temple to be in the course of construction in Harlem soon."

Frank Shaughnessy, president of the International League, reportedly feared the consequences when Robinson played at Baltimore. However, he said, "There is no rule in baseball that says a Negro can't play with a club in organized ball. As long as any fellow's the right type and can make good and can get along with other players, he can play ball."

There were many liberal white writers, of course, who subscribed to that view.

When a statement of opinion was sought from him, Horace Stoneham, president of the New York Giants, replied, "We will scout the Negro leagues next year, looking for young prospects." There was irony—irony of which he was not conscious—in those words, for had the Giants been just a bit more willing to buck the game's Jim Crow tradition, they, years before, could have reaped the international publicity, great players, and increased gate receipts which were to accrue to the Dodgers because of Rickey's move.

Stoneham himself had predicted to the year the admittance of Negro players into organized ball. In 1936, a Negro reporter reminded Stoneham of Jesse Owens's record-shattering performances in the Olympic Games at Berlin. Track had long ago accepted the Negro performer, went the gist of the reporter's argument, when was baseball going to let down its bars?

"In ten years," Stoneham told him, "the Jesse Owenses will be playing in organized baseball."

In 1887, John Ward attempted to sign George Stovey of the Newark, New Jersey, minor league club for the Giants. The Negro pitcher had won thirty-five games in one season, still a record for a Newark hurler. But Adrian Anson, leader of the Chicago White Stockings, put his nix on the move, and so great was his power that Ward recanted.

John McGraw, most famous of Giants managers, first became interested in Negro players while leading the Baltimore Orioles. At Hot Springs, Arkansas, in late 1901 or early 1902, a Negro named Dave Wright told McGraw about a Columbia (Chicago) Giants player named Charles (Cincy) Grant. McGraw watched Grant play, was impressed, and decided to sign him for the Orioles. On April 28, 1902, Grant left the Columbia Giants, who were playing in Zanesville, Ohio, and joined the Baltimore team. He was palmed off to fans and baseball as an "Indian." The ruse worked for a time and

Grant played good ball. But when the team journeyed to Chicago for a series, Negro fans welcomed him enthusiastically, appeared at the park floating a banner inscribed, "Our Boy, Charley Grant," and loudly cheered his every move. McGraw was forced to release Grant.

After he moved to the Giants, however, McGraw hired his friend and admirer, Andrew (Rube) Foster, later to become the most famous of all Negro league executives, as a sort of unofficial pitching coach. One of Foster's "pupils" was Christy Mathewson. McGraw wanted to sign Foster, who earned his nickname by whipping the Philadelphia Athletics with George E. (Rube) Waddell, to his mound staff. But he never did.

In Cuba, McGraw watched José Mendez, a summer-time star with the Monarchs, pitch two fine games against major league opposition. He tried to figure a means of "smuggling" Mendez into the National League, but gave up the idea, the story goes, after spending considerable money in a campaign to transform Mendez into an Indian.

Though the Giants had missed these opportunities, they were perhaps the first club to begin considering Negro players after Rickey signed Robinson.

Strangely, in spite of Rickey's straightforward statements, there were observers who questioned his motives in signing Robinson. They made a point of the fact that Jackie had been signed to a minor league contract. If he had intended to hire a Negro for the Dodgers, they inquired, why hadn't he signed Jackie to a Brooklyn contract? Rickey replied that if he had believed Robinson was ready for major league ball, he would have signed him for Brooklyn. He expressed doubt that Robinson, or any other Negro player, was capable of playing in the majors.

Then came the most surprising objection of all. Tom Baird, white owner of the Monarchs, complained that Rickey had taken Robinson from his club without making any payment whatsoever.

Threatening an appeal to Commissioner A. B. (Happy) Chandler, he heatedly promised, "We won't take this lying down!"

In further explanation of his feelings on the matter, Baird added, "Robinson signed a contract with us last year and I feel that he is our property. If Chandler lets Montreal get by with this, he's really starting a mess."

Baird also revealed that Robinson had been paid $500 a month (also quoted as $400 a month; according to Jackie, $100 a week), was twenty-six years old, and had batted .345 during the 1945 season with Kansas City.

When Rickey was informed of Baird's statements, he replied, "There is no Negro league as such as far as I'm concerned. Negro baseball is in the zone of a racket and there is no Negro circuit that could be admitted to organized baseball."

Objections such as Baird's died a natural death, squeezed out of life by the weight of public opinion. In a few days, Negro team owners read Negro newspapers, ascertained that they were driving the wrong way on a one-way street, then recanted. And Baird announced that he would not interfere with Robinson's chances for a career in organized ball.

In Chicago, Dr. B. Martin, Negro American League president, and Frank A. (Fay) Young, secretary, issued a joint statement. "We feel," they announced, "that it (Robinson's signing) is an elevation of Negro baseball." They said they were glad the Dodgers had signed Jackie.

And out of the South, somewhat startlingly, came a prediction. Writing in the Norfolk (Virginia) Virginian-Pilot, sports scribe W. N. Cox stated, "I guarantee that if Jackie Robinson hits homers and plays a whale of a game for Montreal, the fans will soon lose sight of his color."

3

ROBINSON AT MONTREAL

In the week or ten days immediately following October 23 and the announcement at Montreal, nothing was more obvious than this: Jackie Robinson had hoisted for himself a heavy load. By releasing the news of his signing in the early fall, Rickey had provided a whole winter during which the loudly argued pros, cons, and speculations could build up tremendous pressure for the player. The early announcement was a fortunate circumstance, however, in that those of most heated objections had time to cool off a bit and accept the fact that a Negro had his foot in baseball's doorway. An announcement at spring training or at season's opening would, perhaps, have been infinitely more difficult to handle, for the opposition might have marshaled more damaging forces. Besides, the intervening months gave the opposition, or a portion of it at least, time to take temporary refuge in the hope, the belief even, that the player wasn't good enough to make the grade. After all, the full extent of his pro experience was about a hundred games in Negro ball and Negro ball, many "experts" figured, was just a short step above sandlot play. If Jackie failed. . . . One easily got the drift.

There were many questions about Jackie in those days. Most of them, one way or the other, boiled down to this: What are his chances? Or, can he cut the mustard? The question of his athletic ability, at the time, was neck-and-neck with, was possibly subordinate to, the question of Jackie's "inside" qualities. People wanted to know: is he a good boy?

The record said he was. Born at Cairo, Georgia, on January 31, 1919, he had been transplanted to Pasadena, California, at an early age. His mother Mrs. Mallie Robinson, missing the support of a dutiful husband, raised her brood of six in a religious environment, attempted to give her children the best education within her resources, worked hard, long hours as a domestic to provide a home. Just as had the older children, Jackie chipped in to help as soon as he was old enough, selling newspapers, running errands, performing any honest job which promised a few bucks. He grew up strong, healthy, clean in personal habits, and God-gifted in all the sports he tried.

Following graduation from Muir Technical High School in Pasadena, Jackie entered Pasadena Junior College, where he gained his first slice of national fame by broad jumping 25 feet 6 inches, and reaped state-wide applause for his accomplishments in basketball, football, and baseball. His track feats were reminiscent of his idol and older brother, Matthew (Mack) Robinson, a star of the 1936 Olympic Games.

In the fall of 1939, Jackie entered the University of California at Los Angeles (UCLA), where he greatly enhanced his fame. Oddly, however, he did not stand out in offensive ability in baseball. His records in football and basketball, on the other hand, were superlative. An all-around athlete with so much talent, sports writer Harley Tinkham of the Los Angeles Mirror was to rank him ahead of Jim Thorpe, Robinson was good in at least five sports, including tennis.

Wilbur Johns, UCLA's basketball coach during Jackie's student days, now the school's athletic director, attributed Robinson's athletic prowess to "beautiful timing and rhythm and the ability to relax completely whenever he wished." Jackie always was in perfect physical condition, due largely to the fact that he was always playing in some game and that he never drank or smoked.

The UCLA baseball teams of 1940 and 1941, UCLA publicist Vic Kelley related, were not even mediocre, so it is possible that

Jackie did not have the incentive to pour on the coal as he did in other sports. He played shortstop and hit around .200. But he was appraised as a sharp fielder and excellent base runner. The first day he played for the Bruins, he stole five bases, including two thefts of home.

Sports and part-time work, a rugged combination, left Jackie little time for romance and, though he possessed a fine, quick-trigger mind, cut into the elegance of his marks. At times, this fact disturbed his mother because she wanted him to be a professional—a doctor, lawyer, or coach. He liked the last profession. As a youngster, he had traded on it as an excuse to go out and play.

"If I am going to be a coach," he would say to her, "I'll have to keep playing. You can't teach a game if you don't know it."

Jackie left UCLA without graduating, then worked and played West Coast professional football. He joined the cavalry in 1943, and was sent to Fort Riley, Kansas. In April, 1944, he was transferred to Camp Hood, Texas, where his outfit was motorized and alerted for overseas duty. Because of bad ankles, however, he was prevented from going overseas, and was placed instead in limited service. In December, 1944, he was discharged with a lieutenant's rank. The next month he accepted the basketball coaching job at Sam Huston College in Austin, Texas. Five months later, he joined the Monarchs.

Early in 1946, on February 10 to be exact, Jackie followed Rickey's advice to "marry the girl." It was a move destined to become as important to his new career as any of his previous on-field feats. The "girl" was attractive Rachel Isum, like himself a Uclan. Rachel was a nurse, and a resident of Los Angeles. Ray Bartlett, another Bruin athlete and Jackie's good friend, had introduced them one day while the latter was doing janitorial work in Kerckhoff Hall, UCLA's No. 1 building.

Rachel had filled the role of college sweetheart for Jackie; she now became his ever-loving wife, advisor, "governor," and inspiration. In subsequent months she rode with him through the rocky by-ways of organized baseball, heard him jeered, cussed, discussed, and pronounced, as is said on some of the saltier avenues, "everything but a child of God." And, by way of sharp contrast, she felt unbounded joy and pride when she heard fans cheer him, saw baseball and its players accept him, and became herself one of the game's "inner circle"—an official member of the unofficial "Baseball Wives Association," as hardy a group of women as ever lived.

Arm-in-arm, the Robinsons traveled to Florida, where Dodger-owned teams assembled for spring training. Together they faced the unaccustomed slights and rebuffs of those with racial prejudices. Together they were jolted, jolted repeatedly, by the fact that being a Negro pioneer was no easy deal.

On the diamond, however, Jackie had to carry the full load—alone. In addition to the fact of his race, he was confronted by a competitive situation born of World War II.

When the United States entered the war, ball players, like other men, were forced to take up arms. The Bob Fellers, Ted Williamses, Joe DiMaggios, Stan Musials, and other top stars and journeymen as well gave up their salaries and, in many instances, the meat of their careers to help defend their country's ideals. While these players were absent from major league diamonds, veterans, on reprieve from bush leagues, and beardless youngsters, normally years away from the big time, were rushed in as replacements.

After the war ended, the stars returned to reclaim their jobs. Neither the vets nor the youngsters wanted to be displaced. Plus which, there were other minor leaguers due consideration from major league managers.

Thus Robinson, the Negro, began his career at an oddly unsettled time, when competition was unusually keen, when the spirit was dog-eat-dog and only the fittest could survive. Jackie walked into this situation as an outsider—and he walked on-field alone, adopting a policy marked by humility, observing a rule often prescribed for children; he spoke only when spoken to!

Besides his wife, at the beginning Jackie had as off-field "company" John Wright, a Negro pitcher who had been signed by the organization, and two Negro newspapermen, Wendell Smith and Billy Rowe, sports writer and photographer, respectively, of the Pittsburgh *Courier*. Jackie reported at Sanford, Florida, the Dodgers' general training base.

His manager was Clay Hopper, a native Southerner, who was getting his first practical experience in racial integration and, at the time, not liking it overly. His teammates were from all sections of the nation, some of them harboring racial prejudices which had been drummed into them almost since birth. There were others, however, who were not actively biased, a few even who were on his side. Among Florida fans, too, were some who sympathized with him, understood the peculiarity of his position, wished him well, and with cheers attempted to bolster his spirits in early spring days when he failed to hit.

Jackie's early difficulties at bat caused embarrassment. His being in competition as a shortstop with Stan Breard, Montreal's regular short fielder and a home-field favorite, toughened the situation. The natural anxiety to make good forced him to throw hard too early with a natural result: his arm became sore. Then Sanford authorities served notice on the Dodgers that they wanted no Negroes playing there with a "white" team. The team moved to Daytona Beach, where the members were welcomed, and Jackie began his climb.

First, he was shifted to second base. Next came a "thawing out" of several players, especially third baseman Johnny Jorgensen, outfielder Marvin Rackley, shortstop Al Campanis, and second baseman Lou Rochelli. Although the last-mentioned was a boy of promise and Jackie represented competition, he never hesitated to help the Negro master the difficulties entailed in a switch from the left to the right side of the diamond.

Jackie, calling upon his natural abilities, learned fast. Still, his hitting was doubtful. It remained so until one day the Royals met the Indianapolis Indians in an exhibition game. Paul Derringer, once a Cincinnati Reds star hurler and a superb control man, told Hopper he was going to give Robinson a little test. He did, dusting Jackie off twice. Each time, Jackie responded with a ringing base hit.

The second time, Derringer shouted to Hopper, "He'll do!"

Things were getting better, but were far from being all-blue-skies.

An incident occurred at DeLand, Florida, one day. Jackie got a hit and subsequently scored, sliding across home plate in a cloud of dust. As he arose and bent to brush himself off, a cop walked up and said, "Now, you get off this here field, right now. If you don't, I'm putting you in the jail house."

Hopper moved up to see what was wrong. "He didn't do anything wrong, did he?" the manager asked.

"Yes, he did," the cop replied.

"What?" Hopper wanted to know.

"We told you all to leave them 'Nigra' players at home," the cop said. "We ain't having Nigras and white boys playing on the same field in this town. It's agin the law and I'm here to tell you."

Hopper, a Southerner, as related, was stopped by this turn in events. To save Hopper the embarrassment of having to tell him to get off the field, Jackie headed out through the dugout. Wright followed. As they went, they realized gratefully that Hopper was thawing out, too.

Subsequently, several financially valuable exhibition dates were lost or periled because of Jackie's and Wright's presence. But despite the rigors of his assignment, Jackie approached opening day having pretty well proven that he could play second base and that he could take it.

Opening day in 1946 for the Royals was on the road, at Jersey City.

The Jersey City Giants belonged to the New York Giants. On opening day each year, however, they belonged to Mayor Frank Hague, the city's Democratic "boss." A fan of the first water, he used the power of his political position to insure a booming financial beginning for the "Little Giants." Thousands of Jersey Citians were "urged" to purchase tickets for the first game, regardless of their intentions as to attending the contest. As a result, Jersey City each year boasted of a minor league record crowd.

It was on Mayor Hague's day, then, that the Royals, with Jackie at second base, opened their 1946 season. The crowd was reported at fifty-two thousand. Perhaps it would have been more accurate to call it something like thirty-five thousand. This was the day when baseball history would be made, when mixed emotions would clash in boos and applause, when a few disciples of the Dixieland style would warm up against a project they had bitterly assailed. Whether or not they would come out on top was soon answered.

Mississippian Clay Hopper activated the experiment when he Strode plateward to give an umpire his line-up. It included, in the No. 2 spot, Jackie Robinson, Negro. He was officially a part of organized baseball. It was chips down!

After Breard, Montreal's lead-off man, strode to the plate, Hopper turned to Jackie and said, "You're next, Robinson! Get on deck!"

Robinson got up from his dugout seat, in his now-familiar, pigeon-toed gait, walked to the bat-rack, selected a shillelah, and took a kneeling position on deck. Thousands of eyes memorized his minutest move. Breard, the lead-off man, went out, short to first. Jackie took his place in the batter's box, worked the count to 3 and 2, then hit an easy grounder, going out the same way, "6 to 3."

The crowd had booed when he took a toe hold at the plate—booed loudly, insistently. Jackie had felt the pressure; his forehead was moist. But by the time he had run out the grounder, the sound was different. The cheers had come, challenging the boos, wrestling with them, finally taking over as the dominant noise.

Jackie was up again in the second inning. Tom Tatum and George Shuba were on base; Montreal was leading by one run. Again Jackie worked the count to 3 and 2. Then he put everything he had into the next pitch. His bat connected with the ball in a sharp crack and the white pellet took off for the left-field fence, 340 feet away. It was a homer. Three runs scored.

Shuba was waiting at the plate. "That's the way to hit that ball," George said. "That's the old ball game right there." They shook hands.

Jackie came up again in the fifth inning. He fooled the Giants with a bunt, his second hit of the day. Then, he stole second base. When the catcher's throw eluded the second baseman, Jackie humped it to third.

The ball was finally returned to the pitcher. Boldly, Jackie took a long lead off third, dancing up and down the base line in teasing motions. Just as he took his lengthiest lead, the pitcher halted his windup and turned to third. Hopper came alive immediately.

Charging toward the plate, he cried, "Balk! Balk!"

The umpire waved Robinson home.

And, in his box, Rickey grinned.

The crowd roared with delight.

Jackie's next batting chance came in the seventh inning. He singled for his third straight hit, then stole second again.

Up in the eighth, he singled to left. It was his last time at bat that day. Robinson, setting the standard of his career, had come through magnificently with chips down. Everyone agreed on that. The crowd mobbed him.

"Once again," Jackie was to say, "I was convinced that American sports fans are truly democratic."

As soon as she could, Mrs. Robinson gained her husband's side. "You were wonderful today," she said. "I was so thrilled!"

Jackie's first-game summary read: at bats, 5; hits, 4; home run, 1; singles, 3; stolen bases, 2; runs scored, 4; error, 1. Montreal won the game, 14 to 1.

Both player and team had served notice for the season. As the days flew by, Jackie improved at second. By season's end, he was the league's best. He was also the circuit's leading hitter with a .349 average. And he had stolen forty bases.

Montreal clinched the pennant on August 28. Attendance had been boosted throughout the International League. Jackie had teamed with shortstop Al Campanis, who succeeded Breard, to give the Royals an agile, efficient double-play combination. And, through Jackie's success, other Negroes had set their pens to minor league contracts.

Yet success wasn't the whole story. Jackie had been under terrific strain. He had been unable to beef to umpires as white boys did. In Baltimore, he had lived in a Negro hotel, apart from his teammates. At Syracuse, there was prolonged nastiness. Once or twice, black cats were taken to the park, shoved on-field, and Jackie was told to "meet your brother." At one time, Jackie was on the verge of a nervous breakdown.

Still, with the increasing friendliness of Hopper and fellow players, and the invaluable morale boosting and advice of his wife, plus the thrill of being a creator of history, Jackie had played on and on.

Traditionally, pennant winners in the International League and the American Association meet in a "Little World Series." Louisville won the Association flag in 1946, thus was slated to engage Montreal in the post-season classic.

The first three games were played at Louisville. Fans of this Southern city heaped abuse on Jackie. He paid them small attention, but his bat was strangely silent. Montreal lost two games.

As the teams moved to Montreal, the Royals needed three of four games to win. They were more than equal to the task. With Jackie hitting around .400, they won three straight and the Little World Series championship. Louisville's players never had a chance because Montreal fans compensated for the mistreatment of Jackie in the South.

"Mistreatment" is the word, it should be explained, because that's the way Montreal fans figured it. Jackie was their boy, their hero, their favorite player, all of which reflected Rickey's smartness in selecting Montreal as the player's breaking-in point.

There, Jackie and his wife lived comfortably. Little boys were honored at the chance to run errands for them. The Robinsons were celebrities, so to speak.

After the Royals won the series with Louisville, bedlam, joyful bedlam, broke loose: fans swarmed on the field, grabbed Jackie, Hopper, and pitcher Curt Davis and paraded them around the diamond in a mass victory dance. Jackie, overwhelmed, cried unashamedly, tears falling down his cheeks in rivulets.

At every turn were cheering, admiring fans. They chased Robinson, shouted to him, praised him, begged autographs, showered him with affection.

The experiment had worked so far, and baseball was all the better for it, both artistically and financially.

And Hopper was happy, too. "Jackie," he said after the series, "you're a real ball player and a gentleman. It's been wonderful having you on the team."

For the time being, Jackie was completely satisfied. "I don't care if I never get to the majors," he mused. "This is the city for me. This is paradise."

4

EXPERIMENT COMPLETED

Jackie was sincere in his affection for Montreal and its fans. But, while he was honest in this emotion a hundred percent, his musing in the main reflected a temporary saturation of joy, the lull of satisfaction that comes to every man after a job has been well done. It was, so to speak, a pause of refreshment. Soon his mind, his hopes, his speculations were leaping ahead to the next logical assignment— the major leagues.

It was elemental, of course, that Jackie had earned his way to the majors, to a trial with the Dodgers at the very least. It was also imperative that he move up under the big tent. As terrific as his performance at Montreal had been—as thunderous as was his bat, as fleet as were his feet, as gentlemanly as was his manner—the "great experiment" was incomplete. In a sense, his success at Montreal was comparable to the success of a new play in New Haven. The big test, the proving of this democratic formula, had to come on baseball's Broadway.

The edge of the great thrill labeled "Montreal" became duller in Jackie's mind that off-season as he contemplated more and more the 1947 season. The feeling that he had strode through paradise, that feeling which gripped him on the last day of the play-offs, was readjusted to focus on pleasant memories. During the fall and winter, as he relaxed in California, playing golf, earning a bit of spending change with a professional basketball team called the "Red Devils," greeting his brother Mack and his old friends, Jackie often wondered how the chips would fall in the future.

Meanwhile, Rickey was planning, making arrangements "up ahead" like a theatrical advance man. He had the situation as well scouted as was humanly possible. Early in his preliminary work on this project, he had consulted with Dr. Dan W. Dodson, a New York University professor and executive director of Mayor Fiorello H. La Guardia's Committee on Unity in New York City. They had ferreted out the sociological aspects of a Negro's entrance into organized ball. Rickey had been aware of the fact that over-adulation of Jackie by Negroes might make the job more difficult. He had consulted with Negro leaders, taking them into his confidence, seeking their help, briefing them on the roles they were to play in making things easier for Jackie. At one stage of the project, Negro leaders in Brooklyn formed a committee, headed by Judge Myles Page, in which they outlined lectures, sermons, editorials, and pamphlets, all designed to guide the Negro public in restrained behavior at parks where Jackie played. Herbert T. Miller, a YMCA Official, subsequently visited National League cities for the purpose of forming similar committees. At the proper moment, Negro sports writers, notably Dan Burley of the New York *Amsterdam News*, advised Negro fans through their columns, and bars tacked up signs reading, "Don't Spoil Jackie's Chances."

On the baseball side, Rickey now arranged to hold spring training in Cuba, where replicas of Sanford were unlikely. Side trips were set up for Venezuela and Panama. Psychologically, this was an appropriate move on Rickey's part, for Negro players long had been popular in Latin American countries.

Thus, two important problems were taken care of. In the matter of Dodger players, opposing players, and white fans, there was little to be done in advance. Rickey could not, for instance, send letters to Dodgers saying he was going to bring up Jackie and please be nice to him. There was no way in which he could reach opposing players. And he had to trust to the innate fairness of white sports fans, plus the old American fondness for the underdog. Fellow club heads he could count on pretty well: they were in no position openly to throw obstacles in Jackie's path.

One of the questions Jackie probably asked himself during the off-season was this: "What's Brooklyn like?" It was a natural question. Perhaps his wife, who took additional nurse's training in New York while he played with the Monarchs, told him some of the geographical facts. But, admittedly, she wasn't much of a baseball fan, and thus was unable to describe the immensity of the game's popularity there.

For decades, Brooklyn had been a baseball stronghold. The Dodgers were known wherever the meaning of baseball was understood, for this team had provided more hilarious copy than any other; it owned the game's most unique fan tradition; it was a club characterized by the saying, "Everything happens in Brooklyn!"

The first great feat of a Brooklyn team went into the books in 1870, when the team upset the Cincinnati Red Stockings, 8 to 7, ending a skein of ninety defeatless games.

In 1890, the Dodgers won their first National League pennant. They repeated in 1899, 1900, 1916, 1920, and 1941. In 1904, their ace pitcher, Iron Man McGinnity, won thirty-five games and lost only eight. Old Iron Man lived up to his name in one stretch of six days, during which he pitched and won seven games. One of their greatest heroes was Wee Willie Keeler, the master place-hitter, who batted .432 in 1897 and added to diamond lore the advice, "Hit 'em where they ain't." He could do it.

The National League's all-time-best base stealer, Max Carey, spent some time in Brooklyn. One of the game's most illustrious managers, Wilbert Robinson, for years was their leader. Later, they were to employ the most flamboyant, bombastic twosome at the time in the game—Larry MacPhail, for the front office, and Leo Durocher, to manage from the field. Among the more colorful Dodgers through the years were Nap Rucker, a great pitcher; Zack

Wheat, a fine outfielder and top-grade hitter; Lefty O'Doul, later to become the dean of Pacific Coast League managers; fireballer Van Lingle Mungo, whose penchant for fun robbed him of a glorious career; Dazzy Vance, truly one of the great swift pitchers; and Babe Herman, the skilled hitter of whom it was said that baseballs bounced off his head.

Verily, when he aimed at this outfit, Jackie Robinson was trying to move up from the one-night-stand, bus-riding operations of the Negro American League to the fine-hoteled, Pullman-styled life of the big time. In many ways, it was like stepping out of the Sahara, where an existence was possible only through the most diligent of grubbing, to good, green pastures.

Although it was generally believed that Jackie would advance to the Dodgers in 1947, and although Rickey had made up his mind to it, the player went to spring training as a member of the Royals. This was a part of Rickey's overall plan to handle every detail in a way which would stimulate a minimum of adverse reaction. Jackie reported in fine shape.

First problem: where would he play if and when he was elevated to the Dodgers? Jackie had played second base at Montreal, but Eddie Stanky held down that position in the Brooklyn line-up. And, although Stanky's running, fielding, and hitting abilities had been appraised at little more than, if as much as, journeyman, he was called one of the National League's most valuable players. His fighting spirit was the answer to that riddle. Jackie had played shortstop at Kansas City, but Peewee Reese was the Brooklyn short patcher. He was a very good one, and getting better. First and third bases, however, were open to competition.

Dodgers brass considered moving Jackie to third, but the plethora of candidates made this idea seem impractical. Aspirant third sackers included Arky Vaughan, Cookie Lavagetto, and Jackie's Montreal mate, Johnny Jorgensen. Next, and last, first base. Howie Schultz and Ed Stevens were top candidates.

The problem was solved one day when Mel Jones, Montreal general manager, handed Jackie a first baseman's mitt. It was solved, though, over the objections of both Robinson and Clay Hopper. The player's objection was based on his previous experience, especially his second base play at Montreal. Indeed, it was a bit odd that he was being asked to make another position switch, that his way was being made more rocky, When so much had been done to pave the path. Hopper protested not only for the same reasons as Jackie, but also because his plans for the Royals were being upset. He had taken it for granted, so to speak, that Jackie would be promoted to the parent club. That being so, he would be unable to test first basemen for his team until Jackie was out of the way.

Robinson and Hopper might well have been raising an objection with an umpire! Jackie, for better or for worse, was a first baseman.

Now, when racially prejudiced players on the Dodgers heard about Jackie's conversion to first, they correctly surmised that he was being set up for near-future promotion to the Dodgers. Quickly they drew up a petition against him. But, before it was finished, there was a leak, Rickey caught onto the play, halted it, and made plain the fact that they could not prevent Jackie's promotion. Further, Rickey asked two of the anti-Robinson leaders to try playing with the Negro. They agreed. One said, however, that he wanted to be traded at season's end. After the other became more familiar with Jackie, he said he was unchanged in his feelings toward Negroes in general, but that playing with Robinson was all right.

Subsequently, Jackie cinched the promotion in a seven-game series between the Royals and Dodgers, hitting .625, stealing seven bases, and handling first base in fair enough fashion for a novice.

The "big announcement" was slated for April 9, but the plan was upset when Commissioner Chandler startled baseball by suspending Durocher for a year. It was a penalty for Leo's part in a New York Yankees-Dodgers squabble over alleged gambling, or the presence of gamblers, at a game in Havana. For the moment, Rickey was occupied with this unscheduled development.

The news broke the next day. Montreal and Brooklyn were engaged in an exhibition game at Ebbets Field. Jackie was on first. Arthur Mann, Rickey's assistant, went to the press box with a batch of papers, distributing them to the writers covering the game. They read the simple announcement;

"The Brooklyn Dodgers today purchased the contract of Jackie Robinson from Montreal."

Under the same rules of conduct he had observed at Montreal, Robinson, wearing uniform No. 42, played his first major league game on April 15 against the Boston Braves at Ebbets Field, with some twenty-five thousand fans watching. The Brooklyn line-up was: Eddie Stanky, second base, and leading off; Jackie, first base, batting second; Pete Reiser, center field; Dixie Walker, right field; Gene Hermanski, left field; Bruce Edwards, catcher; Johnny Jorgensen, third base; Peewee Reese, shortstop; and Joe Hatten, pitcher. The Dodgers won, 5 to 3, but Jackie failed to hit, grounding out to third, flying out to left, hitting into a double play. He was safe on an error when his bunt was booted. In the late stages of the game, he was removed from the line-up for defensive reasons.

The next day, he beat out a bunt for his first major league hit. Subsequently, he hit his first major league home run against the Giants at the Polo Grounds. But he soon fell into a serious slump, which tested the patience of his well-wishers, including Rickey and new manager Burt Shotton. For five straight games, Jackie couldn't get a hit.

George Sisler, Brooklyn scout, was to recall something about Jackie's early hitting habits. "Jackie's biggest hitting fault when he joined the Dodgers was being a lunge hitter," Sisler said. "At that time, he was so anxious to make his move that changes bothered him quite a lot."

How was it going sociologically?

Fan reaction at the park appeared to be in his favor. There were scattered boos, but white fans and Negro fans alike applauded him, the Negro fans, despite the fine-point planning, cheering his every move. Crank letters came through the mail. But there were others like the one which said, in essence, "Hope you make it, Black Boy," signed "White Boy." And there were all sorts of individuals and organizations who wanted to capitalize on his publicity. No less than five thousand requests for personal appearances, endorsements, et cetera, were received during his first week as a major leaguer. These were passed along to Rickey, who said nix to most of them.

Opposing bench jockeys were rough. When the Dodgers opened a series with the Phillies, at Brooklyn, the visiting club shouted a greeting, "Hey, you black Nigger!" Then followed the kind of epithets Rickey had anticipated the day he told Jackie how rough things would be and that he couldn't fight back. Ben Chapman, the Phillies manager, was criticized for the jockeying tactics of his players, but Chapman, a Southerner, protested to the press that it was only the kind of jockeying he had received when he came up, the kind any rookie might get. Robinson, he claimed, was being treated just like any other rookie. It was reported, however, that the Phils received a warning against this raw jockeying from Commissioner Chandler. The first time Brooklyn appeared in Philadelphia, Chapman and Robinson posed together for a picture. Still, opposing teams got in their "digs." Pitchers threw dusters. Infielders made unnecessarily hard tags. And, there were gestures.

On the Dodgers team, Jackie was pretty much a loner. Clyde Sukeforth and Shotton and Sisler encouraged him, especially during the tough days of his near-disastrous slump. Stanky helped him solve the intricacies of first-base play. He and Jorgensen were friendly. Yet he was far from being a member of the club, in the fullest sense. In Philadelphia and St. Louis, he was barred from the Dodger hotels. Most of the time, he ate alone or with Negro friends. He shunned card games. He wore, as Rickey had advised, the "armor of humility," fitting well the time-worn description of Negro athletes: "He is quiet and unassuming."

Jackie gradually eased himself out of the slump, and his teammates began to thaw out, just as had the Royals the previous spring. But it was all a sort of lull before the storm. The heaviest blow of all fell suddenly like loosely mortared bricks in an earthquake.

Stanley Woodward, sports editor of the New York *Herald Tribune*, reported the details in a scoop on May 9:

"A National League players' strike, instigated by some of the St. Louis Cardinals, against the presence in the league of Jackie Robinson, Negro first baseman, has been averted temporarily and perhaps squashed.

"In recent days, Ford Frick, president of the National League, and Sam Breadon, president of the St. Louis club, have been conferring with St. Louis players in the Hotel New Yorker. Mr. Breadon flew east when he heard of the projected strike. The story that he came to consult with Eddie Dyer, manager, about the lowly state of the St. Louis club is fictitious. He came on a much more serious errand."

Woodward said that the strike, though organized by certain of the Cards, had been instigated by one of the Dodgers! The plan, he said, had been to strike on May 6, the day of the season's first meeting between the two teams. Players, he said, at one stage had conceived the idea of a general strike within the National League. Woodward's story was quickly denied by the Cardinals.

A wire service reported that the strike leaders were Marty Marion, shortstop, and Terry Moore, center fielder, of the Cards. Again, denials.

But Woodward reported National League president Ford Frick's flat warning, certainly an unnecessary act if there had been no strike plans.

"If you do this," Woodward quoted Frick as saying, "you will be suspended from the league. You will find that the friends you think you have in the press box will not support you, that you are outcasts. I do not care if half the League strikes. Those who do it will encounter quick retribution. All will be suspended and I don't care if it wrecks the National League. . . .

"The National League will go down the line with Robinson, whatever the consequences. You will find if you go through with your intention that you will have been guilty of complete madness."

The strike never materialized.

Robinson declared that he was surprised to hear that St. Louis players had planned the strike, for, he said, of all the teams he had played against, the Cardinals were the friendliest.

By June 15, Robinson was on his way, both at bat and afield. He manufactured a twenty-one game hitting streak and showed considerable improvement at first base, though he was not destined either to become a great first sacker or to have a particular liking for the spot. Some observers concluded that Sisler, one of the all-time first basemen, had helped improve Jackie's fielding, just as Robinson said he had contributed to his rising batting average. Sisler said no.

"I did nothing to improve his fielding," Sisler explained. "It was a case of lack of experience. Robinson was of the type that could learn to play any position, regardless of what it was."

He added, "My work with Jackie brought out very forcibly that he had great aptitude and body control. He could learn to do anything and, of course, his record in sports would indicate just that. He was a very appreciative fellow and one who would take instruction willingly and well."

Jackie's confidence was bolstered when Schultz and Stevens were disposed of to other clubs.

Jackie stole home for the first time in National League play against Pittsburgh, at Forbes Field, on June 24, previewing a feat which inspired the late Bill Robinson, tap dancer deluxe, to call him a "Ty Cobb in Technicolor." The victim of the steal was pitcher Fritz Ostermueller, who napped just that fraction of a second necessary for execution of this difficult maneuver. The batter at the time was

Dixie Walker, who leaped out of the way at the last moment as Robinson went hurtling home in a neat, tricky slide.

That game at Pittsburgh also proved that Jackie's relations with the team were fast improving. Before the game, he conversed freely, and apparently jocularly, with outfielder Carl Furillo, reportedly one of the most rabidly anti-Robinson Dodgers in the beginning. He used his bat to show Peewee Reese the proper swing for a golf shot. He smiled easily and played confidently. There was little in this public show to indicate that things were as tough as they had been or, for that matter, as tough as they were, in certain instances.

Jackie was the butt of an incident in Cincinnati, a "rough-riding town," which was tragic in aspect, yet comic in retrospect. Tall, lean Ewell Blackwell, the Reds' hurler with the hide-and-seek delivery, had been throwing a no-hitter until Stanky got one. Blackwell took out his disappointment by loosing a stream of profanity on Jackie. Finally, Jackie said, "Pitch the ball!" Blackwell did—and Jackie rapped a fast ball to right field for another hit.

Proof that Brooklyn players had "thawed out" came again one August game when Enos Slaughter, the Cardinals' hustling outfielder, spiked Jackie while running out a ground ball.

The incident angered the Dodgers, and Ralph Branca, their pitcher, was of a mind to "stick one in his ear" the next time Slaughter came to bat. But Jackie asked him to forget it. After the game, the Dodgers talked it over in more detail, convinced that Slaughter, a North Carolinian, had spiked Jackie intentionally. They didn't like it because Jackie was defenseless. He couldn't fight back.

Slaughter denied that he had intended to spike Jackie because of his race, and Robinson later indicated that he had accepted Slaughter's denial. "I think Slaughter would cut his mother if he thought it would help win a ball game," Jackie said.

There were other indications that Jackie was a full-fledged member of the team. He played cards with other Dodgers. Occasionally, he golfed with them. And the crank content of his mail was almost nil. Most letters, and there were many, contained requests for autographs and/or pictures.

There were opposing players, too, who had accepted Jackie. Typical of them was Hank Greenberg, the Pittsburgh slugger, later general manager of the Cleveland Indians. One of the biggest names in the game, Greenberg advised Robinson to "stick in there," made friendly small talk with him, even invited him to his home. They had something in common, for Hank, a Jew, knew something about racial prejudice.

As the season wore on toward its nub, the pennant race settled down to a round between the Dodgers and the Cardinals. They played a "crucial" series in September, and Jackie batted .462. The Dodgers won two of three.

At season's end, Jackie was made as a major leaguer. He had stolen twenty-nine bases (three of home) to lead the National League and batted .297. A dozen of his hits were home runs. The Dodgers won their first pennant since 1941 and met the Yankees in the World Series. They lost again. Jackie hit .259.

One of the most significant factors of the season, financially and in impact on other club owners, was the emergence of Negro fans in great numbers. Jackie, in one season, proved himself to be a fitting rival for Joe Louis, till then the race's athletic idol. They—the Negroes—had joined with the curious, the students of race relations, the countless ones who cared little for baseball but who wanted to sit in on history and, of course, the regular fans to make Brooklyn's season a whopping success at the gate. Their attendance at Ebbets Field increased 400 percent. On the road, their presence at games was even more noticeable. League statistics revealed that the Dodgers had attracted 1,807,526 fans at home, a National League record and simply phenomenal for a park hardly designed to seat 35,000 fans comfortably; 1,863,542 on the road, another league record; and set attendance marks in New York, Boston, Pittsburgh, and St. Louis. Conservatively, it was estimated that Jackie had increased attendance a half million. He had been paid, it was said, $5,500.

That the experiment had been completed, successfully, was proven in the words of G. Taylor Spink, editor of the *Sporting News*, baseball's bible. Awarding Jackie rookie-of-the-year honors, Spink said:

"In selecting the outstanding rookie of 1947, the *Sporting News* sifted and weighed only stark baseball values.

"That Jack Roosevelt Robinson might have had more obstacles than his first-year competitors, and that he perhaps had a harder fight to gain even major league recognition, was no concern of this publication. The sociological experiment that Robinson represented, the trail-blazing that he did, the barriers he broke down, did not enter into the decision. He was rated and examined solely as a freshman player in the big leagues—on the basis of his hitting, his running, his defensive play, his team value.

"Dixie Walker summed it up in a few words the other day when he said: 'No other ball player on this club, with the possible exception of Bruce Edwards, has done more to put the Dodgers up in the race than Robinson has. He is everything Branch Rickey said he was when he came up from Montreal!"

Walker's view coincided with those who voted for the National League's Most Valuable Player. Bob Elliott, Boston Braves third baseman, was first. Edwards was fourth, and Jackie was fifth.

The honors had been earned.

"Only those on the team know the great patience and self-control he exercised continuously throughout the season," Rickey said. "For this exemplary conduct, displayed both off and on the field during the entire season, he deserves the commendation of everyone."

5

DOBY INVADES CLEVELAND

A strange kind of restlessness allected certain sportive-minded citizens of Chicago's South Side on Sunday morning, July 5, 1947. The air about them was charged with expectancy, filled with a busy buzz not totally unlike the droning of a bee pack, a constant reminder that "something was up." This atmosphere extended into churches, even, as some members yawned their impatience with verbose ministers whose sermons were running dangerously close to game time at Comiskey Park.

The reason for all this was Cleveland's signing, that morning, of the American League's first Negro player. His name was Larry Doby. He had been purchased from the Newark Eagles of the Negro National League, for whom he played second base and batted something like .458. The Indians had signed him in the office of the Chicago White Sox and were to put him on display that afternoon in one or both games of a doubleheader.

Doby, a trim, collegiate-type youngster, had the willies that day, with reason. He had been jet-propelled, so to speak, from the congenial atmosphere of the Eagles' dugout to the strange, new world of major league ball. Apparently the strong, silent type, the kind of person by nature liable to take the hurt of a rebuff on the inside rather than explode in an extrovert's display, Doby was unable to bluff the situation with a hearty smile or quick quip.

One interviewer had observed, following the contractual ceremonies in the White Sox office, "His voice is so low, you have to lean over to hear him talk!"

Doby and Jackie had one thing in common: they had gone up as second basemen and had been handed first baseman's mitts. But, whereas Rickey had planned Robinson's entrance as carefully as a man would plan building a house of matchsticks, Doby knew less than twenty-four hours before he played his first game that he was on his way to the majors. Basis for the difference in the handling of the two Negroes may well be said to have been these considerations: Rickey didn't believe that any Negro player was talented enough to crash the majors "cold"; the Indians' president, Bill Veeck, wanted a Negro "good enough to play major league ball." Doby was the selectee.

In the second game of the doubleheader, Cleveland manager Lou Boudreau sent Doby to play first base; and he made a typical freshman's debut, handling eight fielding chances without the recording of an error, scratching out one hit in four trips to the plate. That was his only full-game performance of the season. In pinch-hitting roles, he batted .156. Before the half-season wore out, he heard himself called a "Class-D ball player," and learned the lyrics to those "I-Am-a-Failure-in-the-Major-Leagues Blues," a ditty not unfamiliar to many a rookie before him.

Doby's advent, of course, was a direct result of the Robinson-Rickey move. Fact is, the Dodgers had let Larry slip through their fingers so Cleveland could get him. Since Jackie had proven that the mere browning of skin on a person's body was in no way related to his ability or inability to hit and field; that a Negro could help improve a ball club; and that one like Jackie could blast repeated homers in a team's cash balance, Doby's advent was a logical development. It was also logical, in retrospect, that effervescent Bill Veeck was the first American League club president to follow Rickey's lead.

The very challenge of the move had been enough to whet his interest. A man whose open-necked white sport shirts were worn as trademarks, revealing a hairy chest in fair or foul weather, he was already in his own right a pioneer: he had proved, through booming action, that he was most decidedly not to be restricted by the staid promotion methods of many of his predecessors in the baseball business.

For example, when he assumed control of the Indians in 1946, the team was a stable, going concern. But it wasn't going fast enough! He immediately pepped up operations with circus-type entertainment, created headlines at the drop of a thought and, on the serious side, worked like a Texas red ant which had the word that a tough winter was ahead.

Negro writers soon recognized Veeck as a person likely at least to give ear to the proposition of Negroes playing in the American League. Perhaps they had heard the unsubstantiated story that Veeck once shocked baseball's late commissioner, Judge Kenesaw Mountain Landis, with a proposal to buy a major league club and transform it into an all-colored aggregation.

After Veeck added a Negro to his public relations staff (Louis Jones, ex-husband of singer Lena Horne), they anticipated an early break for their cause. Several of them, seeking to speed progress, made pertinent suggestions:

William (Bill) Nunn, Sr., managing editor of the *Courier*, discussed Negro performers with Veeck early in 1947. According to a subsequent story in his newspaper, among the prospects he had suggested to Veeck was Larry Doby of the Eagles. Ham Burley suggested Doby as a major league bet through a letter to his friend and Veeck's aide, Harry Grabiner. The letter gained Veeck's attention.

Veeck himself became involved in a discussion with another Negro writer which, if not directly responsible for activation of the

Doby-signing idea, at least gave it more than a small breath of life. This is what happened:

On one of his spring appearances, in a small Ohio town, Veeck was asked for an appraisal of Jackie Robinson's chances. Forthrightly, Veeck replied to the effect that Robinson was not of major league caliber, an opinion expressed earlier on the West Coast by the Indians' ace hurler, Bob Feller.

Soon after Veeck returned to his office, he was contacted by Cleveland Jackson, then sports editor of the Cleveland *Call-Post*, that city's leading Negro newspaper. Jackson took issue with Veeck's appraisal of Robinson. What facts, Jackson wanted to know, did Veeck have to support his statement? Had Veeck ever seen Jackie play? Veeck admitted that he hadn't seen Jackie play.

One word led to another, not in anger, but in constructive discussion of the issue. Eventually, Jackson, in effect, asked whether, if a Negro player of major league promise was available, Veeck would sign him for the Indians. Veeck said yes, he would. Jackson named Larry Doby.

Within a few days, Veeck's scouts went into action, searching for Negro players of major league promise. They returned with favorable reports on Doby. One of them, Bill Killefer, said Doby appeared to be an extremely solid prospect.

Veeck, a man of action, lost no time following through. He contacted Mrs. Effa Manley, general manager of the Eagles, and as she related:

"Veeck told me he wanted to buy Larry Doby. I asked him how much he would pay for him. He said, '$10,000.' I told him, 'Mr. Veeck, that is perfectly ridiculous. But, I want Larry to have a chance. If you will promise me he won't earn less than $5,000 per year, I'll let you have him.' "

They agreed on details. Later, Veeck added five thousand dollars to make the total purchase price fifteen thousand dollars.

The announcement that Cleveland had signed a Negro ball player gave birth to partial repetition of the earlier episode involving Robinson. Questions popped up incessantly. Who is Larry Doby? Is he a good ball player? What team is he with? Will the Indians play ball with a Negro? Will any white player lose his job, or be sold, to make room for him? Will there be other Negroes after him?

Veeck made a casual statement for Cleveland consumption. Doby, he said, was going to be a great player. He had been an outstanding star with the Eagles. He was a nice fellow.

That Doby's advent had presented something of a problem for manager Boudreau was evident the first time Larry appeared at Cleveland. Doby was a second baseman. The Cleveland midway guardian was Joe (Flash) Gordon, one of the all-time-great fielders; at short, of course, was Boudreau, likewise perhaps entitled to ranking with the best; on third was another solid performer, Ken Keltner; and at first, where Doby had played in Chicago, was Eddie Robinson, a home-run hitter of considerable ability. On his first appearance in Cleveland, Doby worked out somewhat awkwardly at second after Gordon had finished his practice. He fielded grounders well enough, but his throwing motion appeared a bit unsuited for the infield and he needed smoothing on the pivot play. When he didn't see action in that game, many fans who had attended the game because of him were disappointed.

One of them, a white man, grumbled on his way out of Cleveland Stadium. "If they're not going to use him," this fan asked another, "why did they sign him?"

At season's end, "experts" said the Doby proposition was a flop. They prescribed a good long dose of minor league play for him. However, in those days of almost total despair for the sensitive, twenty-two-year-old Doby, a lad given to tenseness and introspection, he made a move which was to affect his whole career favorably: he went to kindly, baseball-wise Deacon Bill McKechnie, an Indians coach and former major league manager, for advice.

"Will you tell me frankly, Mr. McKechnie," Doby asked in sober voice, "whether you think I have a chance to become a major league ball player?"

McKechnie was prepared for the question.

"Larry," he said, "you have a fine chance, but you'll have to get rid of some bad habits you picked up with Newark. That wild, desperation swing at any pitch near the plate may have been a crowd pleaser there, but it won't help you in the majors. You have youth, a strong arm, speed, power, and quick reactions, all of which are important for success in baseball. However, I don't believe you can make the grade at second base. Your best bet is the outfield, where you can capitalize on your speed."

(The idea of making an outfielder out of Doby had been suggested to McKechnie, it was said, by Raleigh [Bizz] Mackey, catcher-manager of the Eagles.)

Doby went home to Paterson, New Jersey, where he had been reared as an only child and grew up to be a four-letter man at East Side High School, and pondered McKechnie's advice. Friends, attempting to boost his morale, made light of his failures.

He kept himself in shape, and ate, slept, and drank baseball all winter—through books, newspapers, and "hot stove league" discussions. Even while he performed a portion of that winter as the first Negro in the American Basketball Association, baseball was on his mind. As a result, he was in top shape when Boudreau called the first spring training session of 1948 at Tucson, Arizona.

In many ways, Doby had been the perfect choice for the pioneering job in the American League. In others, as in his tendency to tighten up, he was a puzzler, a lad who not infrequently confused his closest friends. It might be said that the major difference between Jackie and Larry was this: Jackie, as time was to prove, dressed himself in the cloak of humility and made it into a perfect fit through one of the greatest acting jobs in baseball history; Doby wore the cloak as a gift of nature. There was little need for Veeck to caution

Larry, "You can't fight back." Still, there was lacking in Larry the great gift for coming through, the thing which made Jackie, as Rickey put it, "a combative competitor. And yet the fact had long been apparent that Larry's sports destiny lay in stardom. It had been taken for granted, even, by people who knew his parents and had watched him play and grow as a kid in Camden, South Carolina, where he was born on December 13, 1924. David Doby, his father, was a semi-pro player of considerable ability and his mother, Mrs. Etta Doby, was a long-time sports fan.

After Larry's father died, Mrs. Doby moved to Paterson, New Jersey, where she worked as a domestic as did Jackie's mother, saving all she could from her meager pay to insure a happy childhood for the eight-year-old boy. Larry ate from no silver spoon as he grew into his teens, but Mrs. Doby always could point with justifiable pride to the fact that he never had to "work out."

Larry grew up as an only child, in strong resemblance to his mother. From her he inherited seriousness of carriage, neatness of person, and cleanliness of character. Even before he was old enough to join the "big boy" teams, he followed them around, wide-eyed as he watched their play, many times serving them as a water boy. Eventually, he played with the Paterson Smart Sets baseball team and became a sports hero—track, football, basketball, and baseball—at Paterson's East Side High School. He was a multiple letterman, team captain, and an all-state selection in football, basketball, and baseball.

It had been asked in the half-season of 1947: "Since Larry spent most of his youth in the North and since he was a star with white boys in high school sports, why is he made so tense by his association with white boys on the Indians?" It was pointed out, too, that in the way of physical equipment, Doby, at twenty-two, was on a par with Robinson, who was twenty-eight. Why, then, was he so tight? A large portion of the total answer was this: Doby for the first time was a symbol. For the first time he had been made aware of "being different" by the initial coolness of the Indians dressing room, by the teeming sports writers who sought to grill him, by the boos of some fans, and by the markedly accentuated cheering of Negro fans.

That *the problem* was playing havoc with his natural abilities was noted by one veteran observer who said, in effect, "When Doby doesn't have time to think about a play, he's a star. He shows his innate athletic greatness. Let a batter drive a line drive his way and he's off with the crack of the bat. And, he'll pull the ball down with a sensational catch. But, let the batter lift a lazy pop fly his way. He's got time to think about it, to stand out there and pound his fist in his mitt. The fact that he's a Negro in the majors comes home to him, he knows all eyes are watching him. Chances are he'll muff the ball."

Unlike Jackie, Doby had not been a big-time college hero. He entered Long Island University, one of the basketball capitals, in 1940, but soon transferred to Virginia Union University, a Negro school at Richmond, Virginia. His college education was cut short when Uncle Sam sent the usual "greetings." He chose the navy and, subsequently, was shipped off to Great Lakes Naval Training School, near Chicago.

"Doby was a loner at Great Lakes," a friend has recalled. "Many times, I tried to get him off to Chicago with me, but he didn't want to leave the base. He was always interested in sports, though. . . ."

At that time, Mickey Cochrane, former all-time-great catcher for the Philadelphia Athletics and Detroit Tigers, was coaching the No. 1 (the white) Great Lakes baseball team. He had occasion to see Doby in action with the all-Negro nine, was impressed, and was quoted as voicing the usual lament, "If he were only white. . . ."

It was following his discharge from the navy that Doby joined the Eagles, a team slated to produce pitcher Don Newcombe and outfielder Monte Irvin for the majors before it passed out of existence. With the Eagles, based in his home state, playing with and against fellows he knew, free from pressures and causes, Doby was simply great. It was that greatness, or a reasonable facsimile thereof, which Doby hoped a winter of mulling over McKechnie's advice, of studying baseball techniques, of making up his mind to heed the advice of friends and "get in there and play the kind of ball you're capable of," would bring him in the year 1948.

Outwardly—off the field, that is—Doby appeared in 1948 spring training to be the same humble person he had been the half-season of 1947 in Cleveland. Still reserved, a loner, he said nothing when informed that the swank Santa Rita Hotel at Tucson had refused to house him—that he would have to live in a private, Negro home some two miles removed from the ball park. But, on-field, he was a new man. On his third day in camp, he blasted a 380-foot homer. He made several nifty, running catches in the outfield. Aided by Tris Speaker, the best center fielder of all time, and encouraged by Hank Greenberg, who had gone to Cleveland from Pittsburgh, Doby made rapid strides. Some of the "experts" backed off their previous opinions. Veeck wagered that he would make good. Boudreau conceded that Larry would be with the club on opening day.

When the Indians began their homeward trek of exhibition games with the New York Giants, Doby was batting .341. Boudreau made another concession: "Doby can play any outfield position," the manager said, "but he needs polish." Specifically, he had to polish off some of his Negro league roughness.

During this transitional period, Jim Crow was not so rough on Doby as it had been on Robinson; yet, there were incidents. In Los Angeles, Doby was erroneously informed that the Biltmore Hotel would not accept Negro guests. The player was sent to the Hotel Watkins, a Negro establishment. An investigation by Leon Washingson, publisher of the Los Angeles *Sentinel*, revealed, however, that the Biltmore would accept Negro guests, that it had accepted them for years, that, in fact, three Negroes were living there at the very moment Larry lived in the Watkins. At Lubbock, Texas, Doby discovered that it was not always profitable to be an early bird.

When he arrived at the park fifteen minutes ahead of practice for an exhibition, an attendant refused to let him enter. The arrival of traveling secretary Harold (Spud) Goldstein straightened out this mix-up.

Still, Doby was uncomplaining. And he was rewarded. Joe Gordon proved himself a real friend. Catcher Ray Murray, a jolly-good fellow, relieved tension with his hearty greetings and witty sayings. Thurman Tucker, who most assuredly would have prevented Doby from eventually landing the center field position if he could have hit major league pitching, was another fellow of warm feeling.

The Giants' bench-jockeys rode Doby a bit, but it wasn't raw, or raucous. When Larry spiked shortstop Eddie Pellagrini of the St. Louis Browns in an exhibition, absolutely nothing untoward happened.

By the time the Indians arrived in Cleveland to finish off their exhibition schedule and open the season, Boudreau had named Dale Mitchell for left field and Tucker for center. Right field was open to either Doby or Pat Seerey, a rotund home-run slugger of in-and-out abilities. A special Veeck project, too, Seerey had spent the winter reducing in California at the club's expense.

Doby played right field on Saturday, April 17, hitting safely twice in four appearances at the plate. His final spring training average became .354. Seerey played the position on Sunday and went hitless, striking out twice.

Boudreau and Veeck held a meeting Sunday night. Monday's newspapers announced that Doby, erstwhile .156 hitter, would open the season in right field.

Opening day was April 20. The game: Cleveland versus St. Louis. That Veeck and his staff had done their promotional job well was proved when 73,163 fans went through the turnstiles. Many of them, especially the cheering Negro contingent who flooded the right-field seats, were out to see what the "new" Larry Doby would do. The overwhelming majority of fans present were charitable, handing Doby an encouraging ovation as he strode plateward to try his luck against Fred Sanford, pitcher for the Browns.

Three-for-four, two-for-five, including a homer; or two-for-three, including a double and a sensational catch would have made good fiction. What actually happened was this: Doby struck out his first time at bat—with the bat on his shoulder and the ball speeding across the heart of the plate. For the game, he went oh-for-four. He was inept in right. It wasn't good.

Following the Browns series, the Indians went to Detroit for games with the Tigers. There, Larry hit with a vengeance (.384), fielded well, and was accorded a hero's praise. But all this was only a flash in the pan, for in the final game of the series he struck out five times in five at bats. Hal Newhouser gave him the business three times. Virgil Trucks fanned him once. And a hurler named Gentry made it a perfect day in reverse.

"I wouldn't want you to print this without Doby's okay," Boudreau told Cleveland writers after the game, "but Doby's been worried for the last few days. You can't have two things on your mind and play baseball. His wife had a miscarriage."

Doby admitted the circumstance, but refused it as an alibi. "Yesterday," he said, "I felt like a ball player. I don't know what I felt like today."

That was the pattern for the early season: one day he was "up," the next he was in the dumps. When he was up, he was interesting, exciting, near-great. When he was down, the "anti-Doby" experts played a powerhouse coda in "I-told-you-so's." Finally, Boudreau decided to use Larry only when right-handers were pitching, a bit of strategy heatedly objected to by a white fan who claimed that a "system" he'd worked out proved conclusively that Doby would hit left-handers better than he would right-handers.

On Boudreau's indefinite schedule, Doby's progress was slow. Two of his lucky spots, it seemed though, were Boston's Fenway Park and Washington's Griffith Stadium. He hit well in Boston and rekindled fond memories of Babe Ruth at Washington by hitting the longest home run of twenty-two years. But nothing success-wise was permanent until June 14, when the Indians played an exhibition game against the Brooklyn Dodgers at Brooklyn.

That night, Doby talked things over with Jackie Robinson, by then a veteran of the Negro's strange life in the majors. Robinson gave him advice, hoisted his spirits, and instilled a new supply of confidence. Their meeting at first base at one stage of the day's game had provided a bit of comedy relief. With Doby on first, Dodger pitcher Rex Barney attempted a pick-off play. Robinson was so engrossed in conversation with Doby he never saw the ball. It hit him in the chest and bounded away.

When Doby returned to Cleveland for an American League game the night of June 15, he made his first bold statement. "I don't give a damn now if they do send me to the minors," he told this book's author. "I know I can hit major league pitching!" Around midnight, this writer sent Veeck a telegram, saying: "I respectfully submit that Doby is now ready to do his best."

Gradually, Doby proved this appraisal to be right. Yet his rise was temporarily halted when he twisted an ankle rounding second base. This injury turned out, oddly, to be a kind of blessing, for it brought his teammates closer to him. "I can lick you now," outfielder Hank Edwards kidded. Pitcher Sam Zoldak concernedly advised the trainer on how Larry's ankle should be bandaged. Indians, by this time, had come to respect Larry for the fight he was making; they hated to see him receipt for bad luck when things had been tough enough without it.

The second game of the Dodgers-Indians home-and-home exhibition series was played at Cleveland on the night of July 14. By this time, the Indians had added Satchel Paige to the roster and the

Dodgers had called up Roy Campanella from their St. Paul farm club. It was the first time as many as four Negroes were slated for action in one game, a game which provided the most graphic proof of how popular these players were with fans of their race.

Total attendance was 64,877. As usual, regular Indians fans represented greater Cleveland and such outlying cities as Buffalo, New York; Erie, Pennsylvania; Columbus, Toledo, Dayton, Akron, and Cincinnati, Ohio. Negro fans not only journeyed from those cities, they went to Cleveland Stadium from such far-away places as Nashville, Tennessee; Louisville, Kentucky; Atlanta, Georgia; Detroit, Michigan; Washington, D.C.; Pittsburgh, Pennsylvania; and Chicago, Illinois.

An official of the Indians, whose eyes were trained by years of experience to estimate crowds accurately, rambled through the aisles, gazed at the filled seats in wonderment, then concluded, "Fully forty percent of this crowd is made up of Negro fans!" "Let's see," said a feverishly figuring writer, "forty percent of 64,877 is . . . more than 25,000 . . . 25,951 to be exact!"

The Negro population of Cleveland was estimated at 125,000. Some 3,000 Negro fans were out-of-towners. That meant that between 21,000 and 22,000 Negro fans in the park were Clevelanders. In other words, about one in every six of Cleveland's Negro population was present. An imaginative mind enlarged upon this fact for dramatic effect:

If the Indians could make a proportionate draw on Cleveland's metropolitan population alone, they would require a park seating close to 200,000 fans. If the New York Yankees could duplicate this ratio, they would have to enlarge Yankee Stadium to a seating capacity in excess of one million!

The major leagues had tapped a hitherto largely inaccessible source of new fans. Here was solid argument for the furtherance of democracy in baseball.

After his ankle had fully healed, Doby was made a regular, moving to center field. He supported the fan's theory that he could hit left-handers. He improved, game by game. In August, his bat got red hot. He carried a twenty-one-game hitting streak into September. And, for that month, he hit close to .400. His hits often meant ball games won as the Indians fought for the pennant, grabbing the lead one day, losing it another, then bouncing back with resiliency almost beyond human ken. The season ended with Cleveland and Boston tied for first place.

The Indians traveled East knowing that if they won the play-off game, they would be champs, and that they would remain in Beantown to open the World Series with the Braves, who were National League winners. Boudreau chose the knuckle-ball artist, Gene Bearden, as his hurler. Joe McCarthy, managing the Red Sox after a glorious career as a Yankee helmsman, decided to pitch Denny Galehouse, a veteran.

Result of this game was not long in doubt: Bearden, a battle-scarred war vet, held the hard-hitting Sox in check, taking his twentieth victory of the year, as the Indians scored eight runs to three for McCarthy's men. The season's tally sheet on Doby read: batting average, .301; home runs, 14; runs batted in, 64; runs scored, 80. His fielding, although not of the best by average (.955), had improved tremendously, and base runners with larceny of heart had learned not to trifle with his rifle of a throwing arm.

For the Indians' fandom, the pennant meant no more ifs, buts, or inhibitions—they celebrated the event with hilarious madness. And, as noted in the figures above, it was the culmination of Doby's climb from the status of a raw, sometimes-resented rookie to the high level of full membership in a major league pennant winner.

To one accustomed to the Cleveland brand of love for baseball, Boston's World Series air seemed quiet, sober, almost funereal. A fellow wanted the Tribe to get those games over with so the teams could switch to Cleveland, where a real-honest-to-goodness World

Series binge was on tap. There was no disappointment when the switch was made.

The morning the Indians arrived home, some 300,000 fans lined Euclid Avenue, a primary thoroughfare, to greet them. All was joyous, shouting, grinning, wild acclaim. And with good reason— this was Cleveland's first Series entrant in twenty-eight long, despair-filled years. Every man connected with the team was a hero, even bat boy Billy Sheridan. A parade was arranged and the full squad, on-field and front-office, in open-top convertibles of garish hues, crawled down the avenue. There were Boudreau and Veeck, up ahead; Hegan and Feller, Satch and Gene, Warm friends; Kennedy and Gordon; Keltner and Tucker, kings all. Likewise in a convertible, likewise a king, seated with left fielder Dale Mitchell and Mrs. Mitchell, was Doby, a wide smile splitting his face. He had made the long haul.

The Series, known for its ability to make monkeys of some of the greatest stars, could not halt Doby's momentum. He batted .318, hit a homer off Johnny Sain to help win a game for Steve Gromek—and the post-game picture of Doby and Gromek hugging each other in glee was perhaps the sports photo of the year.

Excepting Feller's failure to win a long-cherished Series game, there was no damper; the Indians beat the Braves, four games to two.

Doby pocketed $6,772.07 for his Series efforts, paused a moment to breathe the rarefied air that swirls around a hero's head, then announced that he and wife Helyn were going back to Paterson to buy a home.

"And," he added, "we need everything from knives and forks on up!"

On the basis of his fine showing in '48, Larry was expected to blossom among the greats in 1949. The author, caught up in the natural flow of optimism at Cleveland, wrote for *Sport* magazine an article entitled, "Is Larry Doby the Successor to Tris Speaker?" As fantastic as the idea sounded, it was not far-fetched to those who appraised the player's natural talents and saw him bat with wild abandon that pennant year.

But into every life some rain must fall. Ball players are not exempted. There are games in which Ol' Debbil Jinx clutches them tightly in the palms of his hoary, heavy hands and nothing;—nobody—can purchase their release.

The year 1949 was like that for Doby. No single incident dramatized his failure to improve—his fallback, in fact—more than his attempt to steal home against the Yankees. It happened at Cleveland Stadium on July 20. The Indians were in second place, the Yanks in first. It was the eighth inning, Yanks leading 7 to 3. The Indians were at bat, starting a rally, bases loaded (Doby on third, of course), the count 2-and-2 on batter Bob Kennedy. Following the pitch from Joe Page, which established the 2-2 count, Yankee catcher Yogi Berra turned to converse with the plate umpire, and Page stepped off the mound to relax; Doby, alert to the possibilities of the situation, "lit out" for home. Berra, a great talker, continued his conversation. Page leaped out of his relaxed state and shouted to Berra that Doby was coming home. Berra didn't catch on. Page shouted again. Berra caught on! And Doby was out by an embarrassingly large margin of base line!

Ol' Debbil Jinx, figuratively laughing his head off, fired the situation. Fans and writers howled. They wanted to know what had "gotten into" Doby. And, the final touch: Page walked Kennedy, meaning Doby could have waltzed home. Page then retired the side with no additional runs.

From orthodox baseball's point of view, it was clearly a bonehead play. First, the no-out, bases-loaded situation promised that the Indians would score. Two properly placed long flies, for instance, would have driven in two runs, making the score 7 to 5. A double might have cleared the sacks. A homer would have tied the score. But to gamble on a steal of home could produce only a 7 to 4 score and would involve the risk of helping the Yankee cause with an out. Such things just weren't being done in major league ball, observers pointed out, especially when two teams were contending for the pennant.

Doby was the target of many cracks:

"He's a showboat," someone said, and the description made the press.

"He's been reading too much about Jackie Robinson," another said, and that, too, was recorded for public consumption.

Doby's bonehead play killed the rally which might have won the game—virtually everyone agreed on that.

Manager Boudreau was incensed. He reportedly fined Doby.

Yet, the player had a side, too. He had attempted the unexpected. He had shown initiative, albeit he ignored the fact that initiative doesn't always pay off in baseball when the manager's signal hasn't gone out. Had Doby been successful, things might have been different. Page might have blown up; the Yankees, though old pros, might have become rattled. Doby's steal might have led to a rousing victory. This kind of victory—if one wants to play conjecture to the hilt—might have fired the Indians to a pennant. But Doby was out. The game was lost. Doby was in the doghouse.

This incident was the crusher in his 1949 performance. Although he hit 24 homers, drove in 85 runs, and performed in 147 games, it was a "down" year. His batting average shrank 21 points to .280 and his fielding was marred by costly lapses. It might have been a pretty good year, boner and all, for another player. But it wasn't anything to write home about for a player who was expected to follow the path of the one and only Tris Speaker. In that light the year 1949 was assessed against Doby.

The next season, 1950, he bounced back, being in the upward phase of his elevator-like (up-and-down) career. He hit .326, clouted 25 homers, drove in 102 runs, and scored 110 times. Yankee manager Casey Stengel paid Larry a high compliment by assigning him to center field for the entire All-Star game. In six at bats, Doby hit safely twice and handled nine chances flawlessly. It was by far his best year in the majors.

At the annual "Ribs and Roast" banquet at the Hotel Hollenden in January, 1951, Doby was named Cleveland's "Man of the Year" in baseball. A crowd of seven hundred, gathered for the occasion, watched as he accepted the honor and assorted gifts, then cheered unreservedly as he made an acceptance speech eloquent in simplicity and sincerity.

"Gentleman," Doby began, "this is indeed a great honor. I'm so happy I just don't know what to say. You know I have been selected as 'Man of the Year' and I'm proud of it.

"However, I stand before you tonight as Larry Doby. There are quite a few that I would like to mention as responsible for my being here.

"I first want to thank the Lord above that he gave me the ability He did in order that I might earn my living playing baseball. . .

Larry then paid tribute to Boudreau, to Veeck, to Ellis Ryan, Cleveland president, to Bill McKechnie, to coach Mel Harder, former Cleveland pitching great, to Hank Greenberg—to everyone who, he felt, had helped him find success in the game. His teammates were included.

"I can't say too much about my teammates," he continued, "because, as I said before when I was selected as your 'Man of the Year,' as I accept these gifts that you have given me and my family, there is a place in my heart for the men who have worked along with me.

"I don't want to accept these gifts alone for my family, but I accept them for the entire Cleveland organization, from park policemen to the Bossards (grounds keepers), from the ball players to the president, from the men who work with me daily to the people and fans I come in contact with every day.

"I hope that in the near future, after all my teammates have been on this stage, I will be able to come back."

But Doby's elevator was due to go down again in 1951. His batting average fell off to .295, his runs batted in dropped to sixty-nine (only a few more than a dozen against first division clubs), and his homer total was lowered to twenty. It was in these figures, in this failure of Doby to be consistent, that Cleveland again lost out to New York.

Yet, in the off-season, Doby bristled at repeated criticisms of his play. Once he said, "I tried to carry the whole ball club on my back." He admitted this effort had been foolish. But when it was announced that Greenberg planned to cut his twenty-five-thousand-dollar salary by some five thousand dollars, Doby became a holdout. His 1951 season hadn't been that bad, was the gist of his contention.

Eventually, as most ball players do, Doby came to terms, for 1952. The year began slowly. lt. began, in fact, as if it were the make-it or break-it year for him. In this his sixth year as a major leaguer, he was faced with criticisms of his personality, of his "problems." There had been off-season talk of trades, which of course did not materialize, and his salary squabble with Greenberg had contributed to involved public discussions of the pros and cons. After play began, there was a hint that a portion of Cleveland's top brass believed the player was sulking, that his attitude could be improved. Manager Al Lopez, successor to Boudreau, who had moved to Boston in 1951, benched Doby one game for what he called "sulking." The player denied that his attitude was bad.

Doby, however, was dissatisfied with himself. With the Indians generally favored to end the Yankee skein of pennant victories, he was unable to maintain steady performance offensively. (Defensively, he had no peer in the American League.)

It was along about mid-summer that he visited Washington Park on Chicago's South Side, following a game with the Chicago White Sox at Comiskey Park. With him were Buddy Young, professional football star; Sherman Howard, Cleveland Browns back; the author, and several other fellows. It was an informal meeting.

Larry was off duty, so to speak, and he seemed to be enjoying himself immensely. It was a lazy sort of late afternoon. The sun was hot, yet Washington Park was fairly cool. The wide expanse of neatly manicured green grass, the beautiful trees, the gentle chirping of the birds—all were a far cry from the feverish activity of a ball park. A player had a chance to be himself, to relax. Doby, who might easily have been mistaken for a college lad on vacation, appeared not to have a care in the world as he laughed and joked.

"You looked real good out there today," someone said, referring to the Indians-White Sox game.

That was true. Larry had blasted a 415-foot homer and his defensive play was characterized by finesse, by grace, which reminded one of Joe DiMaggio and made one suddenly wonder, with all due respect, how come Joe's brother, Dom, happened to be the starting center fielder in the summer's All-Star Game.

Doby let the comment, pass.

"I've been sick," he said.

"What's the trouble?" the author wanted to know.

"Something's wrong with my kidney or gall bladder," he replied. "They want me to go to a hospital. Some days, I feel great—real good. Everything's right. Then, other days, I feel sluggish."

"But, you looked great on the field," someone reminded him, trying to be cheerful. Another agreed, "You sure did."

"That wasn't my best," Larry protested. "I know how good a ball player I can be. For someone else, that might have been good. But, it wasn't my best. I don't know about this thing. I took some pills. I may have to go to the hospital. . . . Then, maybe I can play the kind of ball I'm supposed to play—the kind I know I can play."

Small talk wedged into the conversation. A remark about Minnie Minoso. A gag about Jackie Robinson. Someone chided Buddy Young about his excess weight.

Then Larry picked up the thread of the conversation:

"There have been a lot of stories about me," he said. A listener sort of figured he was talking about the mass of words written to put him second to Ted Williams as the most frequently analyzed (psycho, and otherwise) player in the game.

"They talked about my legs," Doby continued. "They said I had football muscles after I had trouble last season (1951). But, I never had trouble with my legs before. Seems as though, if something were wrong, the muscles would have gone bad before. Well, I went to a trainer-friend. He told me I had been doing a lot of headfirst sliding, hitting my knees. He said there were blood clots around the knees which hampered blood circulation in the legs. He worked the clots out and I haven't had any trouble since."

There was a pause in the conversation. Someone started a bit of verbal byplay with Buddy Young. Doby turned to the author.

"I've got a lot of talent," he said with quiet confidence. "Maybe more talent than any other player in the game. I know how good a player I should be. But, this trouble holds me back now. For a while, I was hitting real good—went up to a .317, was up in the 'big 10,' where I should be. Then, I had some bad days. As soon as I get this thing cleared up, though, I'll be the player I should be."

Larry was unable to bat .300; he did not escape the plague of inconsistency; he could not lead the Indians to a pennant, for in spite of three twenty-game winners and the hard-hitting Doby-Easter-Rosen axis they finished second again. But, on the final day of the season, Larry broke a 31-31 home run tie with teammate Easter to become champion of the American League. Later figures revealed that he was slugging champion of the majors, compiling a .541 average to lead Stan Musial by three points. Although his batting average fell to .276, he drove in 104 runs.

In the wake of the season, there was evidence that Doby was not yet rid of stories that tended to bedevil him. It was announced by press from Cleveland that the Detroit Tigers were dickering for his contract. There appeared to be quite some haste to lend credence to the story, which, at best, appeared to be speculative. "Doby," it was remarked in one quarter, "probably would benefit from a trade. He hasn't been happy here since Bill Veeck left."

Withal, there was evidence of official confidence in his ability to become eventually the player he should be, the player he wanted to be. General manager Hank Greenberg minced no words in replying to queries about a possible deal with Detroit.

"I wouldn't trade Doby for any player in the American League," he said.

A few weeks later the subject of Doby's 1953 salary became an issue between the player and the general manager. Feller, a nine-game winner in '53, had already signed a contract reportedly calling for $40,000. Second baseman Bobby Avila and pitcher Early Wynn were balking at their salary offers. Over in the National League, Ralph Kiner was resisting Branch Rickey's efforts "to cut his $90,000 pay the full, allowable 25%. And Doby—home run and slugging champion of the American League, as fine a defensive player as the circuit could claim—asked Hank for $35,000. Greenberg thought the request was exorbitant. Doby held out. They negotiated by telephone without success as spring training opened. Doby stayed home in Paterson. Greenberg threatened him by telegram: "Report to Tucson in 24 hours or negotiations will revert to your 1952 salary." Doby flew out, but as he did so there was new talk of a trade. The Chicago White Sox, this time. Another year had begun with uncertainty, and one wondered, "Where goes the elevator now? Up or down?"

6

OLD MAN MOSE AIN'T DEAD

While Larry Doby, personally, his being a Negro in the American League, his play, his difficulties, and his development all were marked with dead seriousness, relieved only on rare occasions by bits of comedy which were embarrassing to him, all around him in 1948 were people and events which combined to produce what was, in many respects, baseball's most stupendous season.

The whole of it, in Cleveland, was like a prolonged day at the circus. Ringmaster Veeck was in his glory. Night games were marked by thousand-dollar displays of loud, stadium-shaking, glittering fireworks. Day games (and night games, too) featured clowns like Jackie Price, a smallish fellow who made a business of catching balls while hanging from his feet, standing on his head, and assuming other odd, assorted, contortionistic positions. Two bands paraded around the Stadium, playing jazz, pop tunes, and gay songs from the not-so-smug nineties. There were special nights for players—or things. A fan named Joe Early suggested to Veeck that a night be held for a patron, since players were receiving so many honors. And Veeck, ever quick to grab the sensational, promptly announced "Joe Early Night." Joe became a town hero and, on his night, received presents ranging from an old, spavined horse to quick-dissolving blocks of ice.

To top off this production, the Indians, as related, were always in the thick of the pennant fight. Fans loved the show and good baseball, and they proved it by spinning the turnstiles 2,620,627 times during the regular season. No club in history had attracted so many fans.

If baseball was the main course, the circus show the dessert, then the champagne was delivered when Leroy (Satchel) Paige arrived on the scene, stepping out of legend like an ancient character intent on proving to some bellowing jazzman that Old Man Mose ain't dead!

For years lost to absolute count, there had been a standard headline which guaranteed to send baseball fans, hicktown and bigtown alike, scurrying for ball parks. That headline began, "Satchel Paige to Pitch. . . ." It was the pre-game announcement for the strangest, most colorful and, perhaps, most efficient piece of pitching machinery in history. In years prior to 1948, it was the advance notice of baseball's biggest side-show attraction, its greatest nomad.

In contrast to the cases of Robinson and Doby, the signing of Paige was not connected with pressure movements, nor was it cloaked as a symbol of racial integration. But it was a surprise—to baseball itself, to baseball writers, and to baseball fans. One of those most surprised was this book's author, who visited Veeck's office one day in June.

The writer sank down on a soft, leather-covered long-seat, across from Veeck, and talked about the latest developments in the "Wigwam." Every so often, the writer glanced around to note the chart of Indian minor league farms on the wall to his left, to glimpse, through a window, Cleveland's grayish stone downtown, to be mentally disturbed by the leg stub propped on Veeck's neatly littered desk (Veeck had been injured in World War II), to observe, in a corner, Veeck's wooden leg.

As the conversation drew near to its end, Veeck stated that he was working on a new and interesting idea. "I don't know whether or not I should tell you about it," he said. "Only three men know about it now."

The writer, sensing an eventual scoop in the making, reminded Veeck that he was trustworthy with off-the-record information.

"Well," Veeck said, thoughtfully, "if I hear about it, I'll know who told it." Then, off-hand: "I'm going to sign Satchel Paige!"

The writer laughed. Later, he explained this silly. "I couldn't do anything but laugh. That, for some unknown reason, was my first reaction. It just hadn't crossed my mind that anyone would think of bringing Satch to the majors. You could have kayoed me with a feather. . . ."

Many others laughed, too, when they heard the news. A few became angry at Veeck and ridiculed him for making "a farce out of major league baseball."

The idea to sign Paige was based on the Indians' need for pitching help. Although they were doing well in the pennant race, Boudreau repeatedly had asked Veeck to obtain additional mound strength. One day, Abe Saperstein, owner of basketball's fabulous Harlem Globetrotters and part-time scout for the Indians, listened as Veeck remarked about this pressing need. Saperstein, who had been associated for many years with Negro baseball in general and Paige in particular, suggested that the ancient right-hander be given a chance. Veeck was skeptical, yet he told Saperstein to work on the idea.

Paige was contacted in the Far West, where he was barn-storming with an "all-star" club. He liked the idea, although he once had been the only Negro on record with the opinion that Negroes could not succeed in organized baseball because of the "social angles." He had suggested an all-Negro major league team.

The entire deal was handled as a well-kept secret. Thus, when Satch arrived in Cleveland on July 4, he was able to put over a story which later became a large joke.

Shortly after his arrival by Cadillac sedan, Paige visited League Park, former home grounds of the Indians, where the Cleveland Buckeyes were playing a Negro American League game. He quietly went up to the press box and watched the contest.

Afterward, Wilbur Hayes, general manager of the Buckeyes, saw Paige and inquired, "Satch, what are *you* doing in town?"

Straight-faced, Paige replied, "I came here to see if I could get a job with the Buckeyes."

This was more good fortune than Hayes, who was being pressed to the wall by the lack of good gate receipts, could withstand, especially since, so to speak, it came from the clear blue sky. He joyously announced to friends and associates that Paige wanted to play with the Buckeyes. He visualized Satch as the sure-shot means through which he could lift the Bucks out of the red.

After he learned the truth, however, all he could do was take the general ribbing with good sportsmanship.

On July 5, the author took Paige and a mutual friend, Cleveland Buckeyes pitcher Chet Brewer, down to Cleveland Stadium. He introduced Paige to Rudie Shaeffer, business manager of the Indians. Shaeffer and Paige conferred privately, then we left the park.

The clincher in this chain of events came a day later when Paige "tried out" for the team. With Boudreau, Veeck, and Greenberg watching through critical eyes, Satch ran around the Stadium's greensward to limber up. Then, he put on a startling pitching exhibition.

Boudreau was at bat. Paige went through his elaborate wind-up, and threw. The youthful manager, having his best year at the plate, clouted a few of the pitches for what would have been legitimate hits in a game. Yet, he found out what Paige could do: of fifty pitches made, forty-six were strikes!

"Now," Boudreau said, "I can believe some of the stories they tell about his pitching."

On July 7, the announcement was made.

"INDIANS SIGN SATCHEL PAIGE" was the headline. And a startled fandom was ready to wonder, "What next?"

Paige's arrival on the major league scene caused few reactions stemming primarily from racial prejudice. For one thing, Robinson and Doby had broken the ice. Many objectors were reconciled to the presence of Negro players on major league diamonds. For another, Paige was known to many major leaguers, against whom he had pitched in exhibition games. Paige also had a "way" with people and was great, most humorous, copy. There were many fans (and players) who were curious to learn whether or not this fabulous pitcher could win in the best of competition.

Perhaps the most vehement critic of Paige's advent on the scene was the *Sporting News*. "To bring in a pitching 'rookie' of Paige's age," it said, "casts a reflection on the entire scheme of operation in the major leagues." It should be noted that the objection was based on age, not race.

Writers, many of them cynical, asked Paige if he thought he could win in the big time. The pitcher reminded them that he had faced many big league batters in exhibition games. He admitted that these contests were not similar to big league games, but concluded, "Home plate's the same size!"

The question of his "real age" became Cleveland's hottest topic of discussion. Paige said he was thirty-nine. He told one writer that he had been born on September 18, 1908. He told another writer, a few moments later, that he had been born on July 22, 1909. A news service representative asked Paige's mother, down in Mobile, Alabama, how old her son was. She replied, "Forty-four!"

Trying to prove Paige older than thirty-nine became great sport. Someone pegged his age at forty-seven, another at forty-one, and still another at fifty. There was one fan who estimated that Paige was at least sixty-five because, the fan said, he had watched Satch pitch a game back in 1916!

A writer asked Paige when he had begun his career. Satch said 1927, with the Chattanooga Black Lookouts. Many readers scoffed at this. Why, it seemed as though they had been reading about Paige all their lives. That he had been pitching only since 1927 was preposterous.

The Cleveland News, then running a feature series on the pitcher, reported that Paige would pay anyone five hundred dollars who could prove that he had pitched a game of baseball prior to 1927.

A Cleveland fan named Carl Goerz produced a photostatic copy of a boxscore from the Memphis *Commercial Appeal* of May 17, 1926. It listed Paige as the pitcher for the Black Lookouts in a game with the Memphis Red Sox. Confronted with the boxscore, Paige said, "I must have slept a year."

He agreed, however, to put the question to Alex Herman, owner of the Lookouts in 1926. Herman said he had signed Paige in April of 1926 and that Satch had helped his team win the first-half pennant. (It was common practice in Negro ball to divide the season into halves. The winner of the first half played the second-half winner to determine the league champion.)

Goerz was paid the five hundred dollars.

"How much did that photostat cost you?" Satch asked Goerz.

"Two dollars," Goerz replied.

Satch considered the figure, then commented, "Five hundred for two! Maybe I ought to quit pitching and look for suckers like me!"

Subsequently, it was pretty well established that Paige actually had begun his career in 1924, as a Birmingham semi-pro.

The Cleveland Indians and St. Louis Browns played a game at Cleveland on July 9, attended by a crowd of 34,780 fans. By the fifth inning, the Browns had racked up a 4 to 1 lead on starting pitcher Bob Lemon. In the last half of the inning, Boudreau replaced Lemon with a pinch hitter. Then, he gave an underhanded signal and Paige slowly arose from his seat on the bullpen bench.

Thus, Satch began his first major league appearance. He shuffled moundward, his spindly legs moving above liver-flat feet which appeared to be the biggest anyone had ever seen. (They were size 14!) Fans laughed as the public address man said, "SATCHEL . . . LEROY . . . PAIGE. . . ."

Paige settled himself on the mound, surveyed the situation. His windup was a baffling combination of legs, arms, and the aforementioned large feet. If he was nervous at all, he did not show it. He seemed nonchalant.

Jim Hegan was Paige's catcher. Bill McGowan was the plate umpire. Satch was slow and deliberate. McGowan walked out to the mound and told him to take Hegan's signals with one foot on the rubber, rather than from a position on the decline behind it. Satch nodded and followed instructions. He pitched two innings, allowing a hit for each inning, and no runs.

In the dressing room after the game, he remarked, "They sure carry you fast up here!"

"You looked very serious out there on the mound, Satch," a writer commented.

"I'm always serious when I pitch!" Satch said.

Frank Duncan, the Negro catcher, was to corroborate Satch's statement. "Paige," Duncan said, "always was a student of the game, much more than the average player. His life's ambition was to be a success in the game.

"Satch never was out of condition. Fact is, he always was in wonderful condition. He was always busy on the ball field, playing 'pepper ball,' bending down to take three-quarter hops, taking infield practice. That's why he was always warm. He could go into a game, throw eight warm-up pitches and be ready. Despite what some have said, Satch was never lazy. He was always doing something— always keeping his body loose."

Paige had very little privacy in Cleveland. As early as six any morning, he would be called by writers, hucksters, promotion men, product pushers, plain fans, and a myriad lot of other humanity. It was little publicized, but he gave to all of them the cordial treatment expected of any gentleman but not always forthcoming from a diamond dear.

On the road, Satch roomed with Doby. They represented a contrast: Satch was a fabulous name, he was confident, and he was a proven success, regardless of the record he was to make during the twilight of his career in the majors. Doby was young, ambitious, and was fighting, as much as his nature allowed, for a place in the sun. They called each other "Roomie." Sometimes, in the manner of college kids, Satch called Larry his "old lady." But they were never buddy-buddy.

Once Satch asked Larry why most major leaguers did not wear hats. The young player stung the veteran when he replied, "Do as we major leaguers do; don't ask questions!"

That kind of ribbing was new to the moundmaster from the far-away barnstorming hills. Another time Larry told a white writer that Satch was carrying a gun, indicating that he (Doby) was afraid to room with him. It was a jest, but by neglecting to tell the writer that Satch, a collector of antiques, had picked up an ancient firearm, Doby had implied that Satch was a sort of Stepin Fetchit. Satch didn't like it—rightly.

In completing their word pictures of Paige for eager-reading fans, writers revealed that Satch owned a Cadillac car, an airplane, a jeep, and a big truck; that he collected the aforementioned antiques and old firearms; that he was a camera fiend and collector of hot jazz records; that he could sing in his version of English and Spanish; and that he could play the harmonica and guitar.

"Satch," a baseball man was to say, "can intelligently discuss anything from engineering to mule-skinning."

Paige turned virtually every fact about himself into good humor. "When I first went to Cuba," he recalled often, "I didn't understand the language. Someone told me 'higado' meant liver. I ordered liver three times a day for 30 days."

He claimed that the hot and greasy food at many of his barnstorming stops caused him to have stomach trouble. That he had this trouble was proven every few minutes when he belched unashamedly.

Giving vital statistics on himself, Satch said, "When I signed with Herman's team, I was six-foot, three and one-half inches tall and weighed 140 pounds. If I stood sideways, you could hardly see me. Now, I weigh nearly 180 pounds. I've gained 40 pounds in 22 (sic) years of pitching. If I keep it up, I'll die a fat old man."

Charting his pre-major league career was a difficult project. Negro league records were skimpy and not even Paige knew how many exhibition games he had participated in over the years. He said he could remember pitching "regularly" for at least thirty teams. And he said he got his start back in Mobile by knocking cans off tree stumps with thrown rocks, adding, "I was born with control."

In 1927 and 1928, he played with the Birmingham Black Barons. He was a member of the Baltimore Black Sox in 1929. Chicago's American Giants held him briefly in 1930 and, the next year, he toiled for a while with a Nashville, Tennessee, club which played out of Cleveland, Ohio. (This sort of arrangement was commonplace in Negro ball.) The team disbanded in August and Satch joined the Pittsburgh Crawfords, a truly great team owned by Gus Greenlee, where he remained until 1933.

Then Satch speeded up the moving-along business. He was given permission to go to Bismarck, North Dakota, where he was the main attraction for a club sponsored by Neil Churchill, an auto distributor and mayor of the town. Churchill wanted the "best doggone ball team" in the Dakota territory. Paige and his mates gave it to him. With Satch in one stretch working twenty-nine games in thirty days, this club won one hundred games while losing only one during its season. Then Satch and the Bismarck outfit entered the Wichita tournament. Satch and Chet Brewer won the National Semi-pro Championship for Bismarck. Paige called this team, which beat Earle (son of Connie) Mack's all-stars, the best he had ever known.

In 1934, Satch pitched with the "original" House of David club in the Denver *Post* tournament. There is no record, however, of his wearing a beard. Grover Cleveland Alexander managed the club. Satch hurled three games in five days, then got off this observation:

"I sure get laughs when I see in papers where some major league pitcher says he gets a sore arm because he over-worked and he pitches every four days. Man, that'd be just a vacation for me. I had sore arms. Sure enough. But, I just walks around and at night pours hot water on it and it gets well."

The year 1934 was one of frequent movement for Satch. For example, prior to the Denver tournament, he had pitched his first no-hitter against the Homestead Grays. Then, he traveled one thousand miles by car, donned a uniform, and hurled in the annual East-West game at Chicago, yielding the opposition's first hit in the ninth inning, finally winning 1 to 0 in extra innings.

Publisher S. Emory Thomason of the Chicago *Times* was so deeply impressed by the feat that he called Satch "Black Matty," a comparison to Christy Mathewson of all-time major league fame. And major league scouts who had watched Satch work sighed the old lament, "If he were only white. . . ."

Next, Paige rejoined the Crawfords and pitched a 1-all tie game before thirty thousand fans at Yankee Stadium. It was the bottom half of a four-team doubleheader. Also in 1934, Satch beat Dizzy Dean (then in his prime) and an all-star aggregation 1 to 0 in thirteen innings.

"If Satch and I were pitching on the same team," Dean said later, "we'd cinch the pennant by July 4 and go fishing until World Series time."

In California, Satch pitched against major leaguers Babe Herman, Hack Wilson (the National League's champion home-run hitter), Lou Gehrig (the noted Yankee), Pepper Martin, Johnny Mize, Charley Gehringer, and the Yankee-clipper-to-be, Joe DiMaggio. At that time, DiMaggio was literally burning up the Pacific Coast League. After hitting safely off Paige's pitching, Joe was quoted as saying, "Now, I know I'll hit in the majors—I finally (once in five tries) got a scratch single off Satchel Paige."

Satch heard the "call of the wild" in 1937. It came from a slick, Latin gentleman who approached him while he was in spring training with the Crawfords at New Orleans. Satch listened to the lure of gold on them thar pitching mounds of Ciudad Trujillo, decided to go "prospectin' with my pitchin'." Greenlee almost wept when he heard that Paige was leaving his team. He was fit to be tied when he found out that Satch had "stolen" eight of his best players!

This club won a championship for Ciudad Trujillo, then returned to the United States in time to win in another Denver *Post* tournament. Paige returned to the Dominican Republic in 1938, but finished the season in Mexico.

During these days, Satch was strictly a fast-ball man. It was said that Bobo Newsom, himself the major leagues' most active nomad, introduced Satch to the curve ball in California.

"All a catcher has to know," Paige would boast in the pre-curve days, "is when I'm throwing my bee ball and when I'm throwing my jump ball. I throw both with the same overhead motion, only the bee ball goes off my fingers on the smooth hide and rides level and the jump ball goes off the seams and jumps four to six inches."

Tragedy, in the form of a sore arm, struck Paige in 1940. The best account of it, of its effect, of how Satch came out of it, was related by John I. Johnson, sports editor of the Kansas City *Call.*

"The great one," Johnson recalled, "owned a wing that was as dead as a new bride's biscuits in 1940. Satch's great flipper just wouldn't work no more. It was at that time that J. L. Wilkerson, owner of the Monarchs, toyed with the idea of employing Satch, who was nursing the once-poisonous paw in pathetic pity, not with the idea that the great one could put anything over on a batter, but for the name that meant so much to thousands of fans who had heard of the fabulous Satchel Paige.

"Never being one to pass up a good attraction, Wilkerson decided to form a team and sent it to the hinterland under the banner of Satchel Paige and his All-Stars. That, mused Wilkerson, would give the fans something to think about and pay for.

"But, meanwhile, the astute club owner turned to his veteran trainer, Frank (Jewbaby) Floyd, who had been conditioning Monarch players from almost the first time the squad took to the field.

" 'Say, Jewbaby,' said Wilkerson, 'do you think you can work some of your magic on the wing of Satchel?'

"Jewbaby, who had combined his natural healing hand with a course in chiropractics . . . furrowed his lean brow, grinned, and said he thought he could.

"Satchel told Jewbaby all—told how he had been burning over the ball in Puerto Rico and elsewhere, how he had been 'poisoned by that water' they drank in South America and worsened by that hot, greasy food they served there, and how his arm just suddenly went dead."

Jewbaby, Johnson continued, found cold deep in Satch's arm. But he worked diligently. Success came slowly and hard.

" 'Say, Doc, when am I going to be able to throw my over-arm stuff?' Satch asked one day in 1942. 'I'm getting tired of pitching these off-side flings.'

" 'You go down to the bullpen and pitch until you get real hot and then come back,' said Jewbaby, 'and I think you can get what you want.' "

Satch did as he was told, Johnson stated. "He threw and threw and threw. The perspiration was running down his face and his shirt was wringing wet when he returned to the trainer.

" 'Here I am,' said Satchel, 'can I throw over-hand now?' "

" 'Sure, get out on the mound and throw,' said Jewbaby."

" 'You really mean it?' Satch asked, unbelievingly."

" 'Sure, Just throw that ball as hard as you ever did,' Jewbaby said."

"Satchel, skeptically, wound up, hesitated, and let go an over-arm throw. He grinned, stuck out his glove in eagerness for the catcher to return the ball. From that day on, Satchel had his stuff back."

Proof of Jewbaby's artistry was Satch's effectiveness against Dizzy Dean's All-Stars, a group of major leaguers in service, at Chicago's Wrigley Field on May 24, 1942.

More than twenty-nine thousand fans turned out for the game. Paige was pitching for the Monarchs. Dean's team included Zeke Bonura, the one-time White Sox home-run hitter; Cecil Travis, spray-hitting star of the Washington Senators; Heinie Manush, Washington and Detroit; George Archie, St. Louis Browns; and Ken Silvestri, New York Yankees. Satch, in a six-inning stint, let them down with two scratch singles.

Both hits came in the third inning. Joe Gallagher beat out a roller to third and Johnny Grodzicki got credit for a hit on a ball that Satch fielded. The first baseman should have handled the pellet, but failed to cover in time. Meanwhile, the second baseman was sleeping, too—he failed to cover first. As a result of this fielding lapse, the All-Stars scored an unearned run (Gallagher's).

The Monarchs scored three times.

Dean added to his appraisal of Paige. "I have pitched 31 games against that Satchel Paige," he said, " and that guy really has something. If he pitched in the majors, he'd be worth $1,000,000. He's still a great pitcher (1942), but was he some boy a few years ago, wowie!"

Paige continued with the Monarchs through 1947. At times, he hurled for that club on Sunday and pitched other games with all-star outfits during the week. After the 1947 season, Wilkerson, whose sight had been impaired in an auto accident, sold his interest in the team, but continued to handle Satch. With Wilkerson's son at the helm, Paige took to barnstorming in 1948 with his aforementioned team. He was in Bremerton, Washington, when he heard the call to Cleveland.

Without a doubt, Paige was the supreme character of baseball before he joined the Tribe. Many of his antics and feats would have been impossible in the majors—like, for instance, the calling in of outfielders and infielders while he struck out sides. This, Satch hastened to explain, was a bit of showboating reserved for special occasions. "I never pulled any of that stuff in serious games," he said.

Satch pitched the year around, in all climates, under a wide variety of conditions. He was one of the first to hurl night games— under illumination furnished by portable generators mounted on a Wilkerson-invented contraption. Pitching, to him, was a full-time career. And he made it pay off.

Probably the best description of the conditions under which Paige worked, before he moved into the Cadillac class, was supplied by Bunny Downs, one-time bus driver for the barnstorming Cincinnati Clowns.

"Shucking corn, hoeing potatoes, picking cotton," said Bunny, "ain't no tougher than this business. No, sir. For a real, hard-working business, day in and day out, you gotta take this here whatchacallit, tourist baseball."

While major league pitchers, in many instances, kept card files indicating strengths and weaknesses of batters, on numerous occasions Paige faced strange batters. He worked out a formula for beating them.

"In a tight one, I give 'em my No. 1 pitch, the fast ball," he said. "That's my best weapon. Old Bill Gatewood, a great pitcher at Mobile, told me once that a good fast ball pitcher didn't have to have anything else that was real good. Just enough so the hitters knew he had more'n one gun to shoot. Make 'em look for more stuff and they'll miss the fast ball more."

Another time, when asked how many games he had pitched during his career, Paige said, "I never kept track of them. Maybe it's just as well. Nobody would believe the total anyway." On another occasion, he said he had pitched 134 games (twenty less than a full major league season) in one year and had hurled a "hatful" of no-hitters. His strikeout record for a single game, he said, was twenty-one.

As related the record books are skimpy. More accurately, there are no records on the career performances of Satch and his diamond generation in Negro ball. Yet, it is logical to assume that Paige worked in upwards of twenty-five hundred games. By major league standards, he probably would have earned at least fifteen hundred decisions. The record for major league victories is 511, held by Denton T. (Cy) Young.

One day in Cleveland, a fellow moundsman asked Paige, "So, you throw the slider, too, eh, Satch?"

"Is that what you call it?" Satch inquired. "I've been throwing it for 20 years!"

Paige wasted no time proving that he would be of assistance to the Indians in their pennant fight. He was of greater assistance as they racked up their attendance record. On July 14, he faced the Dodgers at Cleveland in the aforementioned exhibition and pitched four scoreless innings. He struck out the side once. During his first month, he hurled 26 2/ 3 innings of relief and allowed twenty-three hits, struck out sixteen batters, walked ten, and gave up seven earned runs.

He drew 201,829 fans to the first three games in which he was an advertised performer. A record night throng of 78,383 saw him pitch against the White Sox at Cleveland; 72,434 returned to see him work against the Senators; and 51,013 jammed Comiskey Park to see him in another go with the Sox. Ten thousand were turned away that night. The turnstiles broke down, in fact, as eager fans stormed the park. A mere rumor that he would pitch in Detroit sent some forty thousand fans scurrying for Briggs Stadium.

August was Paige's best month. He shut out the White Sox 5 to 0 on five hits at Chicago, on the thirteenth, then white-washed them, 1 to 0, on three hits at Cleveland one week later. He went the distance against the Senators, winning 1 to 0, on August 30. In that game, he was twice a victim.

Once, umpire Bill Summers saw him wiggle the fingers of his gloved hand before making a pitch with men on base and promptly called a balk. Summers explained that Paige's finger-wiggling was capable of deceiving base runners, to which Paige said, "I thought it was my job to deceive them—if I could."

And, a Washington batter, unable to hit Satch's stuff, called the elongated Negro "a black bastard." Paige felt the full sting of the epithet, made a slight move toward the player, but had the presence of mind to keep the peace. It was one of the few times the race problem came up with Paige as its target.

September wasn't his month, mainly because the Indians were making their furious push for the pennant and Boudreau entrusted his regular starters with most of the work. As related, the Indians won in a play-off.

Satch's record was six games won and one lost. He had saved others. His earned run mark of 2.47 was second best among Tribe hurlers. Everyone agreed that his contribution was necessary to the winning of Cleveland's first pennant in twenty-eight years.

The Indians themselves recognized the value of Satch's contribution by voting him a full share of the World Series money. Otherwise, the Series proved anticlimactic for him.

"It's my life ambition to pitch in the Series," Paige said. "And, Mr. Veeck says it's his ambition to see me out there on the mound. The Series is my dream."

But he only got a little taste. With a record crowd of 86,288 on hand at Cleveland, Paige relieved Feller on October 9. The Braves were running away with the game. Paige went in, pitched to two men, got them out, and was replaced by a pinch hitter.

Despite this bit role, Satch said, "It was a great thrill to get in there."

After the Series, he went on an exhibition tour. Los Angeles observed "Satchel Paige Day" on October 24. Satch was given a special Helms Award honoring him as an outstanding athlete, then he pitched three innings against Bearden's all-star team.

Satch had won over virtually all of his critics. The only "out" was the fact that after years and years of doing just about what he pleased, he found it difficult to follow major league schedules. He was late for the first Sunday home game after he joined the club. In New York, he failed to go to the park because, he said, "I knew it was going to rain. My corns hurt." It rained, but the Indians arranged an early getaway. Satch missed the train and was fined fifty dollars.

Gossipmongers invented wild tales about his personal activities. Some claimed he was an extreme adventurer with the women. Others said he drank to excess. The truth was: Satch was frequently in his hotel room when someone reported that he was seen elsewhere at a late hour with a girl. He was never intoxicated, not even during the post-season party when virtually everyone got giggly and two Indians got mad and threw fists.

And almost all of his publicity suggested that here was a Stepin Fetchit counterpart. Nothing was ever further from the truth. Satch had legends to prove that he'd never been lazy.

Nor was he stupid. Bill McKechnie was to say, "Satch would make a good businessman. He probably hasn't had much education, but he is very smart. People would be surprised to learn how much he knows about this country and other parts of the World." It was that smartness which forced him to accept gags about his age, laughs about his feet, and the wild tales told about him. A man with a keen sense of showmanship, Satch never squawked, not even when his name was misspelled, as it was more than once.

He was around in 1949, but did not enjoy the same sparkling success. With a change in administration, he was let out in 1950. The next year, he joined Veeck with the St. Louis Browns. In 1952, he again was mesmerizing American League hitters. "If my legs hold out," he said that year, "I can stay up here another 10 years. Man, I'm a hundred years old and I can still strike these guys out."

It was his 1952 record—twelve wins against ten losses, including several superlative efforts—which caused writers to launch a campaign for Satch's inclusion among all-time stars honored in the Hall of Fame at Cooperstown. The movement had been started in 1950, when Joe Williams, sports columnist of the New York *World-Telegram*, suggested that Satch be made a "write-in" candidate for the highest honor in baseball. The Associated Press followed Williams's lead in 1952. Then, in its November issue, same year, *Sport* magazine provided the biggest boost in an article entitled, "Let's Get Old Satch into the Hall of Fame!"

Ed Fitzgerald, author of the article and editor of the magazine, wrote, "Although organized baseball didn't get a first look at his pitching magic until 25 years too late, the venerable Leroy Robert Paige has proved he belongs in Cooperstown."

But, he advised readers, "If you believe (he) belongs in Baseball's Hall of Fame, you had better start writing to your favorite sports columnist about it right now. Satchel will be eligible for election to the Hall the year after he retires as an active player, but he won't have a Chinaman's chance of making it if you don't turn on the heat and turn it on good. . . .

"The men who hold in their hands the power to open or close the Cooperstown door to Satch are all those members of the Baseball Writers Association of America who will have held their memberships for ten years when it comes time to vote on Paige's qualifications. . . .

"The thing is, it isn't Satchel's fault he was born 25 years too soon to fully exploit his rare talents. He has been a towering figure in the mythology of the game for a couple of decades, and if the words Hall of Fame can be taken at their true worth, he should not be excluded from admission merely because the color of his skin kept him out of the major leagues until he was—take your pick—39 or 42 or 46 years old. If Satchel Paige isn't a famous baseball figure, then Babe Ruth was an unknown."

7

CAMPY

Although the Negro leagues—National in the East; American in the West and South—had served, and were to serve for some time, as primary showcases of prospective colored major leaguers, the foundation of baseball's new democracy was eventually to be laid in the national association of minor leagues. This was, of course, logical, fortunate, and imperative.

The minors were natural feeders of the majors. If the program was to remain wholly democratic, then Negroes had to be channeled the same routes as other youngsters. And this channeling was the easiest method of assuring democracy as an easy-flowing thing at the major league level.

White boys and Negro boys who played against each other in the minors, at ages that left their minds pliable, were likely to accept each other, to learn each other's ways, to gain respect for each other, to make camaraderie. Fans, club owners, everyone connected with baseball would be freer and easier with Negro athletes climbing the ladder like other boys instead of jumping in from Negro clubs outside the structure of organized ball.

The first Negro to reach the majors following a fairly extensive minor league apprenticeship was Roy Campanella, the alert, rugged, rotund, hard-hitting, defensively superb catcher who joined the Dodgers in July, 1948. His career in organized ball began at Nashua,

New Hampshire, in 1946, gained momentum at Montreal in 1947, and reached its goal in the final promotion at St. Paul.

Branch Rickey first offered Campanella a chance in the Dodger organization on October 17, 1945, six days before Robinson's signing was announced. But Campanella turned it down!

As Roy later explained, "Mr. Rickey asked me in and asked me if I would like to play for him. I thought he meant for the Brown Dodgers, a new colored team I had heard about. I said, 'No.' I told him that I liked it where I was, with the Elite Giants. He said that he was sorry."

His thinking in the matter was characteristic. He was a big star with the Baltimore Elite Giants. In the winter, he added to his three-thousand-dollar summer salary by playing Latin league ball. It was rugged, sure, but Roy wasn't one to shun work. Once he had caught four games in a single day. Most important: the Elite Giants represented a going concern. He could count on getting the three grand, or more, from them. But Roy had no assurance—in fact, he doubted—that the Brown Dodgers would be successful.

Roy tricked himself in assuming that Rickey wanted him for the Brown Dodgers. He was not told as much. Actually, Rickey did want to sign him for the Dodgers, but after Roy answered in the negative, Rickey let the idea drop for the moment. As Roy left his office, however, Rickey said, "Do me a favor. Don't sign with anybody until you hear from me."

A few days later, Roy got into a card game with Jackie Robinson at a Harlem hotel. Jackie said he'd heard about Roy's meeting with Rickey. Roy admitted the meeting, told Jackie what had happened, and explained why he hadn't signed with the Brown Dodgers.

"Did Mr. Rickey tell you that he wanted you for the Brown Dodgers?" Jackie asked.

For the first time, Roy realized that Rickey hadn't said anything about that team. "No," Roy replied, "he didn't mention them. He didn't mention signing with anybody in particular. But, I told him I wasn't interested in signing with no Brown Dodgers."

Jackie then dropped his big surprise, pledging Roy to secrecy.

"I'm going to play for Montreal," Jackie said.

Startled, puzzled, Roy inquired, "What do you mean, Montreal?"

Jackie explained.

"Well, I'll be darned," Roy ejaculated. "What a dumb boy I am."

Roy had contracted to play winter ball in Venezuela. Before he left the United States, however, he wrote Rickey a letter, informing him of his address in South America. In March, Roy received a telegram from Rickey, saying, "Please report Brooklyn Office by March 10. Very important." This time, there were no mistakes, no jumping to conclusions, no negative answers. Roy had just about forgotten the Brown Dodgers.

After first attempting to place him with their farm club at Danville, Illinois, of the Three-Eye League, where they were turned down, the Dodgers finally assigned Campanella and a strapping-big, fast-ball hurler named Don Newcombe to Nashua. Before the year was out Roy had belted himself into the chicken business, had managed the Nashua Dodgers, and had worked as a scout for the Brooklyn Dodgers!

This is how Roy went into the chicken business: In every baseball town, there is a businessman-fan who likes to reward spectacular feats. This fan at Nashua was Jack Fallgren, a poultry farmer, who offered one hundred chickens for every home run hit for the local team. By slugging thirteen homers during the season, Roy collected thirteen hundred chickens. He sent them home to Philadelphia. Later, when Fallgren decided to quit farming, Roy bought his stock, thirty-two hundred chickens, and, with his folks, was in business.

Roy became acting team manager one night when the regular manager and first baseman, Walt Alston, lost an argument with an umpire. Alston had prepared for such an eventuality soon after he became aware of Roy's extensive knowledge of the game and his leadership qualities. "If I'm ever thrown out of a game," Alston had said to Campanella, "I want you to run things." The opportunity came in a game between the Nashua Dodgers and Lawrence (Massachusetts) Millionaires.

The Dodgers were three runs behind (in the sixth inning) when Roy "took over." They scored once before the inning ended. In the seventh, with a man on base, the pitcher was due to bat. Deciding to use a pinch hitter, Roy called on Newcombe, who was quite some shucks with the big stick. Newcombe responded by hitting a score-tying homer. Nashua went on to win, 7 to 5.

The scouting job resulted from a deal between Rickey and Campanella. When Rickey had decided to send Roy to Nashua, he faced the problem of salary. The catcher was being paid, as reported, three thousand dollars to play for the Elite Giants and was adding to this income in Latin circuits. The New England League maximum, however, was less than two hundred dollars a month. To skirt this maximum, thus allowing Campanella his accustomed pay, Rickey used the old college subsidization play—a job that wasn't exactly a job. A sop job, in other words. Something to keep the money rolling in.

After the season, Rickey summoned Campanella to the Brooklyn office.

"I suppose you've been wondering what we have in mind for you in the way of a job," Rickey said.

Campanella admitted that he had been wondering about it.

"I want you to scout the Negro world series for me," Rickey explained. "I want a report on any boy you consider a major league prospect."

The catcher, just finished with a season in Class-B, scouted the Kansas City Monarchs and Newark Eagles, then turned in a voluminous report. The most impressive players, he said, were Larry

Doby, the Newark second baseman; Monte Irvin, a Newark outfielder; and Earl Taborn, Kansas City catcher.

As related, Doby was purchased by Cleveland, with an assist by Rickey, who did not deal for Larry when he learned of Veeck's interest in him. Irvin subsequently was obtained by the New York Giants. Taborn was signed by the Chicago Cubs organization, but bowed out of their system following a short term at Springfield, Massachusetts, which had become an International League Club.

Campanella had proved conclusively that he was entitled to a promotion. Appearing in 113 Nashua games, he had batted .290. His all-around catching finesse was unquestioned. A fact that was vitally important to the future, he had helped Newcombe post a 14-4 record and 2.21 earned run average. Campanella and Newcombe, in fact, had carried Nashua to a regular-season second-place finish, then to play-off victory over the pennant-winning Lynn (Massachusetts) Red Sox. Campanella was named Most Valuable Player in the league.

The reward for these accomplishments was promotion to Montreal.

The transition, in 1947, from Class-B to Triple-A shaved seventeen points off Campanella's batting average. But, giving a hint of the rugged feats he was to perform, he appeared in 135 games. He fielded .988. And, again, he hit thirteen homers.

Brooklyn, the next stop? Well, maybe yes; maybe no.

The question of whether Campanella would be promoted to the majors arose because, first, the Dodgers already had a fine No. 1 receiver in Bruce Edwards; a promising, strong-armed player named Gil Hodges; and a steadying oldster, Bobby Bragan (who was subsequently named to manage the Fort Worth Cats). Second, there was some doubt that Campanella could hit major league pitching. But, most important, Rickey had another idea: he wanted Roy to break the color line in the American Association!

While Rickey was fomenting this idea, in 1948 spring training at Ciudad Trujillo in the Dominican Republic, Leo Durocher, who had returned from suspension, was brewing one of his own: he wanted to make a first baseman out of Hodges and replace him with Campanella.

When Durocher was informed of Rickey's plan, he objected to it in these certain terms: "I'm thinking of my club, not St. Paul." Rickey countered that he had Edwards and Hodges. Durocher informed Rickey that Edwards had a sore arm. "Oh, that's nothing," Rickey said. "A little soreness. His arm will be all right." Durocher said he wasn't so sure about that. "He (Edwards) says it hurts him real bad. Besides, Campanella is better. Sukey (Clyde Sukeforth) says he's the best catcher in camp. And, Hodges can be the best first baseman in a matter of days."

Durocher might well have been arguing with an umpire. He lost, although Rickey promised him that Campanella could be recalled in mid-season, if the Dodgers needed him.

But Campanella did not go to St. Paul immediately. He joined the Dodgers as an outfielder! This move resulted from Rickey's thinking along these lines: Campanella was due a promotion. It was expected. But he wanted him to open up the American Association to Negroes. To gain an excuse for sending him back to the minors, Roy would be tried as an outfielder with the Dodgers. Naturally, he would fail. Thus, back to the bushes.

All this was explained, in confusing detail, to Campanella. And so it was that he began the 1948 season as a Dodger.

It happened that the Dodgers went badly in their early games. Roy warmed the bench. Durocher chafed at the bit on the Campanella question. Once, in desperation, he bypassed his forced agreement with Rickey and sent Roy in to catch. The next day, on orders, Campanella was on the bench. Eventually, in the middle of May, he left for St. Paul.

"There had never been a colored player in the American Association before," Campanella was to say, "and Mr. Rickey wanted me to break the line. He asked me to. He didn't tell me. He gave me a chance to play big league ball. I went. I didn't know for how long."

His sensational play decided that. At first, American Association officials were reluctant to use Negro players. Top brass said the inclusion of Negroes would "wreck the league." But the "problem" became no problem at all after Campy displayed his ability behind the plate and hit Association hurlers with abandon. Again under the management of Walt Alston, who had been promoted from Nashua, Campanella belted eight home runs in his first seven games at St. Paul. In thirty-five games, his total was another thirteen. His batting average was .325.

On the night of June 30, at Toledo, Alston had news for Campanella: "They want you back in Brooklyn right away," he said.

The catcher frowned, surprising Alston. It wasn't that he didn't want to join the Dodgers; his wife, Ruthe, had just given birth to Roy, Jr., in St. Paul. The question of her condition for travel was solved when a doctor said it was okay for her to fly. She was so elated over the good news she probably would have gone had the doctor said no.

Campy joined the Dodgers while Durocher was composing a line-up for the July 2 night game with the Giants. With the National League cellar dangerously close, the Dodgers, knowing of Campy's St. Paul feats, welcomed him with open arms or, to be more accurate about this thing between men, hearty handshakes. Durocher ordered: "Get dressed; you're catching tonight!"

The game was played at Ebbets Field. Campanella hit two singles and a double that night. But the Dodgers lost another one.

The future was brighter, however. Durocher made an epic move, shifting Edwards to third and Hodges to first. And, Campanella continued his hitting binge. In twelve official at bats, he hit safely nine times, including two homers. The Dodgers got hot, winning nine of eleven games.

The surge carried them to first place. But, in a series with the Giants, then managed by Durocher, who had been canned in a surprising Dodger move and hired by New York in one that topped it, the Dodgers were slugged down to second place. They finished third.

Withal, Campanella had made it. Although his batting tailed off to .258, he caught eighty-three games, fielded .981, and led the league in double plays with twelve. He was especially impressive in his handling of pitchers.

Once, he explained his technique: "Take fellows like Ralph Branca and Rex Barney," he said. "When they get in trouble, they want to start working faster. They snatch that ball when I throw it back to them and they can't wait to fire the next pitch. That's when I start kicking a little dirt around the plate to slow things down. I wait a while before I throw the ball back, and sometimes I go out to talk to the pitcher."

Although he began catching professionally at the age of fifteen, this bit of pro activity washing him out of sports at Germantown High School in Philadelphia, Campanella observed as a major leaguer, "There's plenty to learn about this game." From Sisler, for instance, he learned to improve his batting. By observation, from a distance, he learned to improve his catching during spring training of 1949.

"We went to St. Petersburg to play the Yankees and Bill Dickey (the one-time Yankee great) was showing Yogi Berra how to throw," Campanella was to relate, "how to get the ball away from him in a hurry.

"They were standing so far away from me that I couldn't hear what Dickey was saying. But, I didn't have to hear: he was showing Berra how to pick the ball out of his glove and throw from here" (pegging off the right ear) "instead of away back from here. The first thing I knew, I was doing just like he was telling Berra to do."

In 1949, the Dodgers won the National League pennant again and Campanella became "the king of catchers." His batting average jumped to .287 (.304 days, .252 nights). He appeared in 130 games. He hit twenty-two home runs, drove in eighty-two runs, caught most of the annual All-Star Game, and was named catcher on the *Sporting News*'s All-Star major league team. (As bright as had been his star, however, Jackie Robinson's was brighter. Having the best year in his major league career, Jackie hit .342 to lead the National League, stole thirty-seven bases, and was named the senior circuit's Most Valuable Player.)

In the World Series, against the Yankees, to whom the Dodgers lost again (!), Campanella won the undying admiration of baseball men. With cat-quick movements and an unerring arm, he picked two "old pros," Tommy Henrich and Phil Rizzuto, off bases.

Startled, Rizzuto said, "That's the first time I ever was picked off third by a catcher. What an arm that guy has!"

Campanella's all-around alertness won the praise of Joe DiMaggio. A one-time catching great, Mickey Cochrane, marveled at his finesse. Aspirant receivers had a new "ideel," a guy filled with smartness and gifted with the inborn qualities of a leader, a solid stick man, durability personified.

And he liked the work.

"I can't understand why major leaguers complain about doubleheaders," Campanella said. "At the most, two games a day, you travel first class and you stay at the best places. I'll catch 154 games, if they'll let me."

Campy's 1950 season was consistent with his performance the year before. He continued as an artist with the mask and mattress, he played in 126 games, hit 31 homers, drove in 89 runs, stole a base, and batted .281. It was a prelude to his greatest year—perhaps the best season ever enjoyed by a catcher—1951.

Manager Dressen, in retrospect, might be of a mind to attribute Campy's great '51 season to a diet, but it is to be doubted that the catcher would agree. Dressen, having noted the star's tendency to put on weight quickly when inactive, came up with the diet after Roy's right thumb had been injured during spring training. The daily recommendations in the "Mayo Two Week's Diet" for Campy's eating during the period of convalescence were particularly heavy in grapefruit and eggs. Campy groaned after he read them and asked of Dressen, "On what day do I begin cackling like a hen?"

Whatever the reason for his outstanding success, the season was one in which guts and ability triumphed over pain. Even before he suffered the thumb injury, a mishap at home during the off-season had just about scared him and the Brooklyn front office out of their wits. Campy was lighting the pilot to a water heater one night when the thing exploded, searing his face and blistering the corneas of his eyes. There was much relief all around when a doctor announced that it wasn't as bad as it sounded, that a solution would dissolve the blisters, that his eyesight would be unimpaired.

During the regular season, Campy suffered assorted injuries. In a game with the Cubs, his left hand was cut and bruised by Eddie Miksis as he (Campanella) slid into second base; pitcher Turk Lown, also of the Cubs, beaned him, the ball striking below the protective helmet he wore; Whitey Lockman of the Giants crashed into him, jolting loose calcium chips in his left elbow (Campy said Lockman hit him harder than anyone else ever had "in a ball game"); and he pulled a thigh muscle at the fag end of the season—an injury which might have cost the Dodgers a victory in the play-off series with the Giants, although Bobby Thomson's homer probably was ordained in heaven.

Injuries notwithstanding, this is what the man did: he hit .325, played in 143 games (!), clouted 33 homers, and drove home 108 runs. His slugging percentage was .590. Demonstrating baseball's best throwing arm, he cut down thirty of forty-five base runners who had larceny in mind, an efficiency statistic which worked out to reveal that he was twice as good in that department as other catchers. His thirty-three homers drove in sixty-five runs, the same number first baseman Gil Hodges batted in with forty round-trippers.

There wasn't a month of the season in which Campy didn't contribute a fancy feat. On May 25, he hit safely four times in four trips against Boston. On June 14, at St. Louis, he picked two men off base in one inning! On July 27, he hit his seventh homer in eight games, breaking a tie in the ninth inning to drive home three runs and create a 12 to 9 victory. On August 12, he hit safely three times, twice for the limit, driving in five runs. On September 23, his second day of play following the beaning, he went 4 for 4, including a homer. The Dodgers won, as they did most days when Campy was hot. Besides, he stretched his string of innings in which he had caught National League pitchers in the All-Star Game to twenty-nine.

A twenty-four-man committee of the Baseball Writers Association selected him as the National League's Most Valuable Player. He polled 143 votes to 191 for Stan Musial, 166 for Monte Irvin, and 153 for Sal Maglie. Jackie Robinson polled 92.

Notified of the honor while in Texas on a barnstorming tour, Campy expressed surprise, remarking that he had thought Irvin would be named Most Valuable Player. But he added, "This is the best thing that's happened to me since I got married."

Yet he was dealt a big slice of irony a bit later. Yogi Berra of the Yankees was named most valuable player of the American League and eventually was signed for 1952 at a salary reported at forty thousand dollars. Campanella, generally regarded as the best catcher in baseball, in fact as one of the all-time greats, signed for a salary reported to be twenty-four thousand dollars.

During the winter, when Campy fell into a celebrated hassle about an operation for removal of the bone chips in his elbow, some observers found a connection between the hassle and the startling difference in pay for the two catchers. It was announced that Campanella would enter a hospital for the operation. But Campy refused. It was then said that he used the bone chips to "hold up" the Dodgers for a higher contract, one more like Berra's, or Jackie Robinson's.

He denied this with some vehemence. "If I was not happy with the money I signed for," Campy explained, "I wouldn't have signed. I've never had money trouble with the ball club. I won't have the operation because I don't think I need it. They could offer me a mint to do it and I still wouldn't."

There was considerable pressure on Campanella. Buzz Bavasi, Dodger vice-president, was one who thought Campy should have the operation. But the catcher stubbornly parried all entreaties, all pleas, with lines of simple eloquence:

"It doesn't hurt!"

"It's my arm!"

"If my arm bothered me that much," he said to Dodger president Walter O'Malley, "I'd have the operation."

O'Malley was equally eloquent in simplicity: "Okay," he said, "it's your arm!"

There were no hard feelings between the catcher and his boss.

The arm never figured, publicly at least, in the 1952 campaign; but Campanella, nevertheless, could not duplicate his greatest year. His batting average fell off to .269, his homers decreased to twenty-two, and he drove in eleven fewer runs. His failure to hit in crucial moments, like the failures of Robinson and Hodges, was a tragedy of the World Series, which the Dodgers lost to their old post-season foes, the Yankees. Afterward, Dressen made a remark to the effect that Campy would be put on another diet before the 1953 season was well under way.

The Series had hardly passed from front pages, however, before O'Malley indicated just how highly he rated Campanella. He announced that he had discussed the possibility of the catcher's becoming a coach when his playing days were over. He said he had pointed to Campy's entrance into the liquor business and inquired whether or not Campy wished to be connected with baseball later on. Campy said he wanted to remain in baseball. The offer of a coaching job was made contingent on Campy's career, which O'Malley estimated should last another five years.

"I don't see why Roy can't turn to coaching," O'Malley said. "He's intelligent, level-headed, well-liked by both players and fans, and I think he'd make a fine teacher."

There was every indication that Campy would be around to take up the offer. He revealed in no uncertain terms how he felt about his club when he said, "The day they take the Dodgers uniform off me, they'll have to rip it off." And, when they do that they can bury me."

8

RHUBARBS FOR ROBINSON

During his first year in the majors, Jackie Robinson observed to the exclamation point Branch Rickey's exhortation, "You can't fight back!" While a certain group of players, managers, and fans, especially in the early days of that season, maintained a whirling pace of devilish activity, he said nothing. He was, in fact, the game's counterpart of a good, little Sunday school boy—one taught that to show anger openly was sin, to turn the other cheek was Christian, and to *take this! and this! and this!* was holy.

The second year, however, with things going well, Jackie, who was tired of reining in his combative instincts, began to relax. Oddly, his first involvement, his first "rhubarb," was with Negro baseball, his showcase. It waxed every bit as hot, while it lasted, as later beef sessions with Leo Durocher.

The first rhubarb began to grow when *Ebony* magazine ran an article entitled "What's Wrong with Negro Baseball?"—by Jackie Robinson. This was a vitriolic blast, so specifically vitriolic, in fact, that many observers concluded he was primarily taking a pot-shot at the Kansas City Monarchs instead of Negro ball as a whole.

Pertinent to this conclusion was this Robinson statement:

"Three years ago . . . I reported for spring training with the Kansas City Monarchs. Tom Y. Baird told me I didn't need a contract. He had corresponded with me about playing ball with the

Monarchs . . . and he insisted that the letters were all the contract I needed.

"My five short months' experience in Negro baseball convinced me that the game needs a housecleaning from top to bottom. I found plenty wrong before . . . Scout Clyde Sukeforth convinced me to give up my $100 a week shortstop job with the Monarchs and accept a railroad ticket for a (talk) with the (Dodgers). The bad points range all the way from the low salaries and sloppy umpiring to questionable business connections of many of the team owners."

He denied that the Dodgers had "stolen" him from the Monarchs, as charged by Baird, declaring that "leaving Kansas City was done of my own volition."

Spring training in Negro ball was a farce, Robinson wrote, and "umpiring is unsupervised and quite prejudiced in many cases. The umpires are quite often untrained and favor certain teams. With the Monarchs, I found the rules as far as players (were concerned such) that on many days some (of them) would not go to bed at all. They were allowed to drink whatever they pleased."

His criticisms ranged upward to include the president of the Negro American League, Dr. B. Martin, who was also owner of the Chicago American Giants. Said Robinson: "Regardless of how fair the president may be, such a situation would naturally tend to make other teams feel they are getting a raw deal in cases where their team and the president's team are involved and the judgment goes against them."

Robinson was critical of the Monarchs' owners on another count. As he declared, "I went to the management . . . to get permission to play up until September 21 (1945) in exhibition games and then go home, as I was tired. I was told I would have to play all games or none. The owner's son gave me a lecture and assured me that if I left the club I was through. The 'cooperation' I received that afternoon made me feel glad I no longer had to play with the Kansas City club."

Pronto, Negro sports writers jumped on Robinson. Many said, for example, that even if everything Jackie had said were true, he, having gained his opportunity with the Dodgers as a result of his short term in Kansas City, was biting the hand that fed him. Others pointed out that Negro baseball, as a widespread setup, was the result of discrimination in organized ball and that thousands of Negro players who otherwise would have been bereft of a chance to play professionally had gained employment through it.

It was also pointed out that Jackie had found it difficult to obtain the kind of job he wanted following his release from the armed services and that, at least, he (1) had found employment with the Monarchs and (2) had been paid, for there was no squawk about nonpayment of wages nor talk of bouncing checks.

And, one writer inquired, how long could any league last if players were excused just because they were tired?

Among the first in rebuttal was Tom Baird himself. He declared that not at any time had he written a letter to Robinson, nor had he sent a telegram. The negotiations between the Monarchs and Robinson, Baird insisted, had been carried on by the team's co-owner, L. Wilkerson, and William (Dizzy) Dismukes, club secretary.

In a letter which he mimeographed and made available to all interested parties, Baird reiterated his contentions relative to the manner in which Rickey and the Dodgers obtained Robinson's services.

"Mr. Rickey never paid one cent for Jackie Robinson," he wrote. "Rickey was not even gentleman enough to answer or acknowledge my many letters I wrote him with reference to Jackie Robinson.

"Rickey's acquisition of Negro baseball players reminds me of the fellow who found a rope and when he got home there was a horse on the end of it. I have been informed that Mr. Rickey is a very religious man. If such is true, it appears that his religion runs toward the almighty dollar."

Baird then contrasted the actions of the Dodgers and the St. Louis Browns. "In 1947," his letter continued, "Mr. Jack Fournier, scout for the St. Louis Browns, contacted me personally in Kansas and scouted Willard Brown and Henry Thompson of the Monarchs. After scouting these players, Mr. Fournier asked my permission to speak with the players, which I gladly gave. Mr. Bill DeWitt, vice-president of the St. Louis Browns, called me shortly thereafter and a deal was made for Thompson and Brown. Mr. DeWitt stood by all of his commitments 100%. . . .

"There is no doubt that Mr. Rickey should be given credit for removing the barriers and allowing Negro ball players to get into organized baseball. However, it appears that his unethical methods of obtaining Negro players do not meet with the approval of the public."

(Subsequently, organized baseball recognized the rights of Negro teams and either paid or made other arrangements for the services of their players.)

John I. Johnson, Kansas City *Call* sports editor, observed thusly: "Jackie Robinson can do a lot more good for himself and for Negro baseball by concentrating on maintaining his high standings in the majors than by letting himself be persuaded to pop-off continually about 'What's Wrong with Negro Baseball.' He got his start with (the Monarchs) . . . the owners . . . shot square with (him)."

Mrs. Effa Manley, whose beauty belied her ability to turn on the vitriol, declared, "Frankly, no greater outrage could have been perpetrated. No greater invasion of the good sense of the American people could have been attempted. No greater ingratitude was ever displayed. I charge Jackie Robinson with being ungrateful and more likely stupid."

That rhubarb withered with the passage of time, but Jackie planted another when he reported at the 1948 spring training camp overweight from a winter on the "fried chicken circuit." Durocher was considerably miffed. Jackie did not take kindly to criticism of his weight. That a feud began to brew was declared in a statement.

"My feud with Durocher is real," Jackie was to say. "Sports writers said it started with him because I reported to spring training overweight. A newspaper friend of mine told me then, 'Leo just doesn't like you.' "

It didn't explode until later, however, by which time Durocher, as mentioned, was managing the Giants.

Meanwhile, during the 1948 season, Robinson began to talk back. In August, umpire Butch Henline ejected him and two other Dodgers from a game in Pittsburgh. There had been, in Henline's opinion, too much talk. It was Jackie's first bouncing, but he made light of it, declaring that now he was indeed one of the ball players.

In 1949, the "new" Robinson emerged in several outbursts with players, Durocher, and umpires. In spring training, he and Dodger farmhand Chris Van Cuyk tried to "out-name" each other. A continual rhubarb with Durocher was renewed whenever the Dodgers and Giants met. Once they almost came to blows. And Jackie's arguments with umpires became frequent.

Perhaps the most conspicuous examples of these was his tiff with Bill Stewart, during a vital series at St. Louis. After Stewart had made a decision, Jackie drew his hand to his throat, indicating that Stewart was "choking up." The umpire threw Jackie out of the game, and the incident became subject of national comment.

Later, in the World Series, Robinson tangled with American League umpire Cal Hubbard, a former professional football star. Commissioner Chandler chastened the player, who then apologized to Hubbard.

Robinson had an explanation for his change of demeanor. "I had too much stored up inside of me," he explained. "I would go home at night feeling all keyed up, all tense and irritable. I blamed it on the fact that I wasn't able to squawk when I thought I had a squawk coming. I honestly think I can play better by letting off steam."

He could, of course, cite the record which earned him the Most Valuable Player award to back up his belief.

The Robinson-Durocher feud settled down like the Hatfields and McCoys.

Somehow, Durocher appeared to have discovered the secret of Jackie's base-stealing ability. He worked his gimmick with maddening regularity, every time the Giants and Dodgers met. Jackie fought back through each game—and through the incisive rejoinder. In one game, Leo pantomimed Jackie as a "bighead." The player shot back a stinging inquiry, "Say, Leo, are you still using Laraine's perfume?"

Other than in a few stolen bases lost, perhaps, the feud had no detrimental effect on Jackie's play. Instead, as he said, "The madder he makes me, the better I play!"

In 1951, Robinson became involved in a veritable field of rhubarbs.

On April 17, the Dodgers opened the Ebbets Field season in a game with the National League champion Philadelphia Phillies. The next day, second game of the series, plate umpire Dusty Boggess called Jackie out on strikes and the player disagreed. Jackie kept up a running fire of comment about the call to which third base umpire Babe Pinelli took exception. According to Jackie, Pinelli berated him for shouting at Boggess. (It appeared that Pinelli had heard remarks which failed to reach Boggess's ears.) Robinson said Pinelli was at fault for the argument and complained that the umps were picking on him.

On April 20, Jackie was still seething over his run-in with Pinelli. "I have no doubt that there are some umpires in the National League who are 'on' me," he told reporters.

Although Dodgers' manager Chuck Dressen had asked Jackie to keep out of arguments with umpires, the player contended that he had a right to say something when the occasion arose.

In the sixth inning of the April 29 game with the Giants, Jackie was hit in the side by Larry Jansen's second pitch. Immediately, Jackie set up a beef to Larry. When he reached first base, he paused only long enough to shift gears. He continued to yell all the way around the path as he rode home on first baseman Gil Hodges's homer. And Jackie kept alive the verbal attack after he reached the dugout. Jackie's jockeying evidently jangled Jansen's nerves, for the pitcher lost his customary good stuff. Subsequently, the Giants lost the game.

Later, Oscar Ruhl explained the incident in his "Ruhl Book" column for the *Sporting News*:

"Chuck Dressen was stealing Larry Jansen's signs and whistling to the batter when a curve was coming. Durocher got wind of Dressen's skullduggery and told Jansen to hold the ball for a curve, then change after his hand was hidden in the glove. Result was that Dressen whistled the curve sign to Robinson, but it was a fast ball instead, and nearly separated Jackie from his upper rack. So Robinson started the beanball charges against Jansen, who never threw at a batter in his life."

Whenever there were Giant-Dodger fireworks, Robinson and Durocher put their feud into action, too. Like actors who hated second billing, they broke loose on April 30 to insert into baseball history words which will be remembered as long as the game is played.

That Monday night, with 33,962 Dodger-partisan fans present, the Giants broke out of a long losing streak by jumping off to a six-run lead in the first inning. Throughout the game both teams used the "duster," jagging tempers until the game seemed about to become a fist-fight. After Giants' pitcher Sal Maglie dusted off Robinson in the third inning, Jackie's temper went off. He took his stance in the batter's box and called on a bit of strategy from the rough old days of baseball. With diabolic purpose, he dropped a bunt down the first base line. As Maglie ran over to field the ball on the base line, Robinson, charging for first, jolted him with his shoulder.

Jackie's trick, of course, was to retaliate against Maglie, the duster-offer, by drawing him into a dangerous fielding position.

It worked perfectly. Anger boiled within Maglie. But he was restrained from punching Robinson. Later, Durocher declared that Jackie's play was a bush league trick.

"If it was a bush league trick," Robinson retorted, "then Durocher is a bush league manager. He taught it to me!"

Robinson further blasted Giants' pitchers for throwing dusters, uttered criticisms of National League umpires, and wondered why league president Ford Frick did not take measures to prevent some of the situations which, in Robinson's opinion, were detrimental to baseball.

Frick, in turn, criticized Robinson, saying he was tired of Jackie's popping off "and all that business." He added, "This sort of thing has to stop!"

On May 1, he produced a more formal statement: "I have warned only one person—Jackie Robinson," Frick said. "I am tired of hearing about his popping off . . . if Brooklyn cannot handle the situation, I may have to step in. . . ."

Brooklyn president Walter O'Malley replied, "I have no reason to be dissatisfied with Jackie Robinson. He has the full backing ot the Dodger organization."

Dodgers' vice-president E. J. (Buzz) Bavasi said, "If there is anything wrong which Robinson has done, he can be talked to, and we will talk to him. But, if there is going to be any fuss about the Giant series, we want Durocher on the carpet, too."

Then, referring to the Jansen-Robinson thing, Bavasi said, "Robinson was the one hit and he gets the blame. If Frick wants to know who's at fault, he should ask his umpires."

Robinson's rhubarbs and howls, and the resultant hoots, created much to-do. Relatively little attention was paid to his early-season .435 batting average. At every National League stop, he was asked for his version of the incidents, about his attitude, and what he intended doing in face of Frick's warnings and other criticisms.

"I'm not going to be a sitting duck," he said. "I think somebody ought to step in and stop this bean-balling before somebody gets hurt. It's a dangerous business. I don't like rhubarbs any better than anybody else. As far as Mr. Frick's statement about me and the umpires, I've been quiet all season. I haven't blown off steam at all. Just once I had words with Babe Pinelli, but that was all. I just hope everybody forgets everything and we can get back to the business of playing baseball."

Another time, Jackie said, "Country Slaughter of the Cardinals says, 'I don't care if they throw at me, but the base lines are mine.' And, that's the way I feel about it. Dusting off a player is part of the game, but the batter has a right to get even with the other team, if he can."

The *Sporting News* said in an editorial:

"Jackie Robinson must be beyond reproach. He is still on the pedestal, not only with his race, but with all fans. He remains the hand-picked hero who carried off so well the great experiment which worked a democratic revolution in the National Game.

"Branch Rickey selected Jackie as the pioneer big league player of his race, not because he might have been the most talented Negro star, but because Rickey felt Robinson was ideally fitted with the depth of understanding and the power of will to achieve his goal with dignity and respect. Jackie need only reflect on those high attributes which have served him so well, to adopt a more moderate course at this time.

"So, stop, look, and listen, Jackie. Let us have, once more, pure and unalloyed, the superb and stylish batsman, the deadly double-play dealer, the intrepid base-runner—that and nothing more.

"For that, there is an honored place in the history of the game and perhaps a niche in Cooperstown. For the mean and petty practices of a chronic griper, there is no place, except in shabby, sordid memory."

Jackie's involvements took a different twist when the Dodgers arrived at Cincinnati for a series with the Reds. It was then revealed that crackpots had written several letters threatening Jackie's life. Scrawled in block formations, the letters said that Robinson would be shot by a rifle from a building overlooking Crosley Field, if he attempted to play against the Reds.

(One of these letters had been sent to police, the other to the *Enquirer*, a morning newspaper. Subsequently, they were turned over to the Federal Bureau of Investigation.)

Jackie applied becoming logic to the threat. In conversation with a writer, he said, "I figured that if anybody was serious about trying to shoot me, they certainly wouldn't tell the police about it first. Furthermore, if anybody actually wanted to try something, they could do it when I'm walking down the street. It would surely be a lot easier that way."

His Dodger teammates also made light of the incident. Outfielder Gene Hermanski (later traded to the Cubs) told Jackie not to worry, declaring, "We'll fool them, Jackie; we'll all put No. 42 on our backs. That'll screw 'em all up."

The only trouble with that idea, Jackie quipped, was that they would have to paint their faces, too.

Jackie was held blameless by Frick in another incident, one that occurred during a Dodgers-Phillies game. Jackie was on third base and right fielder Carl Furillo was at bat. Furillo was to "squeeze" Jackie home. But he missed the ball and Jackie, in baseball parlance, was "hung up" between third and home. In a rundown, Jackie ducked and dodged until six Phillies were involved in the play. Finally, he broke for home, which was being covered by pitcher Russ Meyer. Meyer took the throw from one of those in on the rundown, tagged Jackie, but dropped the ball. Angry with himself, Meyer attempted to block Jackie out of the base path.

What had been a fine moment of sports excitement suddenly became explosive as tempers flared. Meyer continued to push Jackie, as though spoiling to start something. An umpire rushed in to halt the sprouting rhubarb. Meanwhile, Jackie held his ground against Meyer. Next, Campanella rushed up and virtually lifted Jackie off his feet, carrying him from the scene, while Jimmy Bloodworth of the Phils did likewise to Meyer. Phillies manager Eddie Sawyer then pulled Meyer out of the game.

Later, from the Phillies' dugout, Meyer invited Jackie to "go below" and settle things, then got up and started out. At that, Jackie darted off the Dodger bench to accept this invitation to a brawl. Quickly, however, both benches emptied, an umpire rushed in, and the fuss ended.

Incidentally, the Dodgers won the game, 4 to 3, and the run Jackie scored amidst the byplay was the deciding tally!

After the game, Meyer went to the Dodger dressing room and apologized to Robinson. Frick fined Meyer fifty dollars, but didn't mention Robinson. The sting of the incident was removed when Jackie sportingly accepted part of the blame.

During the passage of June days, Robinson's actions were above reproach. In its June 13 issue, the *Sporting News* published another editorial:

"For a while this season," it said, "Jackie Robinson appeared to have developed a persecution complex, in which he envisioned enemies among the umpires and opposing players. But now the second base star of the Dodgers apparently has put aside his suspicions and has returned to the restraint and dignity that have characterized his previous progress in the game. . . .

"Many close to Robinson insist that his public presentation is not always his fault, because of the tendency of a small portion of his interviewers to 'slant' some of his always ready remarks and to seize upon any fragment which might reflect on racial relations.

"However, in Cincinnati, Jackie handled the threat on his life in a way that Americans like—lightly, and with wit. . . .

"In the Russ Meyer bumping incident in Ebbets Field, Jackie also won friends. . . .

"The fans of the nation can take pride in Robinson's conduct recently, having returned to his original party—the American party."

Withal, there was one more big blow to come. It came on September 27, in a game won by the Braves, 4 to 3, further to mesmerize the Dodgers in their great el foldo. The teams were tied at 3-all in the Braves' half of the eighth inning. Boston outfielder Bob Addis (later sent to the Cubs) singled. Sam Jethroe drove him around to third with another single. Earl Torgeson then hit a hot grounder to Robinson, who threw to Campanella in an effort to put out Addis. Campanella set up a blockade at the plate, took Jackie's throw, and dived to tag the sliding Addis, rolling over from the impact of their collision. He leaped to his feet still clutching the ball.

But umpire Frank Dascoli spread palms down—Addis was safe! Like a jumping jack, Campanella popped up in front of the umpire to protest the decision. Dascoli reiterated his belief that Addis was safe, whereupon Campanella slammed his mitt to the ground. Simultaneously, Dascoli bounced Campanella from the game. All hell broke loose. Dodgers stormed on the field in boisterous, belligerent disagreement with Dascoli's hasty action. Before the rhubarb died, Dascoli had cleared the Dodger bench of all players and also ejected coach Cookie Lavagetto from the game, leaving only manager Chuck Dressen and coach Jake Pitler in the dugout.

After the game, the Dodgers continued to sizzle. As they filed past the umpires' dressing room, someone splintered its door with kicks. Jackie was fingered as the door-kicker. Pitcher Preacher Roe (said to have been the kicker) swore, however, that Jackie was innocent, as Robinson himself protested. Nevertheless, Frick slapped Jackie with a hundred-dollar fine, took Campanella for another hundred, and fined Roe fifty dollars.

The crop of rhubarbs was smaller in 1952. But the few that grew attracted wide press notice.

The strangest of all these hassles occurred at Cincinnati in May. Jackie sat out the game because of a minor leg ailment. When umpire Frank Dascoli flubbed a call, in Dodger opinion, he was given a rough riding, during which, it was alleged, he was called "dago" and "wop."

Warren Giles, freshman president of the National League (Frick had succeeded Chandler as commissioner), was present and heard some of the jockeying. He sent a note warning Dodger manager Chuck Dressen that his players must "show more respect for umpires." Oddly, Robinson was singled out for mention in the note. This player, Giles said, had been particularly offensive, and his statement led to the highly publicized conclusion that Jackie, the Negro, had been guilty of race-baiting.

Quickly, both Dressen and Robinson denied that Jackie had called Dascoli names. "I would never call anyone a name like that," Jackie said. "I've had too much of it myself."

Subsequently, he carried his denial directly to Giles, and the National League president said he had not meant to insinuate that Jackie was the name-caller.

At St. Louis, in June, Jackie and rookie relief pitcher Joe Black were made targets of racial. epithets reminiscent of 1947. A Cardinal bench jockey with a high-pitched voice, hurled the word "nigger" at both Black and Robinson. Then, after umpire Art Gore called a ball on a pitch to Robinson, Gore was labeled a "nigger lover."

Robinson said he couldn't identify the name-caller, but, while at bat, he told Cardinal catcher Del Rice, "I am sick and tired of that stuff from the bench and you can tell that gutless — that I said so."

Dodger brass declared that an official protest would be lodged with Giles. The Cards' freshman manager, Eddie Stanky, in the earlier manner of Chapman, labeled the jockeying "routine."

As July brought mid-season, Jackie was again voted the National League's All-Star Game second baseman, holding a wide margin over Cardinal Red Schoendienst and rating, in the estimation of fans the nation over, as one of baseball's super stars. It was his fourth appearance in the classic.

It was in this game, played at Philadelphia, that Jackie and Leo buried the hatchet, at least for the time being. Leo, as manager of the National League champion Giants, automatically became manager of the senior circuit All-Stars. Jackie got the National Leaguers off to a 1 to 0 lead in the first inning when he hit a home run. The playing field was muddy, however, and he later bobbled a couple of balls he might have handled easily on solid ground. Fans gave him the boos. The National Leaguers subsequently won the rain-abbreviated game, 3 to 2.

Reviewing the play, Durocher refused to stand for criticism of Robinson's defensive play. "They should boo Robinson!" he said sarcastically. "On a field like that, muddy and slippery? And they boo him because he didn't come up with the ball." When Jackie himself moved to take the blame, Durocher would have none of it. "You were great!" the manager said.

And Dressen and Dodger scout Red Corriden added that Jackie was baseball's greatest performer. "Why, he doesn't even have to hit to help you win," Corriden said.

In September, Jackie became involved in an argument with umpire Larry Goetz, following a game with the Braves. Giles fined the player seventy-five dollars. Jackie, saying he would not pay the fine until he received a personal conference with Giles, blamed Goetz for the post-game set-to. (Jackie paid the fine and talked to Giles.)

"If Goetz hadn't opened his mouth," Jackie said, "nothing more would have been said."

It is, of course, natural to wonder why Robinson was so often the center of rhubarbs. Was he a natural grouch, a troublemaker? Was he being maligned? Was he being "picked on?"

The answer has several parts. In the first place, Jackie never was the soul of humility, as he acted during the first year and a half of his major league career. On the West Coast, as related, he was called a "talk back" guy, but the fact was that had he been white, this "talking back" would have been called the sign of a spirited player rather than something to be criticized. Secondly, much of the editorial criticism leveled at him was due to the fact that even in sports, where democracy has been developed more than in any other field of American endeavor, excepting in some phases of show business, "quiet and unassuming" Negroes are preferred. Thirdly, Jackie, as a big star, was always sought out for opinions whenever any sort of hassle developed. Hardly ever at a loss for words, he would speak up. There were times when his quotes were twisted or employed out of context to fit whatever slant the particular writer desired. And, also, there were times when Jackie's temper got the better of him and he was plainly wrong.

Most important, however, was the fact that Jackie was, is, and will be to his dying day a wanna-win guy. That was the only way he ever knew how to play—to the very hilt. He was out of the mold of Ty Cobb, generally regarded as baseball's all-time all timer. "Just like Cobb," one Dodger official said, "Robbie has an unquenchable thirst for victory. The word defeat is not in his vocabulary."

And what was the total result of this spirit-the wanna-win Spirit of which rhubarbs were a by-product?

At the end of 1952, Jackie stood as one of the real champions of the diamond. He was, as said, one of the very few super stars of the game. He ranked alongside Stan Musial and Ralph Kiner and Phil Rizzuto and Robin Roberts. In many respects, he topped all ball players, as Dressen said.

On the field, he had earned such rewards as Rookie of the Year (1947) and Most Valuable Player (1949); he had won a National League batting title (1949); and his .992 fielding average for 1951 set a record. Through his base-line feats, accomplished with less speed of foot than possessed by Jethroe and Minnie Minoso, he made the late Bill Robinson's description of him—"Ty Cobb in Technicolor"—one of the most appropriate tags ever fastened on an athlete. He had inspired his teammates, had played his heart out under conditions not usually conducive to such play, and he had written into baseball history its most dramatic chapter.

And, the topper, through it all he built himself as a worthy idol—a clean-living idol—to thousands of kids across the nation, kids whose dreams of becoming stars came within reach because of his achievements and kids who might have made it anyhow because they were always of the right pigment. Jackie represented to them a man who reflected the good rearing of a loving mother—a man who was not always right, perhaps not always liked, yet one universally respected. Or, as Milton Gross wrote in the New York *Post*, "He has demonstrated conclusively (that) he is one of the all-time greats of baseball. It is difficult to conceive of Jackie ever playing without inspiration. His background and all he has been through make it impossible."

Branch Rickey, the man who signed Jackie Robinson and opened up organized baseball to Negro players for the first time in more than half a century.

Jackie Robinson as a UCLA football star.

Robinson returned to the UCLA campus in 1951 to serve as Grand Marshall of the university's homecoming parade. He was given a hero's welcome.

Stan Musial, great star of the St. Louis Cardinals, was quick to shake Jackie's hand after he hit a homer in the first inning of the 1952 All-Star game. *(Wide World)*

Larry Doby, after connecting with a pitch.

Satchel Paige, baseball's "Ol Man River," with Tom Baird, owner of the Kansas City Monarchs, and Lefty Gomez (right) former New York Yankee pitcher.

Roy Campanella showed typical concentration waiting for 2 relay throw from Jackie Robinson in a 1951 Brooklyn-Chicago game. He got the throw, tagged out Phil Cavarretta, Cubs' second baseman, who was racing toward home.

Sam Jethroe scored in a double steal pulled off by the Boston Braves at Wrigley Field, Chicago, in 1950. Cubs' catcher Al Walker (left) couldn't catch the throw-in, which was wild.   *(Wide World)*

Henry Thompson handled some hot ones for the Giants, even in practice
sessions.   (Wide World)

Giant manager Lippy Durocher danced for joy as he urged Monte Irvin toward home after Bobby Thomson hit a home run in a 1951 New York-Brooklyn game. Monte hit an eighth inning homer just to make victory sure. The final score—3-1.

(Wide World)

Hustling Willie Mays, who kept the Giants on the go while he was in the outfield. *(Wide World)*

Orestes Minoso slid home safely, scoring a run for Chicago at Detroit in 1951, while Tiger catcher Joe Ginsberg went after the ball.   *(Wide World)*

Big Don Newcombe completing his delivery.   *(Wide World)*

Joe Black warming up before a game. He was called on time and again to relieve and help Brooklyn to a 1952 pennant victory.

(Wide World)

Judy Johnson, all-time Negro league third baseman.

Harry Simpson at bat for Cleveland.

Luke Easter showed Cleveland fans a lot of power.

Bob Wilson, St. Paul Saints third baseman, proved he could hit
Triple-A pitching and looks forward to a major league career.

Gene Baker, Los Angeles Angels shortstop, is one of the most promising minor league stars.

9

THE JET

In the spring of 1950, there appeared in the National League a Negro player highly touted as more of a whiz on the base lines than Jackie Robinson. The year previous, he had stolen eighty-nine bases at Montreal, had, in fact, been press-agented as "the man who made Montreal forget Jackie Robinson," and was, according to pre-season blurbs, the absolute personification of the new jet age. Shades of Cobb and Carey! There was no limit, one was given to understand, to this man's talents in the field of larceny. His name?

Sam Jethroe.

The Jet, as he was to be labeled, represented the effects on Negro league ball of Negro fan interest in organized ball and was, in the financial sense, best testimony yet that baseball in Technicolor was a solid proposition. The Boston Braves had handed the Brooklyn organization more than one hundred thousand dollars in cash and players for rights to Jethroe.

Prior to his stint at Montreal, Jethroe had been the prize star of the Cleveland Buckeyes, a Negro American League club. When Doby began to click for the Indians in 1948, however, the death knell was sounded for the Bucks. Fans who had been loyal to the Negro club journeyed "downtown" to cheer for Larry and the Tribe. Ernie Wright, Erie (Pennsylvania) hotel owner and title holder to the Buckeyes, and Wilbur Hayes, general manager, were worried. As the season wore along, they herded a few trusted friends into open-air meetings in League Park's right field stands. Scanning many empty seats, Wright and Hayes wanted to know, "What can be done to lure more fans into the ball park?"

No one had an adequate answer. Someone suggested that the Buckeyes turn interracial. Another suggested that perhaps Wright should obtain an outstanding local figure to serve as "front man" for the club. The possibility of radio was mentioned. Wright followed through on this by contracting for game broadcasts. A TV station sought permission for telecasts. Wright okayed the deal, making it possible for fans to enjoy simultaneous radio-television coverage for the first time in Negro baseball history. Still, attendance wasn't enough to let Wright put down figures in black ink.

This financially embarrassing circumstance softened up Wright for offers for his players. The payroll was running high on a roster including Quincy Troupe, catcher and manager; Chet Brewer, the vet right-hander; Archie Ware, a slick-fielding, punch-hitting first baseman; Sam (Red) Jones, a fireballing youngster; Vibert Clark, a good southpaw; and the slender, hollow-cheeked, fleet-footed center fielder with birdlike legs, Sam Jethroe. The big star, the gate attraction, Sam was being paid a grand a month.

The Cleveland Indians had taken a look at Jethroe, but evinced no desire to sign him. There was the question of his age. Though he was listed at twenty-seven, the fact that he was a veteran, both in Negro leagues and Latin countries, led many to suspect that he actually was thirty, or more. Another thing, his outfielding was erratic. Jethroe frequently misjudged fly balls, then with great speed recovered and caught up with them. His throwing arm appeared to be weaker than that required of a journeyman major leaguer. And he seemed to daydream of an occasion out there in center.

Withal, he was in several respects Branch Rickey's kind of a player. Especially in fleetness of foot and the ability to hit, from both sides of the plate. The Dodgers scouted him. In July, they purchased his contract for five thousand dollars and shipped him to Montreal.

In a hectic fractional season there, Sam stole eighteen bases, batted .322, and was fined twice. Once a portion of his pay was subtracted because he fell victim to a pick-off play. The other time, there was a disagreement between Jethroe and team officials which led to his being called a "pop-off guy."

Whatever faults he may have had, the charge didn't fit. His former Cleveland teammates seethed at the report. "Jethroe's not like that," they chorused. A nice guy, confident, yes; but reticent almost to the point of bashfulness was the way they appraised him.

After that season, Jethroe headed below the border for the second half of his year-around season.

In the spring of 1949, he went to training camp with Montreal and promptly proved claims on his speed by running 60 yards in 6.1s. But he was no ball of fire at the season's beginning. After one week, he was batting a mere .208; at the end of two, he had slumped to .206; at the end of three, however, he was up to .258; and, on a month's tally, he was hitting in respectable circles—.305.

Once his hitting was straightened out, Jethroe began to run wild on the bases. He'd take an unusually long lead off first (or whatever base he was leaving), watching the pitcher with eagle eyes. If the hurler took a mere split second too long in his delivery, it seemed, Speedy Sam was off like a cannonball express, only more gracefully. He scored from second on infield outs, stole second, third, and home. He literally ran International League hurlers and catchers ragged. The fans loved it, too. They went to ball parks in droves to see this guy writers were calling "Larceny Legs," "The Colored Comet," and "The Jet."

"He's the fastest man in baseball," all who saw him said. How fast was that? What kind of time could he make on a track? Had he ever run track?

The six-foot-one, 178-pound Jet revealed that he had done a bit of running at Lincoln High School in East St. Louis, Illinois. He was willing to test his speed, in baseball spike shoes and full uniform, against the Olympic Games sprinter, Barney Ewell. They ran twice in exhibitions, splitting. Jethroe was clocked in 7.45 for 75 yards.

In describing Jethroe's victory, pitcher Dan Bankhead, a great story teller, said, "Man, The Jet just ran away from Barney Ewell!"

"I'll be damned," a listener retorted. "Maybe he beat Ewell, but nobody—nobody!—runs away from him."

In any case, The Jet was fast. No doubt about that.

Jethroe's base-line feats bothered Paul Richards, inventive manager of the Buffalo Bisons, disturbed him greatly, the fact is. After Sam had stolen against the Bisons in their first eleven meetings with Montreal, Richards cooked up a bit of strategy. Jethroe was leading off for the Royals. Richards had his pitcher walk the Montreal pitcher, thus plugging second base in case Jethroe got on first. The gimmick worked six of seven times. It backfired like this:

Buffalo's pitcher walked Montreal's pitcher, as ordered by Richards. But he lost his control, walking Jethroe and the third batter, to load the bases. Then Montreal's leading hitter, Bob Morgan, doubled to unload them!

As Jethroe approached the final day of the season, he needed two stolen bases to break a thirty-year-old record and two base hits to top a mark in that department. He got four hits and stole three bases. He broke the base-theft mark by stealing home!

His record read: batting average, .326, second best in the league; hits, 207; runs, 154; total bases, 330; triples, 19, a league first—and 89 stolen bases!

The natural conclusion from the record was that Jethroe had earned a major league trial—but where? The Brooklyn roster already included Robinson, Campanella, and Don Newcombe, who had pitched his way out of Montreal. Although Rickey had pioneered baseball's racial integration play, he was of the opinion that the saturation point for Negroes on one club had been reached. For a time, there was talk that Sam would be sold to the Chicago White Sox and that team's manager, Jack Onslow, reportedly hoped rumors were true. He was an admirer of Negro athletes. The rumors were killed, however, when Jethroe was sold to the Braves.

Commenting on the deal, Rickey declared, "It might be the biggest mistake I ever made in baseball."

Being sold to the Braves brought back memories for Jethroe, one pleasant, the other unpleasant. He was happy to go to Boston because Billy Southworth was the manager. In his youth, Sam had watched the Cardinals play and Southworth had become his idol. The unpleasant memory had to do with that day in 1945 when he tried out for the Red Sox. He had skied his hopes that day, but the Red Sox hardly had a "thank you" to say for his trouble.

The Braves, wanting a fresh Jethroe for the '50 season, suggested that he forego winter ball. The player agreed, spending an unaccustomed winter at home in Erie with his wife, infant daughter, and a relative. The idleness was new to him. He tried hunting, but gave it up after a companion sprayed buckshot too close for comfort. He spent much time discussing baseball with his previous owner, Wright, who once had tried to make a bartender out of the center fielder. Wright, incidentally, complained every time he thought of the piddling amount of money he received for Jethroe's contract as compared to the small fortune Rickey realized from the sale to Boston. He resolved never to sell another player to a major league club!

During the "hot stove" season, one of the most frequent queries was this: "Will Jethroe steal bases at Boston as he did at Montreal?"

"I think I can run the bases in the majors just as good as I did in the International League," Jethroe replied. "The bases sure aren't any farther apart!"

Jethroe reported to 1950 training camp at Bradenton, Florida, and immediately discovered that there was a difference between the majors and the minors. On top of that, he had to live with the Negro problem—segregated living, eating, and recreation. There was no doubt about his speed, but critics immediately criticized his hitting and fielding. Too anxious to make a good impression, Jethroe threw hard before his arm was in shape, causing it to tighten up and further accentuate the fact that throwing was a weakness. And, he pressed at the plate. Result: few hits.

Joe Williams, New York *World-Telegram and Sun* columnist, a quick man with the incisive observation, called Sam one of Rickey's "gold-brick specialties." Someone explained that he pushed the ball instead of throwing it. After he made several glaring errors, it was said that he couldn't get the proper jump on fly balls.

Even his speed was used as a deviler when a quipster said, "He can carry the ball in faster than he can throw it in!"

Nevertheless, Jethroe kept plugging, uncomplainingly. A devout Catholic, he prayed for success, and friends prayed for him. Joe Louis, the old Brown Bomber, telephoned to say, "Good luck." Southworth went down the line with him, keeping him in center field, bulwarked by two excellent throwers, left fielder Sid Gordon and right fielder Willard Marshall. On the bench, ready to take over if Jethroe turned out to be a lemon, was Luis Olmo.

It was during these dark days that Jethroe cut a slice of history, becoming the first Negro to play with a "white" club at St. Petersburg, Florida. No objections were raised. Surprisingly, however, Negro fans stayed away from the ball park.

Jethroe opened the season in center field. Again, he was no ball of fire. "What about your base running?" writers wanted to know.

"I'm learning the league," Jethroe replied, reminding them that he had been a slow starter at Montreal in 1949.

But he was to be harpooned repeatedly as he failed to live up to the claims of pre-season touters. Jethroe began to brood. Sympathetic writers, noting his despair and loneliness, suggested that

Boston buy another Negro "to keep him company." Braves traveling secretary Duffy Lewis and Southworth tried to make him feel as though he belonged. But the solution in the end came from Jethroe himself. It was very simple.

"I just stopped reading about how lousy I was," he said later.

Result: his hitting began to improve. In two weeks, he was the only Brave batting .300. And when the club played the Dodgers, Jethroe had a ball-spanking good time, averaging .375.

Subsequently, Southworth placed Jethroe in the lead-off spot. A teammate, Tommy Holmes, supplied valuable hitting tips, explaining that the trick on long-ball hitting was to get the bat around ahead of the ball, thus preventing it from getting up on the batter before his swing was begun. Holmes also showed Sam how to break his wrists smoothly.

The player settled down. In his first forty-six games, he had stolen only six bases. In the next twenty-seven games, he stole eighteen bases. Against the New York Giants on July 9, he ran wild. In the fifth inning, he stole his twenty-second base of the year. In the tenth, he made his twenty-third theft. The duel between Vern Bickford, Braves, and Sal Maglie, Giants, waxed hot. Jethroe led off the thirteenth inning by doubling off one of Maglie's classic slants. Shortly, he stole third—his twenty-fourth theft—beating catcher Wes Westrum's throw to third baseman Hank Thompson by a hair's breadth. Giants manager Leo Durocher howled that Jethroe was out, but umpire Lon Warneke, the old "Arkansas hummingbird," failed to agree. Then, while the Giants completed an infield out, Jethroe raced home, giving Bickford a 3 to 2 victory.

As he scored, however, it became obvious that Jethroe had injured himself on the steal of third. He hopped across the plate and on to the dugout. A hasty examination, followed by X-rays, quieted Brave nerves: it was a badly bruised instep, no broken bones.

The seriousness of the injury was reflected later. During the first-half season, Jethroe had stolen twenty-four bases. In his last sixty-five games, he stole only eleven times. He had hit .280 the first half, but connected for only .258 the second half. Still, his thirty-five stolen bases led the league and more than doubled the total of his American League counterpart, Boston Red Sox center fielder Dom DiMaggio, who pilfered fifteen.

Not exactly shades of Cobb and Carey, but not bad for a freshman. The Baseball Writers Association named Jethroe National League Rookie of the Year, the third time in four years the honoree had been a Negro. It was Jackie in 1947, Newcombe in 1949, and, now, The Jet.

By leading the league in base thefts, Jethroe qualified as an authority on the subject.

"Stealing bases is like a game of chance," he said. "I think that's why I always get such a kick out of it. The pitcher and the catcher must figure out when I'm going to steal and I have to try to confuse them.

"When I want to steal a base," he continued, "the only ball player on the opposing club I worry about is the pitcher. He's the only one who counts. The whole idea of stealing is to get the jump on the pitcher and the best way to get that jump is to know the pitcher. I study him.

"Lots of players use different slides when going into the bag, but I usually slide straight in. In fact, I use the straight slide all the time. I think I get more momentum that way."

With Jethroe made as a major leaguer, Braves publicity man Charlie Sands was free to tell a short story:

"At Braves Field on May 30," he recalled, "Al Dark of the Giants tried to go from second to third on a deep outfield fly. Jethroe threw him out. Later, I said to Sam, 'That was a great throw.'

"Jethroe replied, 'I can't throw. Anyone who reads the papers knows that. The wind just blew the ball in.' "

In 1951, Jethroe had troubles again. First, there was the presence of Luis Marquez, the sweet-fielding outfielder from the Portland Beavers. A natural who, as a rookie, was compared to Dom DiMaggio, he was the first Negro to be drafted by a major league club. The move, incidentally, made Portland manager Bill Sweeney howl that there was no justice in this major-minor league relationship. Marquez, he said, was worth at least a hundred thousand and, here, he had been picked up for a piddling ten thousand. Marquez could field all right, it turned out, but he couldn't hit major league pitching.

Meanwhile, Jethroe's batting wasn't good and his position was shaky. Southworth shifted him about the outfield. "It's the sophomore jinx," observers chorused.

Sam took to brooding again. After he dropped a routine, third-out fly at St. Louis, allowing the Cardinals four runs, he was rock-bottom in despair. On the train trip from St. Louis to New York, he locked himself in his roomette, refused to eat, and barred Marquez from conversing with him. His teammates liked him as a man, but they figured he had lost six games (up to June) by his faulty fielding.

When the Braves reached New York, Jethroe told writers, "I'm ready to quit." But Southworth talked him into better spirits. It was decided that perhaps Sam's difficulty in picking up the flight of balls hit directly to him was the result of poor eyesight. Evidence was the fact that Sam used glasses for reading.

On the team's return to Boston, Sam's eyes were examined and new glasses prescribed. As soon as he got used to them, his fielding and hitting improved. Then Southworth was gone and Holmes became manager of the Braves, making the jump from Hartford, where he had gone to lap up experience in field generalship.

One of Holmes's first moves was to return Jethroe on a "permanent" basis to center field. Things got better. In the last half of the season, Jethroe batted better than .330 to make his season's average .280. Again he led the National League in base thefts with thirty-five. The total wasn't close to the Braves' record of fifty-seven, set in 1913 by Ralph Myers, but whenever The Jet was running to form, he was amazing.

"He uses no cunning, no trickery," a baseball man said. "Instead, he relies on sheer speed, which makes his base-stealing feats all the more remarkable. He doesn't rely on the big leads that made base-stealing so easy for Carey and Milan (a change from Jethroe's early style). He doesn't walk away from the bag, then take off, as Cobb used to do. Instead, he's off like a flash from the bag and it's seldom that they flag him down."

There was another Jethroe joke for the "hot stove" sessions:

One day in the fall of '51, he appeared at Braves Field wearing dark glasses.

"What's the matter, Sam?" someone inquired.

"Hurt my eye," the player replied.

"Which eye?" persisted the interrogator.

"The one I bat right-handed with," said Sam.

Although The Jet's defensive play again showed marked improvement at the beginning of 1952, it was a pretty miserable year, taken as an entity. The Jet, it appeared, just couldn't hit major league pitching anymore. Marquez wasn't around to threaten his position, although first baseman George Crowe, American Association Rookie of the Year for 1951, was there to play and make a twosome.

Perhaps Jethroe and other Braves were mesmerized by the defeatist air. Attendance was terrible and, for much of the first-half season, the team's play was just as bad. Holmes was let out as manager and Charley Grimm was brought in from the Milwaukee farm to see what he could do about pepping up things. He soon brought along Jim (Bus) Clarkson, the Brewers' hard-hitting Negro infielder. But no miracles were to be worked. Both Crowe and Clarkson subsequently went back to Milwaukee, Crowe to insure another pennant for the Brewers, it was said.

As the season drew to a close, Boston was in the second division and Jethroe had batted .232. His base running, while good enough to place him among the league leaders, was not up to the standard of his first two seasons.

Marquez, in the meantime, appeared to have cured his hitting faults at Milwaukee, which was contesting in late season for the American Association lead. Another outfielder, Bill Bruton, also loomed as serious competition for The Jet. As the year closed, there was a strong suspicion that the cumulative effects of Negro and Latin league play, plus three rough years in the majors, had taken their toll. Maybe, it was said, The Jet had run down.

10

THREE GIANTS

Skies over Yankee Stadium were murky as the New York Giants jogged on-field to warm up for the first game of the 1951 World Series. A fellow in the stands, coupling the dreariness of the day with the latest of Leo Durocher's many line-up changes, reached, albeit shakily, for a quip. Nodding to the outfield, he spoke to a neighbor. "Looks a bit dark out there, doesn't it?"

For the first time in history, a major league club had an all-Negro outfield. In left was Monte Irvin, the National League's runs-batted-in champion; in center was Willie Mays, an eager-beaver kid of twenty, a terrific defensive player, the senior circuit's leading candidate for Rookie of the Year honors; and, in right, was Hank Thompson, the year previous a solid third baseman, in 1951 the club's major disappointment. Hank was out there because Don Mueller, the regular right fielder, had sprained his right ankle in the final game of the league championship play-off.

When the first game was over, it appeared that this new outfield might spark the Giants to another miracle: a Series victory over the Yankees. Irvin and Mays already had played stellar roles in the season's first miracle: the Giants' upset of the Brooklyn Dodgers.

Thompson started things rolling for the threesome, wangling a walk from pitcher Allie Reynolds in the Giants' half of the first inning. Irvin hit to right, sending Thompson to third. Then, Whitey

Lockman's ground rule double scored Thompson and sent Irvin to third.

When Reynolds got just the slightest bit careless, taking a windup, Irvin, the big guy, roared up the base line for a sweet theft of home. It was the first "classic" theft of home in thirty years—and Giant hurler Dave Koslo had a 2 to 0 cushion to ride on.

The threesome helped him protect it. In the last half of the first, Irvin leaped into the left field stands sensationally to glove-hand Hank Bauer's "sure" homer. The play saved two runs. Bauer again was the victim in the fifth when Mays raced in to pick his line drive off the grass tips. A moment or so later, Thompson sped deep to drag down Joe DiMaggio's towering fly.

Going into the sixth, the Giants led, 2 to 1. Then a Giant hit a three-run homer to wrap up the ball game.

It was Dark out there—Alvin Dark, the guy who homered.

Although Irvin and Thompson joined the Giants for the first time in 1949, it was not until the kid, Mays, came along that the Polo Grounds tenants had a player to rival Jackie Robinson, et al., in the affections of Harlem fans. Irvin had been an outstanding performer in the Negro National League, but he was the strong-silent-man type, a players' player sort of guy. Inexplicably to some writers following the Giants, he never made the turnstiles whirl as they did at Ebbets Field when Jackie was to play. Thompson, too, had been a standout in Negro ball and also had the benefit of a 1947 trial with the St. Louis Browns. But he, too, was the workman type, not the kind given to creating hysterics in the stands. The fact was, as dealers in the Negro market have learned, Negro fans were choosy.

And Mays had what it took to win them over. His name was catchy. It became even more colorful when someone tagged him Amazin' Willie Mays. He joined the Giants following a big buildup and a tremendous stint at Minneapolis. As a player, he fairly bristled with talent. He was one born for the flamboyant, crowd-delighting play. That Harlem would go for him became apparent at the Polo Grounds when Negro employees began taking a moment off every time he went to bat. Willie's arrival touched off the miracle.

Before the 1951 season was long gone, it was clear that someone or something had come a clinker in Durocher's "kind of team." The Giants, so to speak, were going no place, and all too quickly. No one realized this better than Leo. Never a stand-patter when Lady Luck was smiling at other gents, he unraveled and rewound his fine baseball brain, searching for the answer, the spark to success.

That the Giants had the "stuff" on paper was unquestioned. It just wasn't clicking on-field. Negro players figured in several ways. Irvin was playing first base in a style which proved he was much better in the outfield. Thompson, whom Durocher had described as the best third baseman he ever managed for one season (1950), was about to write another opinion in his manager's mind. And, both of them, plus utility man Artie Wilson, were sports page candidates for the troublesome spot in right—but neither of them fitted. When in the outfield, Irvin was best in left; Wilson's arm was not suited to outfield throwing; and Thompson was then believed to be in a slump from which he would soon bust loose, hence he continued his status as the Giants' third baseman.

Meanwhile, Willie, just a year out of an Alabama high school, was literally tearing the American Association apart. He was hitting as if pitchers were on his payroll, fielding like one possessed of psychic powers, and cutting down theft-minded base runners with pistol-shot throws. More descriptive than wild adjectives was his .477 batting average. Veteran players and managers, their eyes bulged wide with amazement, lavished praise on him.

"The best kid I've seen in years," said Al Simmons, one of the all-time-best hitters. "He's got everything."

Durocher knew about Mays, of course. He knew that Willie had hit .353 in eighty-one games at Trenton (a Class-B club) in 1950. He knew that Willie had batted .400 or better for much of that season. He also knew how Willie had performed remarkably from the early days of spring training. The natural conclusion: Mays might help put the Giants on pennant peak.

Durocher and president Horace Stoneham discussed pro and con the prospect of Mays, the major leaguer. There were three important, interrogative cons: How would Minneapolis fans react if the boy they fairly well loved was suddenly lifted from the Millers' squad? What would the Minneapolis management say on losing its top gate attraction and team sparkplug? Could a kid of less than a year's experience (then his age was nineteen) in organized ball cut the mustard in the majors?

Fortunately, there was a precedent for calling up an inexperienced youngster for Giant duty. John McGraw had set it when he took a chance on an even younger player, Mel Ott—and the player became the National League's premier home-run hitter of all time.

So Mays, who had turned twenty on May 6, was called up. The Giants ran an ad in a Minneapolis newspaper to explain why the move was being made!

Willie arrived in New York on May 24. Behind him was this fantastic batting average, .477, and a sixteen-game hitting streak. Ahead of him was the unsolicited job of being the Giants' pennant assurer.

Mays wasted little time amazing observers: he drove three long "homers" into the stands during his first pre-game batting practice. Perhaps, though, his personality, build, and carriage drew more attention than his hitting. He was, as said, just a kid, an eager beaver. He talked with the urgency of a first-time father-to-be calling for an ambulance to take his wife to a hospital. He was friendly, square-shouldered, five feet ten and a half inches tall, and weighed 180 pounds. Although he wore some shades of the bush league green, he displayed the unmistakable makings of a diamond artist.

Willie's minor league feats hadn't turned his head. "I was surprised when I was called up," he said. "I didn't figure it would be until next spring. I know what I'm up against here. I know I can't hit that .477 I was hitting at Minneapolis. But, I hope I can hit .280. I think I can."

Durocher liked the way Willie stood up there at the plate. He had confidence—and power.

"The fellows were watching him," Durocher said, "when he took batting practice. When they saw him bang three in a row into the seats, you could see them relax. They were satisfied we had a kid who could help us. But, before that, I learned more about him than I could in a week of just watching.

"He came in and introduced himself. I had read in the paper where they were flattering him pretty good in Minneapolis. I said to him, 'Willie, they must dust you off a lot here to see what you're made of.'

" 'Mr. Durocher,' he said, 'I expect that. It's baseball. But, they throw them down in here too, don't they?'

"He made a motion with his hand through the strike zone."

Despite those three practice shots, Mays did not become an immediate hitting sensation. Beginning his career at Philadelphia on May 25, he was called out on strikes, hit a long fly to right center, drove another to left, and was safe on an infielder's fumble. He handled five chances in the field without a recorded error. There was, however, an error of omission.

"That first game," he recalled, "I was playing too shallow. Sisler hit one I couldn't reach because I didn't respect him enough. The next time I played him deep. I was in the right spot. It didn't go over my head."

Durocher liked the way he figured things. "The kid learned the right thing without me telling him," Durocher said.

On May 26, the Giants beat the Phils 2 to 0, and Willie went hitless again. Although he had done little in two games, however, his presence contributed to one of the season's most important moves. It happened this way.

In order to give Mays every possible chance to make good, Durocher placed him in his usual position, center field, and moved Bobby Thomson, the club's prior center fielder, to another position. Before the arrival of Mays, Thomson was hitting only .229. But jolted by the threat of losing his job, Bobby went on a batting spree that netted five hits in eleven at bats. For the balance of the season, he contributed importantly to the team's offense. The spot he was settled in was Hank Thompson's third base.

Twelve times, Willie went to bat without hitting. On his thirteenth try, he homered. But that was his only safety in twenty-six at bats!

When the Giants began a tour of the West, Mays was hitting a puny .038. On the swing through Chicago, St. Louis, Pittsburgh, and Cincinnati, he lifted the average to .316!

Durocher was delighted. "The guy's got so much drive," he observed, "he's infected the rest of the club."

For a relatively small player, Mays showed tremendous power. During a practice session at Chicago, he drove seven of eleven pitches for "home runs." One ball landed in the center field stands, thirty rows up. His power came from strong arms and fluent wrists. A right-handed batter, he also had the ability to hit the ball where it was pitched, thus driving to all fields. His home runs figured strongly in winning games as the Giants made slow recovery from their near-disastrous, early-season slump.

Mays's fielding was simply sensational. Not only did he have the gift of good judgment on fly balls, more than adequate speed, and sure hands; he also possessed a flair for showmanship.

One night in July, he made a startling, meat-hand catch of a hard line drive off the bat of Pittsburg's Rocky Nelson. Instead of playing many liners for "safe" singles, he tried shoestring catches—and made them.

It was Willie's fielding, in fact, that drew from Durocher another round of applause. "This," he said, "is the best looking rookie I've seen in 25 years of baseball."

On August 25, at the Polo Grounds, Willie made The Play of the season. The Giants were playing the Dodgers. It was the eighth inning, score tied at 1-all. The Dodgers had a man on first and another, Billy Cox, on third. Carl Furillo was at bat.

Furillo hit a twisting fly to right center field, and Mays gave chase. Cox, a fast man, tagged up at third, prepared to score the tie-breaking run. As he ran, it appeared that Mays, a right-hand thrower, was in an impossible position to make a throw—he was running with his face to the right-field foul line. But he caught the ball, wheeled in full circle, and rifled a perfect strike, on the fly, to catcher Wes Westrum, who tagged out the sliding Cox. Dodgers muttered in disbelief.

Furillo, himself one of the game's best throwers, commented, "That was the greatest throw I ever saw . . . and I don't think there's a man in the world who could make two identical throws like that."

In the clubhouse, however, Mays said he had made a similar throw at Trenton. "I had it all figured out," he said. "I had to get my full power into it and the only way I could do it was to make that full pivot. Yeah, I guess it was the best throw I ever made."

Mays was the Giants' inspiration. Although his hitting eventually tapered off to .274, six points below the .280 he'd guessed he could hit, he was a season-long sparkler in the field. And he was the kid who could bring a laugh at the darkest moment. Other players had plenty of fun joking with him, amiably making fun of his habit of prefacing every statement with "Say, hey. . . ." All the Giants got to saying, "Say, hey. . . ." They liked his good nature, his bubbling enthusiasm, his naiveté.

There was this funny incident. Willie and another Giant fell into a discussion of speed. Subsequently, one of the players said to Willie, "I'll race you for five dollars." Willie, knowing he could beat the guy, eagerly and quickly assented. They raced and Willie won. But before he could put in a claim for the money, the beaten runner said, "Okay, give me five dollars."

Willie was dumbfounded. It was a half season before Durocher and the Giants could convince Willie that he owed five dollars, that the beaten runner hadn't bet five dollars that he could beat Mays running but, instead, had offered to race him *for* five dollars.

Willie, of course, didn't pull The Miracle off by himself. But, no other Giant was *more* responsible for it than he. At rock bottom in the early days of the campaign, still thirteen full games behind the Dodgers on August 11, the Giants won thirty-nine of their last forty-seven games, ended the season in a tie with the Brooklyners and beat them two-out-of-three in a historic play-off.

The play-off was won when Bobby Thomson, who'd gone to third when Willie went to center, pickled one of Ralph Branca's pitches for a home run.

Withal, Willie couldn't quite believe it. "My father always wanted me to be a major league player," he said. "I wanted to be one, too. But, I didn't figure I'd make it until 1952."

Hank Thompson contributed to the miracle in a negative way. By failing to come through as he had in 1950, he made a weak spot of third. To fill it, as was stated before, Durocher called up Mays and shifted Bobby Thomson. The season before a fine fielder, a good base runner, and as vicious with the bat as any little man (five-nine, 170) in the majors, he was called, as the writer has said, the best third baseman for one season in Durocher's managerial career.

But he tailed off badly, eventually being returned to the minors (Minneapolis). Rejuvenated there (batting average, fourteen games: 340), he was recalled. Shuttled between the infield and outfield, he finished 1951 with a .235 average.

Although he had failed, Thompson had notched a place in the history of baseball: he was the first Negro to play in both the American and National leagues.

He was given his first "chance" in 1947 when the St. Louis Browns obtained him and center fielder Willard Brown from the Kansas City Monarchs. Jackie Robinson was ringing the National League turnstiles and the Indians had signed Larry Doby. The Browns, going badly at the gate, decided to sign Thompson and Brown in the hope that Negro fans would attend games in substantial numbers. But St. Louis was a border town, given in many ways to Dixieland-style attitudes. Only a few years previous had Negroes been allowed to sit unsegregated in Sportsman's Park. They didn't take the bait. The Browns released both players.

Whether or not Willard Brown was of major league caliber was subject to conjecture, for he was not given sufficient opportunity to make or break himself. Thompson, a second baseman, followed a period of orientation with solid performance. His .256 overall average reflected inaccurately his ability, for in games preceding his release, he was hitting well and fielding superbly.

On his release, he returned to the Monarchs, with whom he played again in 1948. The next season, he signed with the Giants as a free agent—after leading the Cuban league in batting—and was sent to their farm at Jersey City. Playing at shortstop and in the outfield, he hit .296 in sixty-eight games, then was promoted, with Irvin, to the parent-club roster. In seventy-five games at second and third, he hit .280.

If Willie Mays was the spirit behind the Giants' miracle of 1951, then big, strong, solid Monte Irvin was the brawn. He was the guy standing up at the plate cool and steady with men on bases and the Giants behind in score. He was the man who swung the mean shillelah. The guy who cleaned the bases. The guy whose natural, major league ability came through for the first time in a chips-down year.

The belated acclaim that rang in Irvin's ears when the season was over sounded doubly good to him because it had been so long coming; because, like Mays and his father, he had dreamed of the majors.

"Ever since I was a kid," Monte was to relate, "it was my biggest ambition to play in the major leagues."

In the Negro leagues, he played like a prospective major leaguer, yet he remained with the Newark Eagles while others, some with lesser promise, were signed to contracts in organized ball. Naturally quiet, in some personality traits a parallel of Doby, he was to reach a point of wondering if fate was against him before the big chance came. And, after it came, he had a tough time proving his worth.

Irvin, like Doby, was another of those wonder athletes from Jersey. At Orange High School, he was a phenom. His coach, Carl Seibert, was to relate that his feats were "legendary." Possessed of a powerful physique as a youth, he earned All-State honors in football, basketball, and track. One year, he hit .666 and also pitched, averaging fourteen strikeouts a game. After a week's practice, he set a high school record by throwing the javelin 192 feet, 2 inches. Boxing was about the only sport in which Irvin didn't excel.

"I tried boxing once," Irvin related. "I thought I was pretty good. Just a kid in Orange. One day, I went to a gym to box a pro, just to see whether I really had anything worth working on.

"We were going along nicely when suddenly he leaves himself wide open. I hit him with my right, giving it all I had. I mean it was my Sunday punch. Everything. My full arm and all my weight behind it. Right on the jaw.

"But, do you know what he did? He just shook his head. Right then and there, I took off the gloves and threw them away. Fighting was no business for me."

After high school, he received a football scholarship from Lincoln University, a Negro college for boys in Oxford, Pennsylvania. He remained there until 1938, when he quit to join the Newark Eagles. Excluding three years of war service with the Army Engineers, he was an Eagle until 1947, during which time he made an enviable record.

In 1941, for example, he batted .422, blasting 44 homers and driving in 141 runs. In 1946, he again led the Negro National League with a .389 average. Illness slowed him up in 1947, decreasing his average to .313. Meanwhile, he had played in Mexico and other Latin American countries.

Recovered from the recurring physical and psychological ills contracted during the war, Irvin was signed by the Brooklyn Dodgers in 1948. Rickey's plan was to send him to St. Paul. The break had resulted from his outstanding play in the Cuban winter league. But he never played a game in the Brooklyn organization. Rickey and Mrs. Manley were unable to reach an agreement, so Rickey dropped him.

The next winter, he starred with the Almendares club in the Cuban league, then was signed by the Giants, for Jersey City. There, he batted .373 in sixty-three games, drove in fifty-two runs, hit nine homers (including one of record distance), and fielded .991. The Giants called him. But playing both the infield and outfield and pinch hitting, his average was only .224. He went to 1950 spring training camp with the Giants, but started the season at Jersey City. In eighteen games, he batted a phenomenal .510, clouting ten homers and driving in thirty-three runs. The Giants called him up again.

This time, Monte was ready. In his first game, he hit a grand-slam home run off Dutch Leonard, Chicago Cubs pitcher. He played every outfield position and third base, then was placed on first near the season's nub. He batted .300.

He opened the 1951 season at first base, but soon as was said, proved himself inept at the position. His fielding was bad and, because of it, his hitting suffered. Durocher finally sent outfielder Whitey Lockman to first and shifted Irvin to the outfield. He played both right and left fields before finally earning a set position in left. Being a regular in a spot he could handle was all the tonic he needed. Henceforth, he was an all-star.

Previously a Joe DiMaggio-style batter, Irvin studied Ralph Kiner's technique of hitting to both right and left fields from the right-handed stance. He practiced the technique until his timing was perfect. And, in the process, he dueled Kiner for the National League's runs-batted-in title. Monte batted .312 for the season and won the runs-batted-in title with 121.

That latter figure does not eloquently tell his worth to the club. That is found only in a study of the games won. How hot he was is reflected in the fact that from June 28, when he changed his stance, to September 5, he drove in fifty-one runs.

In the stretch drive, when the Giants whittled the Dodgers' seemingly insurmountable lead game by game, Irvin, whistling hits with a cut down swing, hitting homers to all fields although concentrating on meeting the ball where it was pitched, frequently stood between victory and defeat, snatching the club from the latter and placing it on the winning side of the won-lost columns.

It was Irvin's single that drove Alvin Dark home with the winning run in a 3 to 2 victory over the Braves on September 30, final day of the regular season. That run preserved the Giants' tie for the National League pennant, depositing them into the historic play-off games, which the Giants won.

When the Giants met the Yankees in the World Series, thousands of fans wondered if the Durochermen would pull still another miracle, make the clean sweep. Irvin grabbed everlasting fame for himself in the first game when he swiped home from Yankee pitcher Allie Reynolds and catcher Yogi Berra. Ironically, it was the first such theft since McNally and Meusel stole on the Giants in the World Series of 1921. Monte also jarred Yankee pitching with his consistent hitting, collecting eleven safeties and tying three batting records with a .458 average. But the Yankees broke the spell, winning again to end an all-time great season.

That Mays would win Rookie of the Year honors was taken for granted. Many were of the opinion that Irvin deserved the Most Valuable Player award. But Campanella (who was an Irvin man, too) won it with 243 votes of baseball writers. Stan Musial was second with 191 votes, and Monte was third with 166 votes. Behind him were Sal Maglie, Preacher Roe, Jackie Robinson, and other top performers.

During the off-season, Durocher emphasized that Irvin was his "Big Man." Said the manager: "Every time I looked up, he was getting the big hit. He was either driving in a run or leading off the inning and getting on base when we needed a man on."

Giants coach Freddie Fitzsimmons brought up the subject of Irvin's speed and base-running ability, which was most impressively reflected in his six steals of home during the year. "I'd rather have him running the bases than any other player in the league," said Fitzsimmons. "He always gets that extra base, and if we need a steal of home, he's the best there is."

In November, Irvin made a swipe at another career: politics. Interrupting a barnstorming tour with Roy Campanella's All-Stars he flew to Orange from Houston to make his first speech as a candidate, on the Democratic ticket, for the New Jersey Assembly.

"Monte, who is over 6 feet tall, unconsciously slipped into a batter's widespread stance as he approached his first campaign microphone in a lunchroom adjoining the storage battery plant of Thomas A. Edison, Inc., in West Orange," the New York *Times* reported on November 3. "The familiar pose brought approving smiles from the 150 Edison employees who were his audience. Monte, however, quickly corrected the stance, fixing himself before the 'mike' and talked extemporaneously about his program, pledging himself to 'fight for better housing, public health and welfare.' "

Although some observers said Irvin was being used by the Democrats in the hope that they could grab Negro votes and snatch victory in a Republican stronghold, Irvin explained his sally into politics thusly: "There'll be a time—not many years from now—when I'll be too old to play baseball," he said. "There's a chance to do a lot of good in politics. I think I'd like to make it a career."

But, the Republicans, unlike Allie Reynolds, took no windup. They had the play beaten before it started. Monte fanned in the political league.

In December, the Giants rewarded Monte's fine play by giving him a twenty-five-thousand-dollar contract for 1952.

"That's the most money I ever made anywhere in my life," said Monte, who had drawn seven hundred dollars a month from the Eagles. "Naturally I am pretty happy about it, but I still can't help but think what might have been for me, if I had come to the majors just after I got out of high school.

"Of course, I guess I've got more sense now and I certainly know more about the game than I did then. But, I think back on it and can't help wondering how it would have been if I had been able to play in the majors all those years."

Then, in a statement fate was to make most ironic, he added, "With the new contract and no business problems, I haven't got a worry in the world."

Bad luck struck at Denver, Colorado, on April 2, while the Giants were playing an exhibition with the Indians. It was the second inning. Monte, who had walked to open the frame, was racing from first to third on a single by Mays. Unaware that Indian outfielder Pete Reiser had elected to make no play on him, Monte made a needless slide into third, grimacing in pain as the spikes of his shoe caught in the ground and held, shattering his right ankle, the one he powered hits off. Cleveland third baseman Al Rosen said later he heard the bones break. Mays, who had been trapped in a run-down, cried salty tears, and tried to blame himself for the mishap.

In the New York *Journal American* of April 4, sports columnist Frank Graham appraised the loss. "Suddenly," he wrote, "everybody was acutely aware that Monte was the strong boy of the club. The leading hitter. The one who hammered in the most runs. The one who, so often, got that extra base when it was so sorely needed. The one who played left field better than any other the Giants had had for a very long time.

"No wonder poor Willie Mays, believing that, because he had been caught in a rundown between first and second, he was responsible for Monte's injury, battered his head against the ground."

Still, Monte, who had fought back from the terrible ravages of war, tried to erase the gloom that settled over the Giants. From his bed in a Denver hospital, his ankle encased in a cast, he smiled wanly and promised, "I'll be back before the season's over. I heal fast."

Doctors looked at the fracture and admitted that the bones were cleanly broken. But, could he play again in 1952? No doctor would stick his neck out far enough flatly to corroborate Irvin's claim. Irvin, however, knew whereof he spoke. The injury healed amazingly.

In late July, a New York surgeon reported, "The bones have knit perfectly. And, in all respects he has made a highly satisfactory recovery. He can play now whenever he feels that he's fit. All I ask is that he exercise normal care and that he not try to do it all at once."

Cautiously, Irvin worked out. Batting. Hitting. Running. His ankle was protected by a football-type shoe. He started out pinch hitting. He could run fairly well in a straight line, but stops and cuts hurt him.

In the ninth inning of a game against the Cincinnati Reds, Irvin stepped up to the plate as a pinch hitter for pitcher Jim Hearn and got a single, his first hit of the season—in his first appearance at the plate! Fans gave him a tremendous ovation, and the Giants slaughtered the Reds 11 to 4.

Finally, Monte worked himself into shape for regular duty and took over the clean-up spot he'd filled in 1951. The Giants began to move. Shades of 1951! The Dodgers were losing again and the Giants were winning. Was another miracle in the works?

It wasn't, although the Giants gave the Dodgers a bad scare up to September 23. Still, Irvin again had proven his worth. He was the difference between a weak second or an unsteady third and a strong second place finish. As Giants said in the clubhouse, "Since he came back, we started to go."

In the meantime, Willie Mays was in the Army, stationed at Fort Eustis, Virginia, where he continued his scintillating play. Willie had been around until May, when Alabama draft officials definitely made up their minds that he was "fit" for army duty. He had "flunked" an aptitude test during the off-season and was at first deferred. The second time, though, he passed the test. A late family hardship plea failed. And Willie, the precocious kid, went striding off to service, predicting that he'd be back in two years, ready to pick up his career in his prime. He was going to heed Durocher's advice, and stay in shape, he said.

Hank Thompson, enjoying a better year, tried to carry on in center field. But the Giants lost eight out of ten after Willie left. It wasn't Hank's fault. He played good ball and hit as he had in 1950. The fact was: nobody could replace Willie Mays.

11

BIG NEWK

The first game of the 1949 World Series, Dodgers and Yankees, was a classic. Don Newcombe, the Dodgers' Negro rookie, and Allie Reynolds, the Yankees' part-Indian hurler, kept 66,224 fans on the edges of their seats in Yankee Stadium as they dueled, 0 to 0, down the stretch. Newcombe looked like an old veteran, one who had been baptized in World Series fire many moons ago. He had confidence and he had stuff on the ball. He had those Yanks eating out of his hand, so to speak, swinging like rusty gates, fanning the thin air as their bats sought out little white baseballs that weren't there when their swings came around. Allie, much maligned during the season because he finished few games he started, was likewise superb.

At the end of eight innings, Newk had struck out eleven Yankee batters. He was just two away from the Series record of thirteen strikeouts set in the long ago by Connie Mack's surprise starter, Howard Ehmke. He had walked none. And only four hits had been credited to those traditionally hard sluggers from "The House that Ruth Built."

Allie, although in trouble more often than Newk, had held the Dodgers, who had hitters like Robinson, Campanella, Gil Hodges, Peewee Reese and Duke Snider, to a mere two hits. World Series games, from a pitcher's point of view, had seldom, if ever, come any better.

Then came the ninth, and Tommy Henrich, an old pro, led off for the Yankees. Although Tommy played tops in right field, he had for years performed in the shadow of Joe DiMaggio. His greatness, especially in the clutch, was not deservedly publicized. But Bob Feller, the Indians' great swifty, was one who testified to his greatness, for Henrich leveled on Bob as if he had discovered him almost every time the two faced each other.

In Newcombe, Henrich was facing another top fast-ball artist, a big man who could powder that ball in there. Newcombe, in turn, knew Henrich was a dangerous man. He was careful with him. It was reflected in the two balls he threw: he didn't want to put a good one across.

Newk went into his windup for the third pitch. It was a low curve. Henrich timed it, then took a full, hard swing. His bat met the ball and the ball took off in a high arc for the right-field stands.

Big Newk watched it fly over the space between first and second bases. Then, knowing it was a homer, he turned, stuffed his glove into his pocket, and ambled for the dugout. The Yankees had won again, on that big blow in the last of the ninth—by the heartbreaking score of 1 to 0.

Despite the disappointment, the loss of that big first game, Newcombe had become one of the best major league hurlers in less than a season. That he was starting a World Series game was like something out of a movie script, for after the season was well underway, he was pitching for Montreal. Called up when the Dodgers staff showed weakness, he had become a big man in a hurry!

Don Newcombe was (and, of course, is) a big man—big enough, physically, to take on a Primo Camera and make the contest look like an even match, big enough on the mound to become, in less than a season, one of the National League's best pitchers, big enough in three seasons to be on his way toward a truly brilliant career when, whammo!, Uncle Sam sent him back into military service, the long streams of questionable red tape still uncut.

Despite his height, six-four, and weight, 235, Don came by success the rugged, the sometimes-complicated, if not the hard way. Born in Madison, New Jersey, on June 14, 1926, he was one of five children of Mr. and Mrs. Iames Newcombe. When Don's sister died at age eight, Mr. and Mrs. Newcombe had a quartet of boys who, as they grew, took to palling around together, playing most kid games as well as the organized sports. Mr. Newcombe had a steady job chauffeuring for a Madison family; thus the Newcombes were always sure of eating three squares a day, with the very good prospect that dessert, too, would be forthcoming.

Despite his size, Don was allergic to heavy work, a facet of his personality which on more than one occasion led observers to call him lazy. But he liked pitching, and he worked at it. When he was only nine, he hurled batting practice for a semi-pro club.

In his tenth year, the family moved to Elizabeth, New Jersey, where Don was to gain considerable notice as a football and baseball player. He pitched two seasons for the Lafayette Junior High School team, winning seven and losing none the second season. Lafayette had played only an eight-game schedule!

He continued his education until he flunked a course, or two, as a high school senior, then quit to enlist in the army. There had been no high school ball to speak of, since there had been no regular team.

Enlisting in the army was easier said than done in Don's case, an ironic twist in view of the way things worked out in 1952. He was okayed by draft officials, but after the induction notice was sent, Mr. Newcombe went to the board and explained things. Don was on a trip to Tennessee at the time, was the first thing. The other: Don was too young for army duty. The army agreed with Mr. Newcombe. Not long thereafter, however, he was old enough to satisfy the navy. He was shipped to Great Lakes, where he served briefly.

On his return home, Don "fooled around" a bit, working at odd jobs, playing a little semi-pro baseball and a lot of amateur checkers.

Oddly, it was through the checker games that he became a baseball pro.

One day in the winter of 1943, he sat down to a game with a friend, Buddy Holder, in an Elizabeth barbershop. As was usual, Holder won all the games. Newk was so bad, Holder had to laugh.

"As a checker player," he said, "you'd make a darned good pitcher." The idea, expressed first in jest, soon sounded reasonable to Holder. "Say," he continued to Don, "have you ever thought about trying to play ball for a living?"

"Shucks, no," replied Don, who thought he was being ribbed again.

But the next day, Holder drove Don to Newark, New Jersey, where friends of his, Mr. and Mrs. Abe Manley, owned the Eagles.

Mrs. Manley, who patterned her club after the Yankees in searching for big players, was immediately impressed by the size of Newcombe. She offered him a tryout in spring camp at Richmond, Virginia. Don accepted, although he was far from convinced that he could cut the mustard.

"In those days," he was to say, "I was lightning fast. But, I seldom knew where my next pitch was going."

Besides his fast ball, he also owned a pretty good curve. The two pitches won seven games for him that season. He lost five. In 1945, he won fourteen and lost only four. He had developed more stuff, stuff Negro National League batters couldn't understand.

In October, 1945, he pitched in an all-star game at Ebbets Field. One team was composed of Negro National League stars, the other of major leaguers such as Whitey Kurowski, the St. Louis third baseman; Frank McCormick, the Cincinnati first baseman; Eddie Stanky, Buddy Kerr, and Ralph Branca. In three innings, the major leaguers scored a run, but obtained no hits off Don's offerings. However, he was forced to retire because of a bad elbow.

Sorry he had to quit, but proud of his achievement, Don ambled off the field while fans applauded enthusiastically. They had liked the cut of his jib, so to speak. More specifically, they had liked his smooth, sweeping motion, his cunning, and the blazing fast ball he powered across the plate right-handedly. In the dressing room, Mr. Newcombe, proud of his son, wanted to know what the trouble was. Don explained that the elbow had gone bad when he had thrown a fast ball to Goody Rosen.

Then, while Don was finishing his bath, the same white-haired, thin man who had approached Jackie Robinson at Chicago, walked up and introduced himself as Clyde Sukeforth, coach for Brooklyn. "Mr. Rickey," Sukeforth said, "wants to talk to you."

Don and his wife, Freddie, whom he had married following a courtship which took place during the spring training at Richmond, went to see Rickey. Don agreed to play with the aforementioned Brown Dodgers, or any other club Rickey might choose. Not until Jackie Robinson was signed did Don, like Campanella, realize that he was in line for a berth in organized baseball.

Subsequently, Don signed with the Brooklyn organization and, again like Campy, was offered to the Danville club of the Three-Eye League. Danville again said nix on Negroes. So Don, with Campy, went to Nashua, where he won fourteen games and lost four, duplicating his Negro National League record.

Don spent the off-season in Cuba, at first pitching winter ball, but after the league folded, having fun with wife Freddie on what was, to all intents and purposes, something of a honeymoon. He returned home for a short visit, then headed back to Cuba, where the Montreal Royals were in training. With Jackie, Campy, and pitcher Roy Partlow, Newcombe lived in a run-of-the-mine Havana hotel while his teammates lived at the Havana Military Academy. The Dodgers were quartered at the swank Hotel Nacional.

Then began a series of unhappy events:

First, Branch Rickey, Jr., decided that Don was overly large and prescribed a lot of running. Anxious to make good, Don ran and ran and ran, until he had reduced thirty-five pounds—and had lost his effectiveness.

"I got so weak," he was to relate, "that I couldn't break a pane of glass from six feet."

He was sent home to regain weight. Fretting at this spring-time inactivity, Don lazed away a few days, then decided to talk to Rickey, Sr., in Brooklyn.

Don had borrowed some money from the Dodger organization and the primary reason for the trip was to tell Rickey, Sr., that he wouldn't be able to clear up the debt as soon as he had hoped. But Rickey, who had been "queered" on Don by some unidentified culprit, mistook the meaning of the visit and Newcombe's talk and quickly brushed him off.

"If that's the way you feel," Rickey said, after hearing Don's initial words, "you can go over to the office and pick up your release right now!"

Don quit Rickey's presence. But on his way, the thought struck him that somewhere skullduggery was afoot. He returned and, this time, gave Rickey a complete explanation of why he had come. Rickey relented. Don went back to Nashua for 1947 while Campy was promoted to Montreal. He won 19 games, lost only 6, and struck out 186 batters in 223 innings. His wins and strikeouts were New England League toppers.

This record, plus a 10-3 winter league mark for the Caracas, Venezuela, club managed by Roy Campanella, satisfied Dodger brass that Don was on the right track. He was promoted to Montreal in 1948, where he won 17 and lost 6, posted a 3.14 earned run average, and struck out 144 batters in 189 innings. High mark of the season was August 15 when he hurled a seven-inning, no-hit, no-run game against Toronto. He beat Rochester 3 to 0 in his next start, missing a second no-hitter only because of a scratch hit to the infield.

Next stop, it seemed logical to Don, was Brooklyn. But he was not yet out of fate's thickly matted forest. First, there was the race question popping up again and, second, Don was far from convincing during winter league play in Cuba.

By this time, the Dodgers had two Negroes, Robinson and Campanella. Don, if brought up, would make three. Rickey was the pioneer in the racial integration movement and, ostensibly, had the right to set whatever precedent he desired or considered the limit. The limit, at the moment, was two. He was fearful that trouble might result if three Negroes were placed on one club, if, in Brooklyn's case, it happened every fourth day that one third of the playing unit was Negro.

The pitching failure was one of those things. "My arm didn't bother me or anything," Don later said. "I just couldn't get the ball over the plate." He worked with two Cuban clubs and flopped with both of them. After the Almendares (including Sam Jethroe and Monte Irvin) released him for his second failure, the Dodgers had what they considered a solid excuse for returning him to Montreal.

Don was ordered to report with the Royals for 1949 spring training at Vero Beach, Florida, the fabulous Dodgertown operation Rickey built after he leased the site from the Government. On reporting, the player tried little to disguise his displeasure. He thought he was ready for the big team; not making it, he sulked openly, currying disfavor with Burt Shotton, the Brooklyn manager, who replied to an inquiry on the possible promotion of Newcombe by saying, "We'll bring him up as soon as he learns to keep his big mouth shut." The idea got around that Don was "too big for his britches," a startling statement any way one examined it. Don reacted to further criticism and unfavorable publicity by going home!

Here were reflected the then-two Don Newcombes. Newcombe, The Real, was just a big, friendly fellow, one a fan could love. A good, clean guy, not overly talkative, who laughed easily, a kid who liked to eat and tap his toe to the rhythm of solid jazz. A man who'd greet a person with sincere, smiling eyes and a warm, strong handshake.

Newcombe, The Dissatisfied, was the typical I-ain't-taking-no-stuff-off-you type. He figured he was getting rooked by Brooklyn, he was sore, he went home. He was actually a kid who hadn't learned tact.

It has been said that the difficulty arose because Rickey had planned to circumvent the possibility of adverse public reaction to three Negroes on one club. He wanted Newcombe to make such a record at Montreal, it was said, that the force of public opinion would work for the promotion of Newcombe. If so, Don had upset the applecart by going home.

Back in Jersey with wife Freddie, however, Don cooled off. He began to think, and he realized that he had little choice, unless he wanted to go back to Negro ball. There was, of course, the almost sure bet that he would make Brooklyn eventually; and the more he thought about things calmly, with the advice of his wife getting an assist, he headed for the conclusion that Montreal wasn't so bad after all. If he had acted like a spoiled brat once, he counteracted it afterward by acting like a man.

Putting through a telephone call to Buzzy Bavasi, the Montreal business manager, the man who had quickly accepted him and Campanella at Nashua after Danville turned thumbs down on both of them, Don asked, "Buzzy, will you take a damn fool back?"

"Anybody who can win 20 games for me, I want him," Bavasi replied in a friendly tone, and Don was back in good standing. But at this juncture, as if the very devil were on his tail, Don's arm became sore. Nevertheless, he made five starts for Montreal, winning two on shutouts and losing two. Late in May, the call came from Brooklyn.

Shotton, remembering the spring, had only this to say: "I think he's decided to keep his mouth shut!"

But what about that arm?

"Mr. Rickey knew it was sore," Don was to relate. "I didn't think they would bring me up with a sore arm."

He didn't say anything about it, though, after getting word of the promotion. Instead, he jumped into his car and drove to Elizabeth.

"As soon as we got home to Jersey," he said, "my wife started working on the arm. She took hot towels and some liniment from the medicine closet. The liniment didn't even have a name on it. She worked on it that night and most of the next day, rubbing it.

"When I reported, I could cut the ball loose. I guess there had just been a cold in that arm, but it bothered me a whole lot. Nothing worked until my wife rubbed me."

The soreness gone, thanks to Mrs. Newcombe's deftness with a hot towel and a bottle of nameless Latin liniment, Don joined the Dodgers. He was given a relief assignment against the Cardinals as a starter, and it was a dilly—for fattening St. Louis batting averages.

It happened in the seventh inning. Rex Barney had been lifted for a pinch hitter in the Dodger half. Shotton, pulling a surprise, called on Don to relieve. He looked good striking out center fielder Chuck Diering. Then infielder Red Schoendienst singled to left, center fielder Stan Musial also singled, and Eddie Kazak loaded the bases with a hot shot to Peewee Reese. Enos Slaughter, the old pro, promptly blasted one of Don's fast balls for a double, unloading the bases. That was all.

The big guy was worried sick in the dressing room. He had failed in his first chance. Would Shotton recommend a return to Montreal? He couldn't help but ask himself that question, for he remembered all too clearly Shotton's vitriolic comments about him. By the time the game was over and Dodgers came straggling in, Don was about set to hear bad news. But Shotton was of another mind.

Walking over to him, the elderly manager looked the kid in the eye and spoke softly. "Don't let it bother you, son," Shotton said. "There's no need to get discouraged. I'm starting you against Cincinnati. You can make up for it there."

That was like having clouds pulled back for cheerful blue skies and a smiling Ol' Sol. And the arm felt good, too.

Don got rolling against the Reds, shutting them out on five hits. He went on to become an important member of the pennant-winning club, winning seventeen games against eight losses, striking out 149 batters in 244 innings, posting a 3.17 earned run average. During a hot stretch of pennant fight, he hurled thirty-two consecutive scoreless innings. Although he had been called up in May, he was named to the All-Star squad by Billy Southworth; and a few weeks after the Series, in which he lost the aforementioned game on Henrich's homer and another in which he had little of his good stuff, he was honored as National League Rookie of the Year.

Verily, Don had become a big man in a hurry. Said one hitter: "When Newk is right, there's no better pitcher in the National League." The appraisal was, at the least, justifiable hyperbole. Although Don had receipted for the All-Star Game loss to the American Leaguers, Ted Williams, greatest hitter of the era, was impressed. Said Ted: "He's about as fast as anybody in our league. Even Hal Newhouser, Virgil Trucks, Vic Raschi, and Bob Feller aren't any faster." And the *Sporting News* doffed its "hat." "Newcombe," wrote Harold C. Burr, "has all the requisites to make him a great pitcher—size, ability, and stamina."

His repertoire? That hopping fast ball; a low, quick-breaking curve; a couple of change-ups; and adequate control. In his skein of thirty-two scoreless innings, he allowed only ten walks. The slight wildness was in his favor; it kept the batters loose. His three-quarter overhand delivery was a thing of beauty, fluent. Besides, Don could hit and field. That first year he garnered twenty-two safeties, more than any pitcher, and handled fifty-seven chances without an error.

The 1950 training season started off roughly, with Don back in Shotton's doghouse, and there was a pause for wonderment: was 1949 a fluke? Don said his arm was sore. Rex Barney and Ralph Branca said the same about their arms. Their claims were taken at face value, but Shotton, a baseball man from way back when players, like boxers of the Jake LaMotta type, took pride in disregarding injuries, said it was only Don's imagination.

A little hassle developed in April. Don was scheduled to pitch an exhibition against the Yankees. Don said his arm was sore, he couldn't pitch. Shotton said he would pitch.

"It's my arm and it hurts and I ain't working Friday (the day of the game)," Don said. "What's more, I think I got a pulled back muscle. Anyhow, I ain't working."

Said Shotton with a shrug, "My pitcher next Friday is Don Newcombe."

Newcombe rejoined, "It hurts. So does my back. What more can I say? If they feel this way Friday, I won't be able to pitch."

"Don Newcombe's pitching Friday against the Yankees," Shotton insisted. "What more can I say?"

But Don didn't pitch that Friday. In May, he was sent back to Colonia, New Jersey, where he'd bought a home, for a rest. When he returned, things were better. He went on to win nineteen games. His most dramatic feat came in September.

The Dodgers were playing the pennant-bound Phillies, at Philadelphia. Don shut them out on three hits in the first game of a doubleheader. It was his second such whitewashing in succession and his sixth straight victory. It was also his fourth shutout of the season and the third in his last four starts. He was hot, and the Dodgers' staff was battered. So, between games, Don went to Shotton with an idea.

"Want me to try it again?" He asked of the manager who had coldly scoffed at his sore arm, had called him a popoff guy, and said he was lazy.

Shotton was for the idea, if Don thought he could do it.

"I don't know," Don said. "I'm game to try. I'll do whatever you say."

"I think you'd be more effective than Bankhead," Shotton said. "Your arm's still warm, but it's up to you."

"Give me the ball," said Don.

It was the first time in ten years that any major leaguer had attempted this iron-man stunt. Bobo Newsom had tried it against the Detroit Tigers back in '40—and failed. For a while it appeared that Newk might do it. He allowed only two runs on eight hits in seven innings, being particularly hard to get to in the clutch. But he couldn't pull it off.

Afterward he said, "I don't know whether I could have finished or not. My arm had begun to tire in the sixth and it was very heavy in the seventh. No pain, but it was very tired."

Nobody ever said anything about Don being lazy after that heroic attempt to clip the Phillies' wings.

Brooklyn had a new regime in 1951. Branch Rickey had moved to Pittsburgh and Burt Shotton had retired to Florida. Walter O'Malley was club president and Chuck Dressen, most recently of the Oakland Oaks, was manager. The Dodgers got off to a fast start and, by mid-season, were rated as one of the all-time-great squads. They were loaded with stars. Jackie Robinson was baseball's best all-around second baseman, perhaps its greatest individual star; Roy Campanella was baseball's best catcher; and Newcombe at his best was unbeatable. Also: Pee-wee Reese was as good as any shortstop in the majors, if not better; Carl Furillo in right, Duke Snider in center, and (following a trade) Andy Pafko in left gave the team a terrific outfield. Gil Hodges, the muscular first baseman, made like a Babe Ruth and Billy Cox, at third, was an unsung star. How could they miss?

But, as said, they missed. During that run just ahead of the stretch, Newcombe floundered like all the rest. But he came on again in the homestretch. On September 26, he won his nineteenth game, a walloping 15 to 5 rout of the Braves, which included five runs driven in and three scored by Campanella, three scored by Jackie, one on a theft of home, and a seven-run rally in the eighth inning. On September 29, Don was back on the mound, hurling against the Phillies. He shut them out, 5 to 0, on seven hits, striking out seven. The pennant race was all tied up. The next day, after Preacher Roe had been hammered off the mound by the Phils, Newcombe went in as a reliefer. The Dodgers fought back from a 1 to 6 deficit to tie at 8-all. The game went into extra innings, and Newk weakened. He was relieved and the Dodgers eventually won, 9 to 8, on a heroic homer by Jackie.

When he went to the mound to pitch the third game of the play-offs, Newcombe was dead tired. He pitched on heart alone. Going into the bottom half of the ninth inning, at the Polo Grounds, Brooklyn led, 4 to 1. They could win the pennant with that one, and so could the Giants. It was, in other words, a rubber game. The first two batters to face Newcombe hit safely. After he forced Irvin, the big guy, to pop up, however, victory appeared close. Two more outs and it would be the World Series, despite el foldo. But Whitey Lockman doubled home a run. The score was 4 to 2, one out, two on. Bobby Thomson was at the plate.

Chuck Dressen pulled Newcombe and sent in Ralph Branca. Although Thomson had homered off Ralph in the first playoff game, Branca was to say, "Thomson didn't worry me at all. I was ready. My stuff was breaking sharply and the fast ball was hopping during my warmup. I felt good." Branca took the mound.

"Get this guy out!" Dressen said, handing Ralph the ball.

"Go get 'em, big boy!" said Newcombe, patting Branca on the back.

Branca went in with a fast ball, chest high, over the inside corner for a strike. He tried the fast one again, up under the chin—and Thomson swung. That was all, brother. The ball game: 5 to 4 Giants.

Why had Dressen pulled Newcombe for a pitcher who was known for his home-run pitches?

"When they got the hits in the ninth inning," Jackie Robinson explained later, "Dressen wanted to know whether or not Newcombe could stay in there and pitch. Don said, 'This is too important a game to take a chance on my arm.'

"At the end of seven innings, Don told Dressen on the bench, in front of the entire ball club, that his arm was dead. He said he didn't know whether he could go out and win for them in this game and that it was too important to take a chance on his arm."

For the second year in a row, Newcombe had tried to be an iron man—in vain.

In six years of organized ball, Don Newcombe had won 108 games, more than doubling his losses in victories. And he had not yet reached his prime. He had just begun to hit the big money class. He had a nice home in Colonia. There was conjecture that when Don really reached his peak, he'd be a thirty-game winner. Immortality ahead. Then Uncle Sam stepped in. Following a hue and cry in public print, he was inducted into the army and sent to Camp Pickett, Virginia.

Noted for red tape, and often criticized for spreading confusion, service officials pulled out all the stops on Newcombe, making what might have been a routine induction, at least as routine as possible with a celebrity, a cause for much wondering, more than a few angered words, and a slightly off-perfumery smell.

In fairness to the army, however, it is pointed out that there was also confusion in the ranks of the Newcombes. No one knew what kind of discharge Don had received after he served briefly in the navy in 1943. The papers had been lost. Don's wife said she thought he had received a medical discharge. Don said he didn't remember. His mother, Mrs. Sadie Newcombe, said she believed he had received a medical discharge because of kidney trouble.

Then draft officials said the records indicated Don had been discharged "by special order," but no one could say what that meant. For instance, by whose order? For what?

In November, Don took a pre-induction physical at Newark. He was classified as a "physical holdover" because of a kidney ailment, then shunted to Fort Jay for hospitalization and observation, pending clarification of his status. Since he was only twenty-five, was married but had no children, Don fell into a group with those reclassified from 3A to 1A, providing they had not served as much as ninety days in service. Nothing conclusive was revealed at Fort Jay.

In December, Don broke the fifth metacarpal bone in his right wrist while moving furniture in his mother's Elizabeth, New Jersey, home. A physician reported that the injury would be completely healed in four or five weeks.

Later the same month, an announcement came out of the Adjutant General's office in Washington. A public relations man for the Department of the Army announced that Newcombe was eligible for military service. It was revealed also that Don probably would be inducted at Governor's Island in New York, at a date to be determined by the First Anny. The chairman of the Elizabeth draft board guessed the call date at around February 1. Subsequently, Don was inducted from Camp Kilmer, New Jersey, and sent to Camp Pickett.

When the Dodgers passed through Richmond, Virginia, during their exhibition game tour, Don visited with his teammates. In an interview, he said that an examining officer at Pickett had "told me that the newspapers and public opinion forced them to take me into the army, even though they didn't think I belonged." The officer, Don said, had "found I have a growth across the opening of my bladder. The doctor said I should have an operation."

In May, Don entered the hospital at Camp Pickett for a physical examination. No reason was given by army officials. Later in the month, a Camp Pickett spokesman said that a decision would be reached on Don's status.

Next, Don was given leave to visit his sick wife, which, a spokesman said, would result in postponement of another examination and announcement of the aforementioned decision. There was a hint that Don might gain his release.

Shortly, another announcement came out of Washington. Don Newcombe, it said, had been examined and found fit for full duty. He must complete two years in service, was the punch line.

12

COMET FROM CUBA

One of baseball's prize Horatio Alger tales is that of a player whose parents were so poor he didn't start school until he was ten, who had to quit four years later and go to work, cutting sugar cane with a machete, to help chase the wolf from the family door; who as a youngster saw a chance for a better life in baseball and hitched his wagon to an old, crafty diamond star; who fought his way up through Negro ball and the minors, with bat, glove, and fleet feet, to establish himself firmly as one of the superior performers. It is the tale of the man who put the "Go!" in "Chicago." His name: Saturnino Orestes Armieta Arras Minoso. At Comiskey Park, everybody calls him "Minnie."

Minnie Minoso became one of the White Sox on May 1, 1951, the first Negro in the club's history. The first time he went to bat, he homered. The last time he went to bat that season, he homered. In between, he was the major sparkplug in the American League's surprise of the year. That, of course, was the emergence of Chicago as a pennant contender, a first placer for a portion of the season.

In going to Chicago, Minnie Minoso was a key man in the season's Big Deal, a three-way transaction involving Cleveland, Philadelphia, and Chicago. The deal actually had its birth in the mind of Paul Richards. While managing Seattle of the Pacific Coast League in 1950, he watched Minoso play whopping ball for San Diego. He vowed then that if he ever got a major league managerial berth, he would "move heaven and earth" to get Minoso on his side.

Actually, after he became manager of the White Sox, he told general manager Frank Lane of his vow, and it was Lane who moved more than a little earth, if indeed not a speck of heaven, to get the player his field man wanted.

This is the way it worked, most important players named. Chicago sent home-run slugger Gus Zemial to Philadelphia; Philadelphia shipped left-hander Lou Brissie to Cleveland; Cleveland dealt Minoso to Chicago. Philadelphia got power; Cleveland got a sorely needed relief pitcher; and Chicago got itself a first division berth. A good deal all around, excepting the fact that many observers believed Cleveland tossed its pennant chances down the drain when it traded Minoso away.

Minoso first set foot on a major league diamond when he reported to the Cleveland Indians' training base in Tucson, Arizona, in the spring of 1949. He was a man heralded, yet unheralded. Joe Vosmik, the old left fielder who had managed him at Dayton, Ohio, said Minoso was ready for the majors. He cited the fact that Minnie had hit .525 in a brief stretch with his club. He described Minnie's great speed, his uniquely strong throwing arm, his third-basing technique, his will to win.

But sober, show-me-type judges of baseball flesh were unwilling to accept Vosmik's word without an on-field endorsement from the player himself. That was not to say they doubted Vosmik's honesty. But there have been literally trillions of great prospects and . . . well, a guy never hit a homer with a clipping nor with the great praise of his well-wishers. Too, Dayton, these judges reminded themselves, was a Class-A club—a long, long stride from the majors. So it was natural that cynicism clouded their observations as the sleek, dark, compactly built player trotted onto the Tucson park diamond for his first practice session.

As a "Negro," he had been tucked away with other colored Indians in the home of Chester Willis, who regularly solved Cleveland's Negro housing problem after the swank Santa Rita

Hotel ran up the Jim Crow flag. Unlike most American Negro players, however, Minoso seemed not the least bit bothered by racial problems. Baseball was baseball; baseball players were baseball players. He like baseball; he was a baseball player like all the rest. Just as simple as that. His only handicap was the language barrier; he could not speak English, a fact which touched off mild humor among writers and camp followers on his first day in camp.

This author mentioned it in articles for newspapers on his freelance list:

"Orestes Minoso, the Cuban Negro third baseman, added a dash of comedy to the grind of things at Cleveland's Tucson camp when he failed to understand instructions during a calisthenics drill.

"Born in Perico, Matanzas, Cuba, he speaks little English, and, evidently, learned no calisthenics with the New York Cubans (the Negro team which sold him to Cleveland). He tried to overcome this difficulty by anticipating what other Indians would do on orders from Manager Lou Boudreau.

"It was comical to watch because Minoso, more often than not, was doing just the opposite of what he was supposed to be doing.

"Yet, when the subject was broached, Boudreau said Minoso knows his baseball. That's what counts. No baseball player ever won acclaim for being the best calisthenics performer with a major league club."

Minoso struck out awkwardly the first time he went to bat. A couple of veteran writers hid laughs behind their hands. But the laughs turned to hmmmmmmmm's after Minoso improved his timing and blasted out surprisingly long drives, drives few men of 175 pounds were capable of, from a solid, flat-footed stance. He stuck with the team throughout spring training. But as the Tribe essayed a defense of their American League title, he played only sixteen regular-season games, hitting .188, then was sent down to San Diego.

Triple-A ball was his meat. As a padre, he played in 137 games and batted .297. Twenty-two of his 158 hits were homers. He played both third base and the outfield, the former better than the latter.

In the spring of '50, Cleveland called him to Tucson for another trial. More solidly entrenched as a prospect, a result of his Pacific Coast League achievements, he was placed in the running for veteran Ken Keltner's third base job. But another youngster, Al Rosen, had the inside track. Cleveland brass contended that Minoso needed more experience. As it was explained semiofficially when the player was returned to San Diego, Minoso needed to "play regularly and get the experience necessary to harness his ample mechanical ability."

Minoso was not pleased at this turn of events. He had solid grounds for griping from the defensive viewpoint, for Rosen was the Zeke Bonura of third basemen. Al had no speed above the ordinary, but his hitting had been sensational at several minor league stops.

As he parted company with the Indians, Minoso's voice was huskier than usual, his manner was that of the determined. "I'll be back," he vowed.

Just how determined he was was reflected in his 1950 record at San Diego. In 169 games, he hit .339, a 42-point improvement over the previous year. In oddly rounded numbers, he clouted 40 doubles, 10 triples, and 20 homers. Also divisible by five were 30 stolen bases, 130 runs scored, and 115 runs batted in. For Minnie, this was the majors, or bust!

Yet there was no open-armed welcome for him in Cleveland. Fact is, there was a tendency to pick apart his play. He threw too hard for a third baseman. His hands were unsure. He'd be better as an outfielder. Then, of course, Rosen had hit thirty-seven homers in 1950. Al had earned a right to third. More ominous, however, was the recurring story that general manager Hank Greenberg and fellows of the brass were fearful of outnumbering an unwritten quota on Negro players for one team. According to these stories, the Cleveland quota was three. Since the roster included Larry Doby,

Luke Easter, sure to stay, outfielder Harry Simpson, and Minoso—one had to go! Which one of the latter two should be kept? Who should be sold, traded, or returned to the minors?

There was food for much argument over the relative merits of the two players, Simpson and Minoso. Cleveland's thinking was at least partially mirrored in the pre-season report of publicist Marsh Samuel.

"On the basis of reports from the Pacific Coast League," he wrote, "Harry Simpson, the Cleveland Indians' young Negro outfield prospect, promises to become the brightest new star in the major league firmament in 1951. Even the fact that he's had only two seasons in organized baseball (Wilkes-Barre and San Diego) failed to dim the enthusiasm of West Coast observers who almost unanimously acclaimed him as the top rookie in that circuit. . . .

"Obviously no rookie could receive the glowing tributes showered on Simpson unless he ranked as a capable all-around performer and this case is no exception. The 25-year-old fly-chaser not only has a strong throwing arm, but his effortless, loping gait covers the outer pasture in a manner similar to the great Joe DiMaggio.

"In many ways, Simpson's performance last summer is even more incredible than his splendid record would indicate. During spring training, he suffered a painful groin injury but was so anxious to play that he never gave it a chance to heal properly."

On the record, a handicapped Simpson batted .323, clouted 33 homers, drove in 156 runs, totaled 225 hits, scored 121 runs, played in 178 San Diego games, hit 41 doubles, and fielded .982. The natural question: if he could make that record with a season-long injury, what would he have done had he been completely well?

Also, if his fielding was remindful of DiMaggio's, as Samuel wrote, then his batting style was similar to Ted Williams's. As Bill Starr, San Diego president, recalled, "The first time I saw Simpson, he reminded me of Ted." The Negro press dubbed lanky Harry the

"Tan Ted Williams." Thus, when Greenberg decided to keep Simpson and let Minoso go, he had solid footing. Minnie played in eight Indians games before he was tossed in the hopper of the Big Deal.

"We didn't want to give up Minoso," Greenberg explained. "He has a chance to become one of the really good ball players in our time."

The Big Deal, like his return to San Diego, was not particularly pleasing to Minoso. He had built up friendships in Cleveland; he liked the town, the Tribe, and his dreams had been founded on a regular berth in the Wigwam. As has been said, he had confidence in his ability to win a job, if given the out-and-out opportunity. But none of this affected his attitude at Chicago. Fact is, he made the most of the new chance, the blessing in disguise.

How much, and how well, he played was best told by veteran Chicago baseball writer, Ed Munzel. "One outstanding player," Munzel wrote in the *Sporting News*, "usually can turn a fairly good ball club into a pennant contender. That apparently has happened in the case of the White Sox. They have rocketed into the American League upper circles on the tail of the spectacular 'Cuban Comet,' Orestes Minoso."

The White Sox ended a lengthy home stand with six victories in eight games against the Philadelphia Athletics, Washington Senators, and Cleveland Indians. Boston was the first stop on their initial Eastern tour of the year. They reversed their usual procedure— whipping the Red Sox twice. In Yankee Stadium, they gave the Yanks their first home licking of the year. In one game, Minoso clouted a 420-foot homer off pitcher Vic Raschi, best of the Yankee moundsmen. Chicago swept the series! Then, surprising all baseball, the Sox made like pennant contenders by cleaning up at Washington, Philadelphia, and Cleveland. Not until they returned to Comiskey Park to play the Athletics again were they to taste defeat. In the interim, they had won fourteen consecutive games!

Enlarged, their victory drive netted twenty-one wins in twenty-five games, and first place in the American League.

On June 14, Minoso was the league's leading hitter, average .362. He was first in runs with forty-eight, second in stolen bases with ten, and high among hitters of triples with eight.

It was his speed, rather than his hitting, which gave birth to the "Go! Go!" chant at Comiskey Park. Minoso, so to speak, really could pick them up and lay them down. Fans delighted in watching him steal or run out a triple. Bill Veeck said the most exciting play in baseball was Minoso hitting and running a triple.

Minoso showed the Indians his speed in May, at Comiskey Park. He hoisted a fly to Ray Boone, Indians shortstop, in back of second base. Boone dropped the ball. When he picked it up, Minnie was sliding into second.

At Boston, another sample. Minoso was on third base when Al Zarilla flied to Dom DiMaggio in short center. Minnie tagged up. Chicago coach Jimmy Adair, familiar with the DiMaggio arm, tried vainly to hold Minoso on the bag after the catch, but the speedster shouted, "I go!" and was off like a streak of greased lightning. He slid safely across the plate in a cloud of dust.

It was in Boston, too, that Minoso showed his courage. Willard Nixon knocked him down with a pitch. Following first aid, Minoso took first base. A few minutes later, he stole second base. But Richards pulled him from the line-up a bit later in the game.

Coach Doc Cramer, seeing Minoso sulking in a corner of the dugout, asked, "What's wrong?"

"Nothing," Minoso replied.

"Oh, yes," Cramer said, "you're sore because Richards pulled you out of the game. I know."

"Yes, I wanna play all time," Minoso admitted. "I no play in Cleveland. I no hit when I no play."

Back in Cleveland, the Indians were getting fancy pitching from Feller, Garcia, Wynn, Lemon, et al.; good management from Al Lopez; but they were not clicking like pennant winners. Perhaps speed here (in a notoriously slow infield, say), a timely hit there, would have been the difference in games that were lost. Say—the speed and hits of Minoso!

An important segment of Cleveland's fandom hinted broadly that the Tribe brass had committed a faux pas in trading off Minoso. Since Simpson had been considered a better prospect, it was particularly embarrassing when writers pointed to Harry's .243 batting average. Minoso was leading the league! It was charged in some quarters that Simpson was being made to pay for the front office "blunder." He was being kept in the line-up, on the club, despite his weak hitting in the hope that he would catch fire and take the front office off the hot seat.

"Cleveland officials are getting the full force of public criticism all over the league," the Pittsburgh Courier said in June. "They thought three Negro players were the social limit at this time. And the theory has backfired on them. It appears likely that when the Indians return home . . . Lopez will have to juggle his outfield again.

"There is nothing like hindsight and officials of the Indians are willing to admit . . . that this is how they should have solved what they considered their Negro problem in the 1951 season: They should have farmed Harry Simpson out for another year of experience in the Pacific Coast League and kept Orestes Minoso for regular duty."

The gap between the play of Minoso and that of Simpson became broader as the season wore along. Although the Indians proved themselves better than the White Sox, finishing second to the Yankees while the Sox finished fourth, Simpson hit only .229. Minoso, sparking the Sox in their surprising first division landing, batted .326, led the league in triples with fourteen, in stolen bases with thirty-one, and, a dubious achievement, in being hit by pitchers sixteen times. He was voted fourth most valuable player in the American League.

Many observers believed he was the junior circuit's rookie of the year, without question. But in one of the oddest poll results ever revealed, a Baseball Writers Association committee chose Gil McDougald, New York infielder, while the writers, en masse, chose Minoso in voting in the *Sporting News* poll. As soon as the committee's choice was made known, controversy broke out, especially in Chicago.

By all angles of appraisal, the selection of McDougald was marked with inconsistency. First, baseball writers had voted Minoso fourth most valuable, as mentioned; they voted McDougald ninth most valuable! Second, coldly impersonal records loudly proclaimed in favor of Minoso. In only one of fifteen departments of play did Gil top Minnie, in homers, 14 to 10. In games played, positions played (6 to 2), at bats, runs, hits, doubles, triples, total bases, runs batted in, bases on balls, stolen bases, and batting average, Minnie was the better ball player. He also topped McDougald in strikeouts, not an advantage, of course, and in being hit by pitchers.

Frank Lane, effervescent, energetic general manager of the White Sox, a man similar in certain characteristics to Veeck, exploded when he heard of McDougald's selection as the committee's rookie of the year.

"It begins to appear," he said, "that you have to be on a pennant winner to capture the rookie award or the most valuable player honor. If that's the way they are picked, both awards might as well be abandoned. McDougald wasn't any more entitled to the rookie award than Yogi Berra deserved the most valuable player prize. Berra had one of his worst years . . . Minoso in my estimation was the most valuable player in the league (and) he's my rookie of the year, regardless of how the baseball writers voted. . . ."

Meantime, Minoso was home in Cuba, playing winter ball. Perhaps he was unaware of the howl being raised about him. Lane spoke again, more emphatically. "Just so there isn't any mistake," he said, "I want it on record that Minoso is Chuck Comiskey's and my rookie of the year!"

Subsequent announcement of the *Sporting News*'s selection helped salve the situation. When a Cuban reporter went to inform Minoso of the *Sporting News* award, the player said, "I'm tickled to death!"

On January 13, 1952, he attended the Chicago Baseball Writers' "Diamond Dinner," heard himself eulogized, and accepted the Sporting News award from the paper's publisher, J. G. Taylor Spink. He was also given an Atmos clock. While in Chicago, where he saw snow fall for the first time, he signed a new playing contract, one calling for sixteen thousand dollars, according to reports.

A flashback into Minnie Minoso's early life in Cuba reveals poverty, squalor and hard work. Coupled with his 1952 salary, which undoubtedly will be topped ere his career is ended, the flashback provides one of baseball's most exhilarating Horatio Alger stories. Also, in a time when there are people who minimize the value of freedom, the Minoso story is an excellent argument against those who would shackle every life to a dictator's whims or a dictatorial government, the state supreme.

Conditions were such in the home of Mr. and Mrs. Estaban Minoso that the boy Orestes didn't get to school until he was ten years old. He quit after four years, to work at cutting sugar cane with a machete, because his salary was sorely needed in the family's never-ending battle with the wolf camped just a few inches outside their door. But when Minnie was fourteen, good fortune smiled on him. She allowed him to glimpse Martin Dihigo. And as Minnie watched Dihigo play ball, he set a goal.

"I say to myself, I want to be like him," Minoso was to recall. "Dihigo great ball player and everyone in Cuba likes him."

Verily, Dihigo was great and beloved—beloved the way America holds the legend of Babe Ruth close to its heart. To speak the name

Dihigo even today in Cuba, Puerto Rico, Venezuela, or Mexico is to generate fond memories of fans who watched him play in the twenties and thirties. Only to a slightly lesser degree was he appreciated in Negro baseball areas of America, where he cavorted as a member of the New York Cubans and Homestead Grays.

An ex-major leaguer who remembered Dihigo was Doc Cramer, one-time Philadelphia and Detroit star, now (as mentioned before) a White Sox coach.

"He was one of the greatest ball players I ever saw," Cramer has said of Dihigo. "One day, I saw him play the infield, the outfield, and then go to the mound in the late innings and stop a rally by the opposing team.

"He had a powerful and accurate throwing arm. In the early innings, he made a throw from deep center that cut down a runner trying to score from second base on a single."

Dihigo, it should be explained, was past his prime when Minoso saw him, yet his consummate skill, his power at bat, his defensive ability were enough to thrill this poverty-stricken youngster who, even then, had a dream that was to come true.

Not long after this incident, while he was still fourteen, Minoso organized a team on the La Lonja plantation where he worked, for play in a Sunday league with other plantation clubs.

"I was the catcher," Minoso has said, "but I wanted to play third. But, catchers you no find—so I catch."

One day Minoso was hit on the elbow by a bat. His mother quickly handed down an ultimatum: give up baseball or give up catching. He gave up catching, playing henceforth wherever his team needed him most in one of the remaining eight positions.

"First year I have team," Minoso recalls with pride, "we win championship. My team won 25 games and lost 10. I watch professionals play and learn about signs. We use signs, too. And, if they miss one costs 50 cents. Nobody miss much. Fifty cents big money."

After several seasons of plantation ball, Minoso went to Havana, where he obtained work in a candy factory and also joined the Ambrosia ball club. He played there until 1944, when he signed to play with a semi-pro team in Santiago.

Recalling those seasons with Ambrosia, Minnie once related, "I play third base first time there. Manager ask me what position I play. I see three good outfielders. Then I see old man playing third. I say I play third. I hit good, so I stay on third. I hit .367."

Despite his lack of formal education, Minoso, whose mother died during his career at Ambrosia, became a sharp man upstairs.

In 1945, he joined the Marianao team of the Cuban winter league, hit .301, was named rookie of the year, and attracted the attention of Alex Pompez, a New York sportsman and owner of the Negro National League Cubans. Pompez signed him to a contract for 1946.

That season, seeing America for the first time, Minoso hit only .252, but came fast in 1947, batting .310 and landing a berth on the East team in the East-West all-star game at Comiskey Park. Continuing to improve in 1948, he attracted the attention of the Indians, was signed and shipped to Dayton. From there he went to spring training at Tucson, was farmed to San Diego and, after two seasons, got his major league break.

Actually, poverty was a blessing in disguise to Minoso. The hard work built his sleek physique and fine muscles, basis for his power, a Dihigo-type throwing arm, and one of baseball's fleetest sets of fleet feet. Also because of those tough, lean days, Minnie never forgets to send money to his less fortunate family, to be thankful for his good luck, and to hustle.

His income from summer and winter baseball and merchandise endorsements has enabled him to purchase a home for himself and his family in Havana, dozens of suits, hats, ties, sports coats, and innumerable gadgets and trinkets. Chiefly because of adoring fans, who presented them as gifts, he owned four cars as the 1952 season began.

Minoso is particularly grateful to Richards. "Paul had a long talk with me that night after I hit a homer off Vic Raschi," Minnie recalled. "He said I was going to be in the lineup every day, because he knew I could make the league. That was more than a relief; it was a pretty good incentive, and every day I went out and played hard, hustling all I could. Paul made it easier for me by doing it that way."

It should be explained here that Minnie is catching on to the intricacies of the English language.

After one season, Richards was no less enthusiastic about Minoso.

"In 1951," he said, "Minnie had to shuttle between third base, left field and right field, with one or two tours at first base, second base, and even shortstop.

"Now, there was the miracle of the summer, not the Sox. When one player can do a major league job at five or six different positions and come up with the record produced by Minnie at the end of the season, it is a miraculous accomplishment.

"On top of his play, Minnie supplied much of the dash and fire that gave the club its tremendous spirit.

"Best of all is Minnie's utter lack of fear. He's afraid of nothing. Opposing pitchers hit him 16 times . . . in the head and all about the arms and legs. He was struck more often than any other player in either league. Yet, up to the very last game of the season, he was in there, crowding the plate and taking every inch the rules allow. No matter how often they knocked him down, they weren't able to stop him from taking his cut."

When Richards tried to explain the "sophomore jinx" to Minoso in the spring of 1952, the player asked, "Sophomore jinx? What's that?" Upon being told, he indicated that he had no fear of this bit of befouling that strikes many a rookie flash. He vowed that he'd keep hustling, playing each game as it came along, doing his best. Richards himself disclaimed any real belief in the jinx, explaining that it was usually the result of a letting down on the part of players.

Jinx or no, the second season was not so sensational as the first. The White Sox got off slowly in spring training. Minnie was injured, and his speed and defensive ability were cut down. Most of the time he played left field, but as the year closed, Richards was making plans for his possible return to third in 1953. Minnie was instructed to play third during winter ball to sharpen himself for that spot on a regular assignment. Incidentally, his prospective return to third shaped up when his countryman, Hector Rodriguez, tired badly in the second half of the season.

Although his batting average dipped below .300, although his base thefts were not so numerous as in 1951, Minnie was a major leaguer, one of the better major leaguers. Casey Stengel rushed him into the All-Star Game before he was permitted to by the ruling which says stars leading the fan poll must start and play three innings. Reminded of his haste, Stengel had to recall Minnie, but stuck him back as soon as the law allowed.

Withal, Minnie had one "record" which seemed safe. He continued to lead the American League in gold teeth, with three.

13

BLACK'S MAGIC

Pitching was Brooklyn's No. 1 problem as 1952 Spring training began at Vero Beach. In eight other positions, the Dodgers, as a unit, were best in the majors. Fact is, Jackie Robinson, Peewee Reese, Roy Campanella, and company could hardly be forced to take a back seat to a major league all-star team composed of players from fifteen other clubs. But, Newcombe, the twenty-game winner, had gone into the army; Preacher Roe was thirty-four and unlikely to enjoy another twenty-two-won, three-lost year; and no one knew to what extent Bobby Thomson's homer in the 1951 Dodgers-Giants play-off had dented Ralph Branca's confidence. If the Dodgers were to beat out the Giants—whose mound staff appeared to be well anchored by Sal Maglie, Jim Hearn, and Larry Jansen—then pitching help had to come from an unexpected source. It did.

It came from Joe Black, a big (six-two, 220) rookie right-hander whose combined records at Montreal and St. Paul the year before showed eleven games won and twelve lost. Plainly, on his record in organized ball, Black did not appear to be the mound savior the Dodgers needed. And when observers began casting him as a replacement for Newcombe, their logic appeared to be weak, except for the fact that Joe, who oddly enough bore a facial resemblance to Jackie Robinson, was almost as large as Don.

However, Black was highly recommended by Billy Herman, Dodger coach and a former standout National League second baseman. Herman had managed a club in the Cuban winter league.

Black pitched for him, winning fifteen games and losing six, a record the hurler was to credit largely to his manager's acumen.

"Billy Herman gave me a lot of good tips," Black said. "And, Ray Noble was my catcher. He used to tell me I pitched a lot like Sal Maglie, with a low outside curve and a high fast ball. Different people kept telling me I was doing well and I guess I began to believe it."

In spring training and in the early games of the regular season, Black nevertheless did not impress some as the successor to Newcombe. Dressen, the manager, was doubtful that he could get by in the majors. Joe's fast ball was excellent, but because the middle finger on his pitching hand was stiff, he was unable to grip the ball properly for a curve. There also was some question of his stamina.

"All I can throw is a little curve that's sort of a cross between a slider and an ordinary curve," Black explained. In conversations with the pitcher, Dressen called it "that funny curve of yours." Certain members of the New York Yankees called it "a dinky curve" after they faced him in the World Series. But Joe said, "It's still a handy pitch. I use it almost as much as I use my fast ball." He proved that he could get major league batters out with it.

In the early weeks of the season, Dressen used Black mainly as a reliefer in games already lost. The pitcher proceeded to tie together a string of scoreless innings which, in due time, impressed on Dressen the fact that, maybe, here was something special after all. He tested him at Chicago one day after Ben Wade faltered in the eighth inning with the score 3 to 2, Dodgers.

When Black went in, the potential tying run was on third base. He struck out Eddie Miksis, Cub infielder, to avert the score. In the ninth, Joe pitched himself into trouble, then showed his courage under fire by striking out first baseman Dee Fondy and catcher Toby Atwell, both left-handed hitters, to come out unscathed. This stint set him up for more important relief assignments.

By mid-season, Joe Black was the most important Dodger moundsman. At season's end, his record was fifteen games won, four lost, and upwards of another fifteen saved for fellow pitchers. But for the rule which says a pitcher must go 154 innings to qualify for the earned run title, Black would have had that honor sewed up. He was named National League Rookie of the Year and ranked third in voting for Most Valuable Player honors. He had come through with the unexpected, and he was a hero to his manager.

"He wants to pitch," Dressen said. "He'll come and ask me to pitch. And when he gets in there, he throws fast and he throws strikes. We couldn't have won the pennant without him."

Joe was another of those natural athletes from New Jersey, Plainfield's counterpart of Larry Doby of Paterson and Monte Irvin of Orange. Born on February 8, 1924, the son of an auto mechanic, he began sports competition as a seven-year-old in short pants. At Plainfield High School, he starred in baseball, football, and basketball. In 1942, he enrolled at Morgan State College, Baltimore, where he hurdled and high jumped. The next year, he went into the army. While he was stationed in New York, he obtained weekend passes to play with the Baltimore Elite Giants.

His debut with the Elite Giants was distinguished only by his failure to impress. He had been recommended by Cal Irvin, brother of Monte, who is now a Negro high school coach.

"I went to the Elites as a shortstop," Black recalled, "but the manager told me I acted too lazy to play that position. He suggested that I try pitching since I had a good throwing arm.

"In my first start as a pitcher (against a New York team), I struck out the first seven men. But then, I couldn't get the side out. I left the game trailing by an 8 to 0 score."

When Joe was released from service, three years of duty behind him, he returned to Morgan and assumed a tough schedule. In the fall, winter, and spring, he attended college. In summer he played for the Elite Giants. One winter, he took off to play ball in Venezuela, postponing completion of undergraduate studies until 1950, when he earned a degree from Morgan. A student of psychology—one who puts little stock in its ability to strike out a batter—he plans to continue his education.

It was in early 1950, while he performed in the Cuban winter league, that Black's contract was purchased from the Elite Giants by the Dodgers. He was part of a deal which included Junior Gilliam, 1952 Most Valuable Player of the International League and heir apparent to Jackie Robinson.

He began the 1951 season at Montreal, where, oddly enough, he performed well as a starter but lost as a reliefer. When Dan Bankhead was returned to Montreal from the Dodgers, Black was sent to St. Paul. His Montreal record was 4 won, 3 lost. His earned run average was 2.25. At St. Paul, he lost nine and won seven, posting a 3.85 earned run average.

Although he owned a losing record during his term at St. Paul, his late-season games were impressive. His early trouble, one almost unbelievable to those who watched him work in 1952, was a kind of psychological quirk about other relief pitchers.

I had a habit of looking toward the bull pen whenever I got into trouble," Joe recalled. "Hopper (Manager Clay Hopper) told me to cut that out because I wasn't going to get any help. I was in there to finish."

He went from St. Paul to Cuba, racked up the 15-6 record, and was subsequently promoted to Brooklyn. He not only replaced Newcombe, but also became this club's greatest fireman since Hugh Casey.

In late September, Dressen began talking about Black in terms of a World Series starting assignment. It was newsworthy because up to that point Joe had worked only as a reliefer. There was, however, recent precedent in the case of Jim Konstanty, who in 1950 was Philadelphia's ace reliever and who started against the Yankees in the

Series. Selection of Black as a Series starter was logical, albeit no one at the time knew whether or not he could go the distance, there being, in fact, a general opinion that he tired in the stretch of full games. Still, the plain fact was: Black was Brooklyn's best pitcher.

When the Dodgers went to Boston for a Braves game, Dressen decided to preview Black as a starter. Black went the distance, turned in his fifteenth victory of the season, allowing but three hits. The final score was 8 to 2. Black would have had a shutout but for two unearned runs. The victory made it mathematically impossible for the Dodgers to finish worse than in a tie with the second-place Giants, even if the latter club won all of its remaining games and the Dodgers lost all of theirs.

Black made another start for the Dodgers, losing his fourth game of the year, but he was nevertheless set as a Series starter. The Dodgers had won the pennant in time to rest the regulars while, in the American League, Cleveland played on a mathematical chance of catching the Yankees. Maintaining their reputation for winning "the big ones," the Yanks came through as American League champions for the fourth successive year. And, as usual, they were favored to whip the Dodgers, just as they had done in 1941, 1947, and 1949.

Betting odds notwithstanding, Black beat the Yankees and Allie Reynolds in the first World Series game. The victory, by a 4 to 2 score, avenged Newcombe's loss to Reynolds back in 1949 when old pro Tommy Henrich slammed his never-to-be-forgotten homer in the ninth inning. Black's magic had been supported by Jackie Robinson, Duke Snider, and Peewee Reese homers. Robinson's had come in the second inning, a left-field clout off one of Allie's best pitches. Gil McDougald homered off Black in the third to tie the game at 1-all. But Snider untied it with a two-run clout in the sixth and Reese hit one for good measure in the eighth.

Meanwhile, Black pitched with the coolness of a veteran. His control was good, although Campanella said he had been faster. Only eight Yankees reached base, six on hits, two on walks. Six struck out. They were: Billy Martin, Reynolds, Hank Bauer, Phil Rizzuto, Mickey Mantle, and Irv Noren.

Black returned to the mound for the fourth game, Dodgers leading the series, 2 games to 1. (Roe had won the third contest.) He allowed only three hits and one run in seven innings before he was removed for a pinch hitter. But the Dodgers could not hit the Big Chief, who struck out ten, Jackie Robinson thrice. The Yanks won 2 to 0. Reynolds had settled the score.

Carl Erskine won the fifth game, 6 to 5, to put the Dodgers ahead in Series games, 3 to 2. But the Yanks, with Vic Raschi pitching, won the sixth, evening the Series at 3-all.

It was Black and Reynolds again in the seventh and final game! Neither pitcher was around at the finish. Black allowed six hits and three runs, all earned, in 5 1/3 innings. He lost his stuff in the fourth when Rizzuto doubled and Johnny Mize singled. In the fifth, Gene Woodling, first batter, hit Black's first pitch out of the park for a homer, putting the Yankees ahead, 2 to 1. The Dodgers tied it up at 2-all in their half of the fifth, but Mickey Mantle homered and Mize singled in the sixth to end Black's Series appearances. The Yanks won the game, 4 to 2, with Bob Kuzava turning in a brilliant relief job. Black was the losing hurler—in another game the Dodgers could have won had Gil Hodges (who went hitless the entire Series), Jackie Robinson, or Roy Campanella come through in their accustomed style.

Thus Joe Black, only the second rookie in history to perform in three Series games (the other was Frank Shea, Yankees, 1947), bowed out with a 1-2 record—and the sincere respect of his conquerors.

The day following the Series, Dressen held a meeting with coaches Cookie Lavagetto, Jake Pitler, Billy Herman, and George Pfister. The subject was 1953. Each coach and Dressen listed, unknown to the others, what he thought the club needed most for the next campaign. Later, Dressen explained what happened:

"We all agreed," he said, "that some pitching is needed—more, that is, than we have had."

One move he had in mind was the conversion of ace reliefer Joe Black into a starter. Dressen said Black needed another pitch to go with his fast ball and dinky curve. He said he was going to show Black how to throw the knuckle ball.

14

THEY TOO ALMOST PLAYED

In relation to organized baseball, the history of Negro play can be divided into three eras, two during which they were "in" and one when they were on the outside "looking in." The present, of course, is the second of the two "in's," the era of Jackie Robinson, Minnie Minoso, et al. The first of the "in's" dated roughly from 1872, when Bud Fowler, the first Negro professional, played with New Castle, Pennsylvania, until 1887, when Jim Crow set in as unwritten policy. In the interim, Moses Fleetwood Walker had become the first Negro major leaguer, with the 1884 Toledo club of the old American Association, then rated as a rival to the National League. A Newark pitcher, George Stovey, was all set to become the first Negro in the National League, in 1887, when Adrian Constantine (Cap) Anson raised his loud objection.

Henceforth, with the exception of a few small minor leagues where Negroes were accepted through 1903, the bar was up. This was the lost era, which lasted until Rickey made his move.

During this era, there were many great Negro players, players who had developed primarily because of the Negro's love for the sport. Just what baseball meant to the race was best described by Edwin Bancroft Henderson in his book, *The Negro in Sports* (Associated Publishers, Inc., Washington, D.C.) .

"Negro players," he wrote, "took to baseball with the vim they had shown for boxing for the best part of a century. The legendary accounts of great feats by Negro ball players ought to have been recorded and preserved. In the past ages of hard work and colorful religion, nothing meant so much to the life of an impoverished people after a day or week of toil as the scene and setting of the country-side baseball game."

It was from the country-side baseball game that the greatest of Negro players came. They were true major leaguers, except for their color. Just a thin skin, or the lack of a messiah, stood between them and recognition. That's how close they were—yet how far away.

In this era, there was Andrew (Rube) Foster, a round, friendly faced, bass-voiced giant who was first a great pitcher, next a superb manager, and finally an outstanding administrator. It was he who lost the most by the Jim Crow bar, for it was he who had the most to offer. There was a tall, lithe pitcher with rhythmic, overhand delivery, a great fast ball, and a big-bending curve who was as fast as, perhaps faster than, Walter Johnson. His name was Joe Williams. Some called him "Smokey Joe." Others called him "Cyclone Joe." And there were others, including Josh Gibson, a catcher who slammed more homers in one season than Babe Ruth, who, according to the same Walter Johnson, would have been worth $250,000 "if he were not colored."

Andrew Foster was big—all ways. As a pitcher, he was big enough to win fifty-one of fifty-five games he pitched against major and minor league teams in 1905 exhibitions. He was the man New York Giants manager John McGraw engaged briefly as a pitching coach, after failing in his efforts to sign him as a hurler. Among Foster's "pupils" was Christy Mathewson, one of the three or four best pitchers in major league history. As a team manager, Foster was tough, shrewd, and cocky. He belonged to the McGraw school of wanna-win guys; and he was smart like "Muggsy," Stengel, McCarthy, and Durocher. As a league president (National Negro Baseball League), he was strong, perpetually in charge; stern, iron-fisted, in fact; imaginative and able.

Foster was born on September 17, 1879, at Calvert, Texas, the son of a preacher. He began his career by playing Sunday ball, attending church first in deference to his father's position. At the turn of the century, he migrated to the Midwest where he began his pro career. His first big break came when he beat the Philadelphia Athletics in the East. The opposing pitcher was George E. (Rube) Waddell, who won twenty-three games and lost only seven in 1902. After Foster downed Waddell and the club which included Harry Davis and Frank Baker, both subsequent four-time home-run champions of the American League, Foster's teammates nicknamed him "Rube," appropriating the tag from his mound victim.

That win made him the kingpin of Negro baseball, which had been started in 1885 by a group of waiters at the Argyle Hotel, on Long Island, New York. Foster capitalized by forming the Leland Giants in Chicago. (Subsequently, they became the Chicago American Giants, a club which is now operated by Abe Saperstein, owner-coach of the Harlem Globetrotters basketball team.) Foster patterned the Leland Giants after major league clubs. In 1907, the club was entered in the otherwise all-white Chicago City League. It became so good that Frank Leland, the backer, agitated for a game featuring the Giants versus all-stars from the rest of the league. Chicago sports writers took up Leland's cry, and the game was arranged. It was played at the old White Sox Park, 39th and Wentworth, Chicago.

Fans overflowed the park, paying fifty cents for box seats and twenty-five cents for grandstand seats. The All-Star line-up included former or to-be major and minor league stars like outfielders Mike Donlin, Harry McCormick, and Jake Campion; first baseman Jake Stahl, Boston's American League home-run leader of 1910; catcher Scotty Ucckerman; former Chicago Cubs star Topsy Hartsel; and pitcher Ed Hughes.

The first game of its kind in Chicago history, the Leland Giants—All-Star exhibition was brilliantly played on both sides. The Giants scored a run early and held onto the slim lead for dear life.

Foster, mixing his stuff beautifully, faced only one crucial moment, that in the seventh inning when the All-Stars loaded the bases after two were out.

By clever use of trickery, Foster dug his way out of the hole. Hartsel was at bat. Foster stared down at his catcher, Harry Booker, and gave a sign. Booker nodded, then moved to one side, behind Hartsel, as if to take the first pitch-out of an intentional walk. (The idea, of course, was to confuse Hartsel, since a walk would have forced in the tying run.) When Foster fired his first pitch, however, Booker glided back behind the plate, just in time to catch strike one! Foster and Booker repeated the maneuver. Strike two!

Seldom one to ride a gag too far, Foster then decided to embellish his trickery with a bit of acting. He fastened his big-eyed gaze on Hartsel and commanded, *"Take your foot off the plate!"* So realistic were his words and actions, Hartsel looked down to see if his foot really was on the plate—and Foster rammed strike three into Booker's mitt. The Giants won, 1 to 0.

Foster broke with Leland in 1910, obtained the backing of a beer magnate, John Schorling, and negotiated for the purchase of the old White Sox Park. He renamed the club the Chicago American Giants and went into business. Another major league friend, Charles Comiskey, owner of the White Sox, predicted doom for the venture and suggested that Foster attempt games only when the White Sox, who then had their present park at 35th and Shields, were out of town. Foster went ahead with his plans, nevertheless. That he was right was proved one Sunday in 1911 when the Chicago Cubs, the White Sox, and the American Giants all played at home. The Cubs drew 6,500 fans; the White Sox drew 9,000; and the American Giants drew 11,000!

During the next decade, Foster's stature grew and his pitching feats became legendary. He took great delight in playing exhibitions with white clubs. And under his management, the American Giants did better than all right.

When his arm was worn out, Foster became a bench manager, transferring his mound color and ingenuity to the base lines and the dugout. He was the only manager to signal his players with puffs of smoke from his corncob pipe; he had great fun winning games by using a bunt offense exclusively; once he told an opposing manager, C. I. Taylor of the Indianapolis ABC's, that the Giants would win by stealing home, then had his runners try it until one crashed through for 1 to 0 victory; and he always maintained a line-up of versatile players, as many as three or four of whom could pitch. In a tight spot, he'd call in an outfielder to get out a hitter, sending the pitcher to the former's spot, then when the jam was over, he would return the players to their original positions. For all of that, however, he was a sound baseball man. He borrowed from the majors and they borrowed from him.

On February 13, 1920, Foster led in the organization of the National Negro Baseball League. A friend, Dave Wright, drew up the constitution, which was closely patterned, on Foster's advice, after that of Ban Johnson's American League. The league was chartered in Michigan, Illinois, Ohio, Pennsylvania, New York, and Maryland, with Foster as president, L. Wilkerson, as secretary, and C. I. Taylor, as treasurer. Clubs included the Kansas City Monarchs, Indianapolis ABC's, Detroit Giants, St. Louis Giants, Chicago American Giants, a traveling squad of Cuban Stars, and the Chicago Giants.

Under Foster's stern rule, Negro baseball enjoyed a golden age. Every club, excepting the Cuban Stars, owned a park. Teams traveled in Pullman cars. They received salaries as high as $135 a week. They played a "Negro World Series." And everybody made money.

Foster, who might have become a great major league hurler, a manager of the stature of his friend McGraw, and an administrator of Johnson's standing, died in Chicago on December 9, 1930. The NNBL folded two years later. And as Joe Greene, owner of the Chicago Giants, said, "When Rube died, the league died with him, although it was in the throes of death for two long, financially-disastrous years."

In 1910, another Texan—this one a six-foot, four-and-one-half-inch tall Texan-traveled North to join the Lincoln (Nebraska) Giants. He was the aforementioned Smokey Joe Williams, who was, by all odds, of major league caliber.

Stretching his career over twenty-four years, Williams racked up sensational pitching feats wherever he went. His mound foes in exhibition games included Grover Cleveland Alexander of the Philadelphia Phillies, whom he beat in a 1915 mound duel; Rube Marquard of the New York Giants, with whom he split two games; Hooks Wiltse, another Giants hurler, whom he beat; and other greats like Joe Bush, Christy Mathewson, and Jeff Tesreau. Like another outstanding pitcher, Satchel Paige, Williams worked virtually everywhere baseball was played. And everywhere he pitched, fans went away awed at the mound artistry of the man with the smoke ball, old Smokey Joe Williams.

In addition to the already-mentioned victory over the Phillies, Williams won another game in 1915 which had far-reaching effects in major league sanctuaries. Once more a game against the Phillies, it was played at Olympic Field, New York City. A few days previous, the Phillies had lost the World Series to the Boston Red Sox. Two members of the regular line-up were absent, but they were capably replaced by a minor leaguer and Joe Judge, the Washington Senators' first baseman.

Williams's club, the Lincoln Giants, scored a run in the first inning, and Smokey Joe held onto the slim lead inning after inning. In the ninth, he momentarily lost control, filling the bases. But as the shadows of twilight spread across the diamond, he struck out three men on nine pitched balls. The score: 1 to 0, Lincoln Giants.

As word of Williams's victory over the National League champions spread throughout the nooks and crannies of organized ball, someone decided that something should be done to end this kind of "embarrassment." The majors passed a rule which prohibited complete clubs from playing Negro teams in post-season games.

In subsequent years, Negroes and whites played exhibitions, but on the whole Negro players did not have the opportunity Williams and Foster had to prove on-field their claims of major league ability. They were further victimized by the lack of meticulously kept records in Negro leagues. Even when these records were kept, they were often lost in the continual shifting of players and clubs and frequent organizing of new leagues.

Yet, unquestionably, the Negro leagues included many "major leaguers." Tops among them (with major club affiliations):

— First Baseman Walter (Buck) Leonard, Homestead Grays.

— Second Baseman Elwood (Bingo) DeMoss, Chicago American Giants.

— Third Baseman Judy Johnson, Pittsburgh Crawfords.

— Shortstop John Henry Lloyd, Lincoln Giants.

— Left Fielder Pete Hill, American Giants.

— Center Fielder Oscar Charleston, Pittsburgh Crawfords.

— Right Fielder Christobal Torrienti, Chicago American Giants.

— Catcher Josh Gibson, Pittsburgh Crawfords, Homestead Grays.

— Catcher Raleigh (Bizz) Mackey, Newark Eagles.

— Pitcher John Donaldson, Chicago Giants, Kansas City Monarchs.

— Pitcher Bullet Joe Rogan, Kansas City Monarchs.

— Pitcher Chet Brewer, Kansas City Monarchs, Cleveland Buckeyes.

— Utility, Martin Dihigo, New York Cubans.

Leonard was a cross between Lou Gehrig and Hal Chase, a fancy fielder and powerful pull hitter. He was steady, smooth, smart, and consistently above .300 in the batting column.

DeMoss was a finished performer of the Charley Gehringer type, fast, intelligent, a good hitter, and a master of the double play. Old timers recall that he fielded his position with grace and ease. Unlike Gehringer, however, he was a "holler guy," a field general.

Johnson, one of Negro baseball's most fabulous players, was equally adept in fielding balls to his right and left, was sure-handed on bunts, and owned a strong, sure arm. His batting was adequate. One of his most serious challengers, perhaps even an equal in his prime, was Ray Dandridge, former third baseman of the Minneapolis Millers and now with the Sacramento Solons. (Johnson now is a Philadelphia Athletics scout).

Lloyd was super. One veteran observer of major league ball, when asked to name the greatest player in history, stated, "If you mean in organized baseball history, I would say Babe Ruth. But, if you mean in all baseball, the answer would be a colored man named John Henry Lloyd." Like Smokey Joe, Lloyd spanned several eras of Negro ball. It is reported that he still plays sandlot ball in New Jersey, although his age is estimated at past sixty-five. His No. 1 challenger was Willie Wells, who played with the St. Louis Giants and Newark Eagles. Strong-handed and fast, Wells covered tremendous acreage. Writer Lloyd Lewis said of him in 1938: "Willie Wells . . . is as good as a dozen men . . . in the majors." Still, Lloyd, equally facile on defense, gets the nod on the basis of his greater all-around ability, and especially because of his superb offensive talents. He was called the peerless place hitter of Negro ball.

Hill, one of Foster's first stars, was the Monte Irvin type.

No other center fielder in Negro baseball history matched Charleston, and it is subject to debate whether Tris Speaker, Joe DiMaggio, or others of major league fame were his superiors. He was a marvelous defensive outfielder who combined hitting ability with tremendous speed and a powerful throwing ann. An old-timer said of him, "Charleston could do anything required of a center fielder. They compared Tris Speaker to *him*!" His top competitor was James (Cool Papa) Bell, who likewise played more than twenty years at his best. Not as powerful as Charleston, Bell, a Homestead Grays star, was on the Ty Cobb order, without the Georgia Peach's temperament.

Torrienti, a Cuban, was thoroughly capable of playing his position in any class ball.

Gibson is rated above Mackey primarily because of his tremendous offensive ability, yet Josh was excellent defensively, too. Walter Johnson, greatest fast-ball pitcher in major league history, watched Gibson perform once, then said enthusiastically, "There is a catcher that any big league club would like to buy for $250,000. He can do anything. He hits the ball a mile. And, he catches so easily he might just as well be in a rocking chair. He throws like a rifle. Bill Dickey isn't as good a catcher. Too bad this Gibson is a colored fellow."

Josh Gibson joined the Crawfords in 1927. In 1930, he joined the Grays, with whom he attained his highest peak. In a 1938 game at Washington's spacious Griffith Stadium, he hit four home runs. In 1943, he hit three homers in the same park during one game and totaled eleven homers to left field for the season, a record no major leaguer, Senator or other, has approached. Gibson, who died in 1947, aged thirty-five, held numerous records for distance clouting. It was reported in Negro baseball releases that he hit eighty-four homers one season, twenty-four more than Babe Ruth's major league mark. In contrast to Babe's case, however, there is no game-by-game record to prove this phenomenal claim.

Mackey, who ended his career as manager of the Newark Eagles and developer of Larry Doby, Don Newcombe, and Monte Irvin, was perhaps a smarter receiver than Gibson, although Johnson's praise raised argument that he wasn't. Big, strong, and relatively fast, he was a switch hitter with above-average power. Defensively, he was a wily handler of pitchers and possessed an accurate, powerful throwing arm. At fifty, Mackey was good enough to hold his own with his juniors in exhibition games.

Donaldson, now a successful Chicago White Sox scout, was the finest southpaw in Negro baseball, possessing speed, a good change-up, a flossy assortment of curves, good control, plus fielding and hitting talents far superior to those of other top-flight hurlers. Perhaps his greatest feat was performed in 1935, when he allowed the Rockford (Illinois) Stars but one hit (a triple by the first batter), struck out twenty-three, and won, 3 to 0.

Joe Rogan possessed as much natural ability as Smokey Joe or Satch, but his control was not up to theirs. Physically rugged, he was toughest when the chips were down.

Although old-timers among Negro league followers list Chet Brewer below the best—Williams, Rogan, Paige, Donaldson—his record is available for inspection and it indicates that he was honestly in their class. Some of his more sensational achievements, however, were racked up in Latin league ball. A scholarly native of Iowa, Brewer, almost a double for Paige in lankiness, began hurling for the Kansas City Monarchs in 1928 and remained with them through 1935. In 1936, he pitched for the New York Cubans. In 1937, he returned to the Monarchs, but quit during the war. In 1946, he pitched for the Chicago American Giants, who traded him to the Cleveland Buckeyes. He remained with them until May 15, 1949, leaving to play in the Provincial League of Canada.

Brewer thus has recited the highlights of his career: "In 1933, I was voted to play in the first East-West game. I won 16 consecutive games for the Monarchs in 1934 and again was voted to the East-West game. In 1935, I pitched in the first National Tournament at Wichita, Kansas, with a club from Bismarck, N.D. (He took off a portion of the season to play at Bismarck.) Satchel Paige and I pitched all the games—seven. I won four. Satch won three.

"I went to Mexico in 1938—the first American Negro to join their leagues. I posted 18 wins against 3 losses. In 1939, I pitched 40 scoreless innings and two no-hit, no run games in the Mexican League. Going back to 1937 in Santo Domingo, I pitched a 4 to 2 victory over Satchel Paige. It was another no-hitter, but two runs scored on errors. Josh Gibson, Cool Papa Bell, and Sam Bankhead were on Satchel's club.

"In 1934, I held the strikeout record in the Denver *Post* Tournament—19. I also struck out 19 men in a game at Kansas City against the Homestead Grays, who boasted such stars as Gibson, Oscar Charleston, Judy Johnson, George Scales, Jake Stevens, Happy Evans, Chaney White, Vic Harris, and Smokey Joe Williams. I lost that game, 1 to 0, in 12 innings.

"With the Buckeyes, 1947-49, I started and finished all 41 of the games in which I played. In my first 15 games of 1951, I walked only four men—which I think is pretty fair control."

Brewer just missed organized ball by a whisker. When Satch worked out with the Cleveland Indians in mid-1948, Brewer was in town. He went down to Cleveland Stadium to watch as Paige made his bid for a contract. Although he was along for that purpose only, someone in the Indians' family suggested that Chet put on a uniform and throw a few.

While Brewer was throwing a few for impromptu batting practice, Hank Greenberg, the old Detroit slugger who became general manager of the Tribe, walked onto the field. Hank had not seen, nor met, Paige. Thus, he mistook Brewer for the more famous Satch. When Greenberg made an observation about "Paige," however, a bystander said, "That's not Satch out there!"

"Well," Greenberg asked, "who is he?"

Following proper identification, Greenberg ejaculated, "That guy has better control than any pitcher on our club!"

Brewer was then in his twentieth season and the Indians' roster included such hurlers as Bob Feller, Bob Lemon, Steve Gromek, and

Gene Bearden, a rookie then hotter than the tin roof on a house hell-bent on burning down.

15

LUSCIOUS AND SUITCASE

Handsome Bill Starr once caught for the Washington Senators, but his record is buried in the limbo of countless hundreds of lesser-light major leaguers. He was, at San Diego, the only man ever to pinch hit for Ted Williams, yet this fact brought only fleeting fame, if any; it became, in the years after Ted made himself the best batter of the times, a point of pride with Starr, a sliver of interesting knowledge to those who learned about it. It was as the president of the San Diego Padres that Starr made his mark in baseball, and one item in his executive record was the signing of the Pacific Coast League's first Negro player. The player was John Ritchey, a home-town catcher, who joined the club in 1948.

The introduction of Negroes to the Pacific Coast League was made with a minimum of fanfare and virtually no advance preparation, and provoked no outward signs of hostility, a tribute to the league, its president, Clarence (Pants) Rowland, and to PCL fans. Perhaps the crux of the matter is to be found in Starr's statement on Ritchey's advent.

"Of course, we were aware of the sociological implications when we signed Ritchey," he said, "but primarily we were looking for good ball players."

Ritchey, rather small for a catcher, was, when signed, a pepper-pot on the field, a hustler, a batter with a fluent swing; and he brought along a .376 average from his previous season with the

Chicago American Giants. But after a couple of years, Ritchey was dealt to the Portland Beavers and they, in turn, sent him lower in the minors. Ritchey had hit well that first season, but in subsequent opportunities he had failed to fulfill his promise.

In 1949, Starr signed Luscious (Luke) Easter, a happy-go-lucky giant of a man, and Luke's accomplishments in a few short months were so sensational that racial integration spread to every club in the circuit. No other league in baseball can show such unanimous acceptance of Negro players.

Easter's advent was something of an accident. The Padres, who had a working agreement with Cleveland, were in need of a right-handed power hitter to team offensively with their left-handed slugger, former major league star Max West. Both president Starr and manager Stanley (Bucky) Harris sought help from Bill Veeck.

"We were fearful," Starr explained, "that if we got too much left-hand power, it would be an open invitation for left-hand pitching and work to our subsequent disadvantage."

Veeck finally suggested that the Padres take the huge, raw-boned Easter, who had hit forty-three homers in the summer of 1948 for the Homestead Grays and followed up with a dozen and a half four-ply clouts in Puerto Rico, whence the Indians had gotten him.

"When Bill Veeck first mentioned Easter to me," Starr continued, "I did not get enthused about him until Veeck said, 'Now, here is a *right-handed* power hitter for you.' I am frank to say that had Veeck told me Easter was a left-hand hitter, I most likely would have turned him down. Anyway, I passed the word on to Harris that he was getting a right-hand hitter to play first base.

"You can imagine my amazement to get a call from Harris about 10 days later (I was in Tucson at the time) advising me that he had the damnedest left-hand hitter, who was tearing the fences apart in spring training. As I recall, Bucky's words were something like, 'Bill, this Easter is tearing the ball park apart!'

"I might add that it was only a matter of days before Veeck was trying to coax me to return Easter to Cleveland . . ."

Easter was an immediate sensation on the Coast. As Starr said, "He was the most phenomenal gate attraction ever to hit the Pacific Coast League, and I am not excluding Joe DiMaggio. Easter drew editorials on the editorial pages of newspapers which is certainly a rare thing for any ball player."

Luke Easter had the same appeal Babe Ruth had: he could hit a baseball farther than any other man living. Even when he missed, the six-foot four-and-one-half-inch, 240-pound giant sent the fans oh-ing and ah-ing. In Los Angeles, against the Angels, he hit a ball completely over the scoreboard which stands some twenty-five feet atop the uppermost part of the right-field bleachers. In Portland, he drove a ball into dead center field, high over the fence, and on over a foundry in back of the ball park.

"I was told," Starr recalled, "that each of those blows was the longest hit in either park. A fair estimate would be that each ball traveled in excess of 500 feet."

Due to a knee injury, which he suffered playing football prior to joining the Homestead Grays and which had been aggravated in a spring training collision with Doby, Easter stayed with San Diego only long enough to play one week's series in every league park. During the four weeks the team played at San Francisco, Oakland, Los Angeles, and Hollywood, the Padres drew 240,000 fans.

"All the ball parks in the league opened their gates a little earlier when we played them so that their fans could see Luke taking batting practice," said Starr.

In summary, Easter played eighty games with the Padres. His ninety-nine hits drove in a sensational sum of ninety-two runs. Forty-eight of his hits were for extra bases—twenty-five for home runs. His batting average was .363. And he fielded .974 at first base, showing unusual agility and speed for a man of his bulk.

After the knee emphatically demanded attention, Big Luke was sent to Cleveland for an operation. Following partial recovery, he played twenty-one games for the Indians; but, the old magic was gone. He hit a meek .222, drove out only two patented pokes.

The next year, 1950, the Indians fell into the rut which was to hold them at least three seasons: they hung their pennant hopes on Easter's broad shoulders. Luke hit .280, clubbed out 28 homers, drove in 107 runs, and fielded .991. But it was not enough. So, in effect, the Indians said, "Oh, well, that was his first full season in the majors. Next year. . . ." In 1951 (next year!), Luke hit ten points less, clouted one less homer, and drove in four less runs. Again, it wasn't enough. Yet it was pertinent that while he was in the line-up, the Indians played .648 ball. In his absence, they slumped miserably to play .414 ball. That was another explanation of Cleveland's being beaten out of the pennant in '51 by the New York Yankees. Luke was one of only two American League players who had driven in more than a hundred runs in the two years. The other was teammate Al Rosen. The Indians put Luke in the "if" category for 1952, still rating him, however, as the difference between a pennant and a runner-up finish.

"If gigantic Luke Easter, the mountainous first baseman could ever stay physically sound for an entire season," publicist Marsh Samuel wrote, "he might easily become one of the greatest attractions in baseball. As it is, he's become one of the game's most colorful figures, but a succession of crippling injuries has so far prevented him from really hitting the jackpot.

"Near the end of the 1951 season, Tribe officials had many misgivings about their big first baseman. He was limping worse than ever and the prospect of surgery was not calculated to stir optimism.

"However, this despair was happily dispelled by a successful operation, an expression of confidence by the surgeon, Dr. George Bennett, and by Big Luke himself. Once out of the hospital and off crutches, the powerful slugger stuck religiously to a vigorous routine of walking, bicycle riding, and special exercises with the result that he reported to spring training ready to go.

"And, that will be plenty good enough if Easter can just sidestep any new pitfalls and have that one full season which could easily catapult him to richly deserved stardom."

There was to be no typographical wishing away of pitfalls for Easter, whose friendly, easy-going manner had all but disappeared in the rigors of major league trials and tribulations. By late June, Tribe brass were wondering what they were going to do about Luke. He was batting only .208, although he had hit a few homers, and his fielding was falling off badly. The Indians were in good running position with the Yanks, but Luke, the Tribe brass felt, was more dead weight than anything else.

On July 1, Luke was exiled to the Cleveland American Association farm club at Indianapolis. The overtones of manager Al Lopez's parting words held out hope. It was just a sort of rest, he indicated. Luke was being given an opportunity to sharpen his batting sights. But, in the undertones, in the limit of three weeks which Lopez gave Luke to make good in Triple-A, there was the hint that this was the end of the line.

Big Luke accepted the exile in good grace. "I'll do the best I can," he said, "and I'll be back."

But as the Cleveland *Press* said on September 9 on its front page, "There was a certain measure of relief among the Indians, particularly among the pitchers, when the decision was announced. Luke was popular, but the feeling had grown that he couldn't cut it any more. Too old and too infirm."

At Indianapolis, Easter immediately set about forcing his reacceptance at Cleveland. He hit well over .300, clubbed out homers with the same frequency he had used at San Diego. The broad grin returned to his face; he gave everything he had; and as the Press said, "He waited for word from the man."

On July 13, the word came. "They (the Indians) finally realized it was a mistake," the Press continued, "and that Large Luke was as indispensable to the Indians as bats and gloves. They wired him to come home, all was forgiven. Luke forgave them, too, and keep this in mind: This attitude is the key to the big man's character."

Luke reported to the Indians in New York, ready to play. In his first game, against the Yankees, he homered. But the comeback was far from complete. After two games, Lopez benched Easter and installed Bill Glynn, late of the Sacramento Solons, on first. Two weeks later, Luke had another chance. He struck out five times in a double-header at Chicago. Back to the bench he went, and this time it appeared that Glynn would finish the season on first.

When the club returned home in mid-August, however, Lopez did a sudden about-face and returned Luke to first. That was it. Luke came alive, banging homers at a fierce, fast pace. In one week, his homers alone won three games for the Indians. Two were shutout victories. It was baseball's comeback of the season.

Despite the slow start following his return from Indianapolis, the record from July 14 through September 8 revealed that Luke had averaged .339 in forty-eight games, had hit seventeen homers, and had driven in fifty-three runs. The Indians, playing at a .568 clip previous to his departure, had played at a .610 clip during this period of his return. Luke had thirty-one home runs at season's end.

Easter was not to go unrewarded for his fine comeback. Taking notice of his excellent offensive play and team spirit following his demotion to Indianapolis, the *Sporting News* named him the outstanding player in the American League for 1952. Philadelphia's little Bobby Shantz was his companion as the outstanding pitcher.

Like Easter, Harry Simpson made his way to the Indians by way of San Diego. If Big Luke, whose real name was Luscious, had been another in a long line of apparent, yet dudish, heirs to Babe Ruth's throne, then Simpson, as related in Chapter 12, was the heir apparent to the throne of Ted Williams, the Splendid Splinter.

Simpson, a lean, bony, gangling man who was as loose as a dishrag at the plate, played baseball with the same singular intensity which Ted displayed throughout his career. Simpson, like Ted, was a student of the game. While with the Philadelphia Stars, he purchased books on baseball. He asked every veteran he met how best to do this or that on the field. He listened, learned, did it, and gained great confidence.

"I don't believe there's a pitcher alive who can consistently throw that ball by me," he said at San Diego in 1950. "That's how I feel about it." It wasn't so much the braggadocio as a simple statement of fact. "Only thing," he continued, "I wish I was bigger. I've tried eating all times of the day, but I just can't get above 170. Shucks, I weighed that much when I was 16. I've tried everything—drinking gallons of milk, drinking beer, eating steaks. Nothing helps. I can't gain weight. Man, if I weighed 190, there's nobody could hit a ball farther than I could. As it is, I'm all wrists."

All wrists, Simpson had, like Luke, hit homers estimated at five hundred feet. Unlike Luke, however, Simpson didn't hit those prodigious pokes so often.

When he first began showing his wares on the Coast, imaginative writers began calling Simpson "Suitcase." There was a vague explanation that he was being nicknamed for a former major leaguer of that name, the same as Negro pitcher Sam Jones was to be called "Sad Sam" after the former Yankee star. But Simpson didn't like it. He figured the name was being hung onto him because somebody thought his feet were large.

"No, I don't like it," he told a writer one day. "My name's Harry Simpson. That's what people should call me. Where'd they get this 'Suitcase' stuff? Hell, I wear a size 7½ shoe!"

Nevertheless, the name stuck.

Luke and Harry had one thing in common which influenced their careers to an indeterminate extent: they were given more unsolicited advice on hitting than perhaps any other pair in baseball. When Easter played his first full season, he was the favorite target of then-manager Lou Boudreau and Greenberg. Others joined in, too. Boudreau's constant exhortation was: "Pull the ball." The record proved that Luke could hit homers to right, left, and center fields, but Boudreau kept plugging the line: "Pull the ball." Some observers conclude that the plethora of advisers damaged Easter's batting confidence and, as a result, lessened his potential.

Simpson, of course, was unable to produce as expected in 1951, thus he was an open target at 1952 spring training. Again, there were many who diagnosed his weaknesses and attempted to correct these faults. For a portion of the '52 season, it appeared that they had succeeded. Simpson, defensively a stable performer, picked up at bat. For a quarter or so of the season, he was in the .300 range. Then he tailed off to settle in the .280's. By the time Luke was shipped to Indianapolis, however, Simpson, too, was in Lopez's doghouse. Harry was informed that he was playing "on probation." Though his average dipped to .266, he remained the Indians' regular right fielder.

For Luke and Harry, the future loomed largely in neon question marks. Despite his renaissance at bat, Easter's fielding in the final weeks of 1952 was poor. Routine ground balls frazzled him. With the *Sporting News* honor, his thirty-one homers, and ninety-six runs batted in, he appeared to be the kind of chattel a club dithered itself about. The Indians' infield was slow and defensively poor. Easter was both. Yet his was the kind of talent on offense which might send another club romping into the World Series. Then perhaps the '52 spurt was just what the doctor ordered to counteract previous rigors in his major league sojourn. As to Harry, the "Suitcase," the "word" began: "If he can just live up to his minor league promise. . . ."

16

QUICK CUPS OF COFFEE

Quietly, with only the fleeting notice of small type, Dan Bankhead slipped out of organized baseball in 1952, writing a rather sad ending to a story which began in the highest of hopes, not only for the player but also for the Dodgers. Dan was the first Negro pitcher signed to a major league contract in modern times. After he had been scouted by Sisler and Sukeforth and given the personal eye by Branch Rickey, he was purchased from the Memphis Red Sox, Negro American League, in August, 1947. Although the Dodgers led the National League by six and a half games at the time, there was no complacency at Ebbets Field. Almost simultaneously another pitcher, Phil Haugstad, was called in from St. Paul.

"I know this boy has the physical equipment to help this club," Rickey said of Bankhead. "It is not my intention to bring ordinary ball players up to the Dodgers at this time. The only question is whether he will be able to withstand the tremendous pressure under which he will work. His problem is greater than Robinson's. All eyes are on the pitcher."

Affable, 26, standing six-three, and weighing 195, Bankhead, who had struck out sixteen Black Barons the night Rickey watched him, came from a ball-playing family, one equal in Negro ball to the DiMaggios in organized ball. His father, a first baseman, had starred in the Cotton Belt until the day he saw a man killed by a slung bat. That finished the game for him. But he did not influence his boys away from baseball. Sam Bankhead, the oldest, became a star shortstop with the Homestead Grays; Fred played with the Red Sox; Joe, also a cager, was a pitcher; and Garnett, the youngest, was a catcher. As Dan said, "There are five of us and we're all in professional ball."

On August 26, Dan made his debut against the Pittsburgh Pirates, a relief stint at Ebbets Field. It didn't go well. In three and one-half innings, the Pirates, beating the Dodgers 16 to 3 that day, clouted Dan for ten hits and eight runs. Dan, a bit wild, also winged outfielder Wally Westlake and, for a moment, breaths were held for fear an incident would develop. Nothing did. The only bright spot in the debut was this: in his first major league at bat, Dan slammed a home run off Fritz Ostermueller with one man on base.

Afterward, Dan explained his miserable performance. "I was scared as hell," he said. "When I stepped on the mound, I was perspiring all over and tight as a drum. I wound up to throw to the first batter and I thought I'd never get unwound."

Dan was of little help that year. He added a bit of retrospective comedy to the World Series by falling down as he rounded third as a pinch runner. It was a somewhat odd by-the-way that Dan was an excellent base runner.

Dan spent most of 1948 at Nashua, where he won twenty and lost six games. He struck out 243 batters in 203 innings and walked 128. Promoted to St. Paul at the fag end of American Association play, he won four games and lost none. At Montreal in 1949, he again won twenty and lost six, this time fanning 176 batters in 249 innings. But he allowed 170 free passes to first.

In the early weeks of 1950, Bankhead was valuable to the Dodgers. Though he was thought to be on the block, there were moments when Dan indicated that he would earn a regular job. In a "crucial" June series with the Cards, he hurled a 9 to 0 shut-out, giving the club a series sweep, and aided his own cause with three hits, one a single which he beat out by fast running.

Such mound displays earned high praise from Rickey. "Right at the moment," he said, "Bankhead is the best pitcher in the big leagues. He played winter ball and is sharper than anyone else. He's faster, too. I must confess that I was surprised to discover on our measuring gadgets that Dan could throw faster than Rex Barney."

In July, however, Dan was felled by arm trouble. An examination revealed extreme calcification of his pitching shoulder. Dan recalled that he had dislocated the joint at the age of seventeen.

Whether or not this was the beginning of the end for Dan cannot be said with finality. The record is that he never became the star he had promised to be, except for a few fleeting successes. And as he failed repeatedly, "analysts" devoted more and more attention to the case, producing odd explanations.

One of the most frequently used items had to do with Dan's "personality problem." Rickey himself had given impetus to its use in the spring of 1950, when there was much speculation as to whether Dan would be sold, presumably to the Braves for "$100,000" as a "roomie for Jethroe," or be retained.

"Dan is a great pitcher," Rickey had said, "when he's 'at home' and at ease. But when he's among strangers he draws into his shell. It might take him a couple of seasons to climb out of that shell with any other team. But with Montreal and with Brooklyn he feels comfortable and among friends. I've advised other owners not to buy him."

A writer who called himself the "Old Timer" pooh-poohed this idea in the New York *Amsterdam News*. "The theory that Southern Negroes have complexes simply because they were born, and perhaps, brought up in a blighted area, or that those born, or raised in the north are totally adjusted, is a mistake. From what we have seen of Bankhead, there is nothing wrong with him in the majors that some help and encouragement will not cure. The only fear is that he'll allow the indictment to affect his own thinking."

Chet Brewer, the old veteran, said Bankhead's trouble was simply this: "He does too many things before he delivers the ball. He has a herky-jerky motion."

Bankhead himself, gifted with an ability to tell a dramatic story, blamed his failure to find full-time success on the fact that he was forced to maintain his family in an expensive, New York hotel suite. The hotel bill ate up most of his income one season, Dan related, forcing him to exist almost totally on sandwiches. He said he was frazzled mentally by his inability to find suitable living quarters.

"I had to live at the hotel," he moaned, "because no one with an apartment would let me bring in my kids. Nobody wanted them. But, I did."

Early in the 1952 season, Montreal, which he had rejoined, decided that Dan no longer would do. He was released, and at the bottom of sports pages was mentioned the fact that he had been the first Negro pitcher in the majors and that he had homered his first time at bat.

Dan went to Ciudad Trujillo, in the Dominican Republic, where he was named manager of the Escogido club. But shortly thereafter, he became involved in a free-for-all slugfest, was fired, jailed, and fined. It was of little matter that the opposing catcher had started the brawl.

Back in Brooklyn, Irving Rudd, a Dodger official and a Bankhead friend, was asked why Dan failed to stick in the majors. He puzzled it in his mind, then replied, "Around here, we feel it was just one of those things."

There were several other Negro players like Dan Bankhead— performers who, like hurried travelers pausing in a wayside inn for a quick cup of coffee, got their chances, flubbed them or were released, and moved on to other places. One of them was Willard Brown, the aforementioned center fielder who was given a short trial by the Browns in 1947. He went along with Hank Thompson on a deal which the Browns brass hoped would salvage a poor gate. Brown never had much chance to make it or break it before he and Thompson were released. He resumed play with the Monarchs and in Latin American countries.

The quickest cup of all was snatched by catcher Sam Hairston, called up from Sacramento by the White Sox in 1951. At the moment, the Sox were short on catchers. Hairston was used in five games. He hit .400 (two hits in five at-bats), then was re-routed to the Sox farm at Colorado Springs.

Then there was the case of Artie Wilson, the player over whom two clubs feuded in 1949. Both the Cleveland Indians and New York Yankees negotiated with the Black Barons for the contract of Wilson, called "The Birmingham Gentleman," an apt label, by Larry Doby. According to the Yankees, Barons owner Tom Hayes agreed by telegram to proposed terms which, the Yanks claimed, gave them ownership rights to the Negro American League batting champion. But, in Cleveland, energetic Bill Veeck claimed he owned Wilson, by reason of an airplane trip to Puerto Rico, where Wilson managed the Mayaguez club during the 1948-1949 winter, and subsequent contract negotiations.

While the Yanks and the Tribe feuded, Wilson managed Mayaguez to a Puerto Rican League pennant, was named honorary mayor of the town, and was generally declared a national hero. While Commissioner A. B. Chandler continued to hold the matter under consideration, Artie went to spring training with the Indians at Tucson. The Indians subsequently sent him to their farm at San Diego, where he managed to hit .304 in irregular play at shortstop. Finally, Wilson was awarded to the Yankees. Immediately, he was released by the Padres and the Yanks, just as quickly, sold him to Oakland. There, under the considerate management of Chuck Dressen, Wilson went on to win the PCL batting title, meanwhile leading the Oaks to second place. Wilson's bat mark was .348—and he was the second PCL player in history to win the title without hitting a home run. He returned to Oakland in 1950 and, although his batting mark fell off, he led the Oaks to a pennant.

There were few major league takers for Wilson, however, chiefly because of his slap-hitting habit of falling away from pitches to get safeties with uncanny regularity in left field, although he was a left-handed batter. In fact, opposing Pacific Coast League managers had devised the reverse of Lou Boudreau's "Ted Williams Shift" to combat Wilson's offensive habit. Also: there was a question of his arm. Following the 1950 season, however, the Giants dealt for him, along with Ray Noble, and he made his appearance with them in 1951. Since there was little chance that he would displace shortstop-captain Al Dark, Wilson was used as a utility man. He appeared in a few pinch-hitting and replacement roles, then was sent to the Giants' farm at Ottawa, Canada. A few days later, Rudie Rufer broke his leg at Minneapolis and Wilson was hurriedly shipped over as a replacement. On Rufer's recovery, he was sent back to Oakland.

Again, the Oaks needed a spirited leader. Oakland fans, thinking that Wilson could fill the miracle man role, cheered him for fifteen minutes on his first appearance back at the old stand in Emeryville. They even brought gifts that first night. Wilson, ever the gentleman, responded by singling in his first at bat. The old form was gone temporarily, however. For the first time in his career, he hit well below .300. After the season, he was sold to Seattle, where he and Bob Boyd became Negro pioneers.

17

JUST AROUND THE CORNER

In contrast to the players who had their "quick cups of coffee" and passed on apparently not to return are the eager, talented youngsters who stand just around the corner from stardom in the majors. They fall into two classes: those who have been tested to varying degrees in the majors then sent out for polishing up, or experience; and the best of the 150-odd Negroes in minor league play during 1952 whose big time trials are close at hand.

In the first group are Luis Marquez, an outfielder belonging to the Boston Braves; Bob Boyd, a first baseman belonging to the Chicago White Sox; Ray Noble, a catcher owned by the New York Giants; George Crowe, a first baseman owned by the Braves; Sad Sam Jones, a pitcher, and Dave Pope, an outfielder, both property of the Cleveland Indians.

Marquez, a fine defensive performer, was carried on the Braves' roster during 1951, but failed to hit. The first Negro ever drafted by a major league club (from Portland, where he hit .311 in 1950), Marquez was sent to Milwaukee in 1952. There the hustling, twenty-seven-year-old native of Aquadilla, Puerto Rico, apparently corrected his faults and finished the season with a handsome .345 batting average.

Boyd, then the second best batter in the Pacific Coast League, was given a trial late in 1951. A .342 hitter at Sacramento, he hit only .167 in twelve games and was sent, for 1952, to Seattle, where he won the PCL batting championship with a .320 average. A defensive genius, Boyd was, like Wilson, a left-handed batter who had a habit of hitting to left field.

A big, cat-quick Cuban, Noble was third-string catcher for the Giants in 1951. In 1950, when he hit .316 for Oakland, he was often compared to Campanella, but was unable to crash in over Wes Westrum and Sal Yvars with the major club. He returned to Oakland in 1952 where, once more playing regularly, he regained his form.

Crowe, American Association Rookie of the Year in 1951, spent a portion of 1952 with the Braves, being used at first at intervals in place of their regular, Earl Torgeson. In the second half of the season, he was returned to Milwaukee, at no reduction in pay, "to insure another pennant for the Brewers," the odd report was. He hit .351 in ninety-four at bats, and the Brewers won the pennant.

Strikeout, shutout, and complete-games leader of the Pacific Coast League in 1951, fireballing righthander Sad Sam Jones was given a trial by the Indians both at the end of that season and in early 1952. A strong-armed, six-four, 205-pound, fair-skinned player who likes to chew toothpicks while pitching, Jones hurled 267 innings (winning sixteen games) with San Diego in '51, then went to Puerto Rico, where he won thirteen games, shooting his innings pitched for the year above 400. Apparently, the excessive work damaged his arm. Ineffectual with the Tribe, he was sent to Indianapolis ('52), where he won four games, lost none, and struck out twenty-four batters in thirty-five innings.

Some baseball observers thought Pope would be the Willie Mays of 1952 after the Indians summoned him from Indianapolis in mid-season. He could hit, field, throw, and run. A former Library, Pennsylvania, softball star, he appeared, on his American Association record, to be the answer to Cleveland's prayer for both power and defense in right field, a sore spot for years. But the first night in the Wigwam, Pope ran into an abutment in right field, injured his chest, and was unable to perform in brief appearances (six games, four hits) as he had previously. Cleveland returned him to Indianapolis, where he proceeded to win the Association batting title with a .352 average. Then, the Association season over, Cleveland recalled him and Pope, full of confidence, announced, "I'll stick this time."

In the second group—players without any major league experience—are Gene Baker, Los Angeles Angels shortstop; Bill Bruton, Milwaukee Brewers center fielder; Bob Wilson, St. Paul Saints third baseman; James (Junior) Gilliam, Montreal second baseman; Vic Power, Kansas City Blues jack-of-all-trades; and Dave Hoskins, Dallas Eagles pitcher.

The only question about Baker, Chicago Cubs property, appears to be his hitting. A tall, slender, long-necked gentleman, Baker affects a wide-open, choked-bat stance and swing which leaves him vulnerable to outside pitches. In 1951, his average climbed to the .280's, but dropped off some twenty points most of 1952. Defensively, however, Baker is rated a solid, if not superb, prospect. Owning a strong throwing arm and the ability to range far to either his right or left and, when necessary, make acrobatic catches, he was rated the best Pacific Coast League shortstop of 1952. Though slender of build, he proved his sturdiness when he completed a skein of 420 games without a miss to set a club record. One of the numerous Monarchs to reach organized ball, he played briefly at Springfield, Massachusetts, and Des Moines, Iowa, before joining the Angels in July, 1950.

Bruton's forte is speed. He is so fast, in fact, that Johnny Mostil, Chicago White Sox scout, was once moved to hyperbole. "He makes Jethroe look slow," said Mostil. Bill was clocked in 3.9's from the plate to first base during the 1952 season at Milwaukee. With the Braves in spring training, he appeared to be defensively solid, but his hitting ability was questioned. After a slow start at Milwaukee, he finally "caught fire," lifting his average above the .300 mark, where it remained throughout the remainder of the season. His final average was .325. Because he is not a power hitter, Bruton's value to the Braves will be similar to Jethroe's, though he is more skilled in defense.

Husky, twenty-four-year-old Wilson was rated "definitely a major league prospect" before half of his first Triple-A season had ended. At Elmira, New York, in both 1950 and 1951, hitting better than .300 both years, Wilson improved his fielding during spring training to rank by mid-season as the best third slacker in the Association. For 1952 he batted .334 (on 209 hits) and drove in 117 runs.

Gilliam, 1952 Most Valuable Player in the International League, is heir apparent to Jackie Robinson's job with the Dodgers. Speculation is that Jackie will be moved back to first base in 1953 or the next season to make way for Gilliam, a fancy-fielding, slash-hitting speedster. His International League honors came in his second season of organized play. Previously, he starred for the Baltimore Elite Giants.

Although Power was used both in the infield and the outfield during 1952, filling in whenever a "regular" was injured, being unceasingly shifted around at other times, he was for most of the Association season a batting title challenger. A fiery Latin, Power finished the season with a .331 average, having driven in 109 runs. He is the property of the New York Yankees.

The story of Hoskins is one of baseball's prizes.

Early in 1952, Richard W. (Dick) Burnett, wealthy owner of the Dallas Eagles of the Texas League, announced that he was willing to sign a Negro "capable of playing Double-A ball." Subsequently, the Eagles promoted a tryout camp at which two hundred Negro players displayed their wares, but the only three signed were rated Class-C. Later, Ray Neil, hard-hitting second baseman of the Indianapolis Clowns, was signed. But he failed to make the grade in spring training.

The program to which Burnett was by this time committed was at a standstill. In scouting the situation, however, Burnett, Hank Greenberg of the Indians, with whom Dallas had a working agreement, and Eagles manager Dutch Meyer thought of Dave

Hoskins, tall, quiet, steady outfielder who had turned to pitching at Wilkes-Barre, Pennsylvania, in 1951 and finished that season with a 5-1 record. Burnett and Meyers opined that Hoskins, who had settled on a full-time hurling career, could win in the Texas League.

Still, Texas was the South. As Greenberg said, "We didn't want to embarrass Hoskins. So, we put the Dallas proposition up to him."

A twenty-seven-year-old native of Greenwood, Mississippi, who had spent much of his life in Flint, Michigan, Hoskins quickly made his decision, saying: "I'd *like* to go down there."

Dave had pitched only eleven games in his professional career. But he quickly established himself with the Eagles. In an exhibition, he held the Red Sox to two hits and a 1-all tie in a rain-abbreviated game. In another exhibition against the Fort Worth Cats, he won, 9 to 1, striking out seven with a tantalizing curve. He showed marvelous control.

Meyer sent Hoskins against the Tulsa Oilers on April 13, his first start of the first season, and Dave returned a winner, 4 to 2. His control wasn't up to par that day. "I don't suppose I put four curves where I wanted them," Hoskins said afterward. Nevertheless, he showed good courage as he worked his way out of holes. And he hit safely twice in four at bats.

Hoskins won three straight before he lost, 4 to 5, to Beaumont on his own throwing error. He righted himself and at season's end showed an astounding first-year record of twenty-two wins against ten losses. He also was among the league's best hitters, had paved the way for two other Texas League Negroes—teammate Jose Santiago and Bill Greason, Oklahoma City—and had been voted to the league's All-Star team.

Hoskins was such a popular attraction at the gate that writers dubbed him "the savior of the Texas League." For example, in twenty-five games (a portion of his starts), 143,935 paid their way to see him pitch. The average was 5,757. In ninety-eight other contests in which Hoskins was not an advertised performer, the Eagles drew an average of 2,157 fans. One of the top crowds was 11,021 at Houston; more than half of the fans—5,954—were Negroes.

Significantly, Hoskins played in Louisiana, Texas, and Oklahoma without incident. Closest thing to one was the attempt of a Louisiana legislator to have laws made to bar Negroes from play in that state, Shreveport being the immediate objective of this Jim Crow idea. But the bill was tabled. Hoskins himself declared that he was treated much better in the Texas League than he had been in the Central League during 1948 when he played at Grand Rapids, Michigan, batting .393.

And, Burnett, who had bucked Southern tradition, was delighted. "I am proud to state," he said, "that our opinion of Dave was well founded. He has done an excellent job for us. He has shown a great amount of ability and determination. And, the reception accorded him by Texas League fans has been tremendous. We are deeply gratified."

"With bat, glove, and ball," said *Jet* magazine, a Negro weekly, "Dave Hoskins has taken his place alongside Texas pioneers of yesteryear who stood tall in the saddle and manipulated six-guns with the speed of a rattlesnake's fangs."

18

THE GREAT LEVELER

In the beginning of the "great experiment," there were two questions: one related to talent, the other was sociological. In effect, they were spoken thusly: "Can the Negro cut the mustard?" "Can he fit in?" There were, as has been said, a plethora of nays to each query.

Since the entrance of Negro ball players into organized baseball was a radical change—a change from "lily-white" to Technicolor—that there would be problems was no more than natural. Adjustments were needed all along the line, from the thinking of prejudiced minds in the game to Jim Crow practices of certain hotels.

One group of observers (perhaps of a stripe that visualizes that one day an atom bomb will set off a chain reaction creating an explosive, swoosh-type doomsday) figured the end of baseball was at hand the moment a Negro set foot on a diamond with intent to play with white boys. Another group, not necessarily affirmative minded, yet calmer than the first, was willing to wait and see what happened. Cautious, so to speak. And there was a group—Negro and white—which hailed the move, predicted that everything would end on up-beat. This group recognized the American Negro's right to play the American game, if he was good enough to make the team.

Since that day in October, 1945, when Jackie Robinson was uncovered for the benefit of Montreal radio and press representatives, baseball has been the greatest leveler in sports. It has leveled the extreme heights of conflicting opinions—leveled the heaps of pros and cons into a solid mass composed for the most part of affirmatives and for the rest of tolerance—for baseball, with the Negro, has been better and certainly more colorful than it could have been these past seven years without him.

To illustrate, had a sage predicted in 1945-46 what is on record today, he would have become the leading candidate for a ninety-nine-year sentence to the strait jacket. At the close of 1952, there were more than 150 Negro players in organized ball. Through 1951, no team which played Negroes throughout a major league season had finished lower than fourth, or out of the first division. Negroes had won Rookie of the Year honors in five of the six years since Jackie made his debut. Jackie and Campanella had won Most Valuable Player awards. The Dodgers, pioneers in the experiment, had won three pennants, including 1952, which they could not have won without Negro stars. Cleveland had won its first pennant in twenty-eight years with Larry Doby one of its leading players.

At least two of the Negro major leaguers, Robinson and Campanella, were entitled to "super-star" ratings. Newcombe, until the army called, was sighting on rank with the all-time winners. And entitled to "star" rating were Doby, Irvin, Minoso, Paige, and Joe Black, the strong-armed, Morgan State College psychology student who, in his freshman year, surprised baseball in '52 by leading the Dodgers to a pennant. Most of the other Negro major leaguers were journeyman performers and one, Edmundo Amoros, a little Cuban star who spent an inactive, final-fraction-season with the Dodgers of '52, was approaching stardom.

All in all, these players had become integral parts of the game, important cogs in the wheel. Their careers had whirled like those of other major leaguers. Some players climbed to the dizzy heights and stayed; some climbed and slumped, then came on again; some hit a happy gait and kept it going. A few flopped. Negro players, like others, were sold and traded, cheered and booed, praised and criticized—all with primary emphasis on their baseball ability, not the color of their skin.

As spectacular as was the Negro's performance in the major leagues, the feats of Negro minor leaguers, plus the changing attitudes in certain Jim Crow strongholds, were almost colossal.

For instance, when Jackie was signed, Alvin Gardner, president of the Texas League, said with funereal finality, "I'm positive you'll never see any Negro players on any of the teams in organized baseball in the South as long as the Jim Crow laws are in force." That Hoskins, Jose Santiago, and Bill Greason played in his league in 1952 was more proof of baseball's leveling influence than was it a rebuke to, or a proving wrong of, president Gardner.

A player named W. Wingate played with the Lamesa, Texas, club in 1951. Danville, Virginia, signed a home-town Negro boy, who played without serious incident. Several major league clubs had Negro players in training with whites in Southern cities.

In 1952, progress marched on Johnny Lee Williams, a right-handed pitcher, was signed by Galveston, Texas, of the Gulf Coast League. Longview, Texas, of the Big State League signed Bill Mitchell and Jabe Brazzle, two pitchers from Texas College. Texarkana, Texas, of the same league signed pitcher John Willis. New Bern, North Carolina, of the Coastal Plains League signed Charley Roach, a twenty-two-year-old outfielder from Winston-Salem (North Carolina) Teachers College. And the Savannah (Georgia) Baseball Club obtained Albert Israel, a former Interstate League player, for 1953 delivery.

Action at Savannah proved that there were no lasting adverse reactions to a bit of Georgia byplay during 1952 which was, in a sense, filled with comedy. It happened in a game between Statesboro and Fitzgerald of the Class-D Georgia State League. Statesboro was ahead 10 to 0 when the Fitzgerald manager, Charley Ridgeway, sent in the team's twelve-year-old Negro bat-boy, Louis Ralford, as a pinch hitter. Ralford grounded sharply to third base and was tossed out. Later, he took his place in the outfield and made a sensational catch of a line drive off the bat of Jim Shuster, one of the league's best hitters. Georgia fans cheered the kid. Repercussions came thick and fast. Ridgeway was suspended by league president Bill Estroff. Umpire Ed Kubik, who had allowed Louis to play, was fired. And Fitzgerald was placed on probation for making a "travesty of baseball." Yet the Negro boy had been cheered and—however odd or humorous the whole situation appears in retrospect—that, too, indicated that baseball had leveled a few more attitudes.

Throughout the nation, the Negro ball player was accepted in 1952, although Utopia was still some distance away. He was not making his way as a curiosity, as the last straw grabbed by clubs drowning in the sea of poor attendance. He was making it on ability.

Baseball had leveled off the young, athletically inclined Negro's interest in boxing. Jackie Robinson replaced Joe Louis as an idol. Hundreds of Negro youngsters were dreaming of the big time from berths with Little League, American Legion, high school, and sandlot clubs. One of them, Grover Jones, an eighteen-year-old White Plains catcher, was honored as the American Legion player of 1951 and his name was inscribed on the Legion's honor roll in the Hall of Fame at Cooperstown, New York.

And the game also meant a great deal to Negro players. Because of it, a Jackie Robinson could purchase a fine home in St. Albans, Long Island, become an international hero, and be insured as to financial success for life. How different from the days of long, tiresome bus rides, fleabag hotels, four-team doubleheaders and, for many, poor wages. Year-round baseball, although it may have been the secret to the longevity of a Satchel Paige, was no longer a necessity.

Another myth was smashed in 1952. The loudest opponents of Negro entry into baseball had predicted that the first time there was interracial rough stuff, a riot would result. There was rough stuff aplenty at Oakland on July 28. It started when Lorenzo (Piper) Davis, Oakland third baseman, objected to San Francisco pitcher Bill Boemler's hard tag-out at home plate. Coming to violence, Boemler and Davis wrestled, kicked, and punched each other as players from both benches charged onto the field and jumped into a free-for-all. Oakland catcher Ray Noble was one ot those. As he was quoted by Sam Lacy in the *Afro-American* of August 23:

"They heet Piper and when our team go out to help, I go along too. One teller say to me, 'You don't like eet, eh?' He heet me on the back of my neck. I heet heem, he fall down. Another guy swing at me. I heet heem, same theeng. So it go; that's all there was to eet. My manager say I do all right. I don't need worry. He don't need say that. I don't mind nothing!"

When the fracas was ended, the game resumed. Umpires tossed out no one because ejection of the belligerents would have left the game without players. Without going cornball, one might say that at Oakland there was "democracy in action."

The success of the entire movement of introducing Negroes into organized baseball—from Rickey's first move to the point where every major league club with the exception of Boston's Red Sox, Detroit's Tigers, and the St. Louis Cardinals, owned Negroes at various stops in the organized game—was wrapped up in a statement Luke Easter once made to Bill Stan.

"I was explaining the 'situation' to Luke, shortly after he joined our team," Starr said. "I told him that a few fans might not like him because of his race, that he must overlook their boos. But, Luke explained the whole thing to *me* when he said, 'Mister Starr, everybody likes me when I hit that ball!' "

APPENDIX: FACTS AND FIGURES

FIRSTS

FIRST NEGRO TO PLAY WITH A "WHITE" CLUB:
Bud Fowler, with Newcastle, Pennsylvania club, 1872.

FIRST NEGRO TO PLAY IN A MAJOR LEAGUE:
Moses Fleetwood (Fleet) Walker, Toledo club of the American Association (then a rival of the National League), 1884.

FIRST NEGRO SIGNED FOR ORGANIZED BALL IN MODERN TIMES:
Jackie Robinson, Montreal Royals (Brooklyn farm), October 23, 1945.

FIRST NEGRO MAJOR LEAGUER OF MODERN TIMES:
Jackie Robinson, Brooklyn Dodgers, 1947.

FIRST NEGRO PITCHER SIGNED TO MAJOR LEAGUE CONTRACT IN MODERN TIMES:
Dan Bankhead, Brooklyn, 1947.

FIRST NEGRO PLAYER IN THE AMERICAN LEAGUE:
Larry Doby, Cleveland, 1947.

FIRST NEGRO PITCHER IN THE AMERICAN LEAGUE:
Leroy (Satchel) Paige, 1948.

FIRST NEGRO MANAGER IN ORGANIZED BASEBALL IN MODERN TIMES:
Sam Bankhead, Farnham, Quebec, club of the Provincial League, 1951.

FIRST NEGRO UMPIRE IN ORGANIZED BASEBALL:
Emmett Ashford, Southwest International League (California, Mexico, Nevada, Arizona, Texas), 1951.

Negro Major Leaguers, 1952

Six of sixteen major league rosters included Negro players in 1952. Clubs and players were:

BOSTON BRAVES, NATIONAL LEAGUE:
* James (Bus) Clarkson, infield
* George Crowe, first base
Sam Jethroe, center field

BROOKLYN DODGERS, NATIONAL LEAGUE:
* Edmundo (Sandy) Amoros, outfield
Joe Black, pitcher
Roy Campanella, catcher
Jackie Robinson, second base

CLEVELAND INDIANS, AMERICAN LEAGUE:
Larry Doby, center field
Luke Easter, first base
* Sad Sam Jones, pitcher
* Dave Pope, outfield
Harry Simpson, outfield-first base
* Quincy Troupe, catcher

CHICAGO WHITE SOX, AMERICAN LEAGUE:
Orestes (Minnie) Minoso, infield-outfield
** Hector Rodriguez, third base

NEW YORK GIANTS, NATIONAL LEAGUE:
**** Monte Irvin, left field
*** Willie Mays, center field
* Ray Noble, catcher
Hank Thompson, outfield-infield

ST. LOUIS BROWNS, AMERICAN LEAGUE:
Satchel Paige, pitcher

* Players who were not regulars but who performed during a portion of the 1952 season.
** Began season as a regular, but was demoted later.
*** Was regular when he left club for the Army in May.
**** Was injured most of the season, but was club's "regular" left fielder.

Success of Clubs with Negro Players

From 1947 through 1951, no major league club which employed Negro players throughout a season finished out of the first division.

Boston (National League) and St. Louis (American League) broke the string in 1952.

In only one season since 1946 and through 1952 was there a World Series without Negro performers. That year was 1950, when the Philadelphia Phillies and New York Yankees were champions of the National and American Leagues, respectively.

Negroes in World Series

1947—BROOKLYN:	Jackie Robinson, first base; Dan Bankhead, pitcher, used as a pinch runner.
1948—CLEVELAND:	Larry Doby, center field; Sachel Paige, pitcher.
1949—BROOKLYN:	Robinson, second base; Roy Campanella, catcher; Don Newcombe, pitcher.
1951—NEW YORK GIANTS:	Monte Irvin, left field; Willie Mays, center field; Hank Thompson, right field; Ray Noble, catcher-pinch hitter.
1952—BROOKLYN:	Robinson, second base; Campanella, catcher; Joe Black, pitcher; Edmundo Amoros, pinch hitter-outfield.

Principal Honors Won by Negro Major Leaguers

MOST VALUABLE PLAYER:	Jackie Robinson, 1949 Roy Campanella, 1951
ROOKIE OF THE YEAR:	Jackie Robinson, 1947 (Sporting News) Don Newcombe, 1949 (Sporting News, Baseball Writers Association) Sam Jethroe, 1950 (Baseball Writers Association) Willie Mays, 1951 (Sporting News, Baseball Writers Association) Orestes Minoso, 1951 (Sporting News) Joe Black, 1952 (Sporting News, Baseball Writers Association)

BATTING CHAMPION: Jackie Robinson, 1949 (.342),
                                     National League

HOME RUN CHAMPION: Larry Doby, 1952 (32), American
                                     League

SLUGGING CHAMPION: Larry Doby, 1952 (.541), both leagues
BASE STEALING CHAMPION: Jackie Robinson, 1947 (29), National
                                     League; 1949 (37), both leagues
                                     Sam Jethroe, 1950, 1951 (35 each
                                     year), both leagues
                                     Orestes Minoso,1951 (31), 1952 (22),
                                     American League

RUNS BATTED IN CHAMPION: Monte Irvin, 1951 (121), National
                                     League

NATIONAL LEAGUE FIELDING   Jackie Robinson, 1951 (.992), second
RECORD: base

BATTING CHAMPION,   Monte Irvin, 1951 (.458)
WORLD SERIES: (By odd coincidence, James (Bus)
                                     Clarkson, Milwaukee, led Little World
                                     Series batters, 1951, with .458
                                     average.)

NATIONAL LEAGUE DOUBLE   Jackie Robinson, second base, 1951
PLAY RECORD, ONE SEASON: (137)
                                     Hank Thompson, third base, 1950
                                     (43)

Little Known Facts

— There were more than 150 Negro players in organized baseball
  in 1952. There were approximately 25 Negro players in
  organized baseball in 1887.

— Foremost Negro scout for a major league club is John
  Donaldson of the Chicago White Sox.

— Largest bonus ever given a Negro "phenom" was the $65,000
  which Stockton (California) College fast-ball pitcher Wilmer

(Big Mo) Moton said the Cleveland Indians promised him over a three-year period, beginning in 1953. He has a ballplaying brother called "Little Mo."

— Shinguards for catchers were invented in 1902 by Chappie Johnson of the Chicago Giants. Nig Clarke, Cleveland, introduced them to the majors in 1905.

— In 14 games at Minneapolis in 1951, Willie Mays hit .607—34 hits in 56 times at bat.

— Three Negro major leaguers attended Negro colleges: Joe Black, Morgan State College, Baltimore; Larry Doby, Virginia Union University,

— Richmond, Virginia; and Monte Irvin, Lincoln University, Oxford, Pennsylvania.

— Monte Irvin turned down a chance to play football at the University of Michigan for want of $100 expense money.

— Only Negro major leaguer to wear glasses as a regular was Sam Jethroe.

— George Crowe, Braves' prospect, likewise wears spectacles.

— Jackie Robinson has been the subject of two books, a Hollywood movie, and a song.

— In off-seasons, Larry Doby, a non-drinker, is public relations man for a beer concern.

Statistical Story of Negro Big Leaguers

KEY TO ABBREVIATIONS:

PITCHERS:

G	Games pitched
IP	Innings pitched
R	Runs scored off
ERA	Earned run average
HO	Hits off
BB	Bases on balls
SO	Struck Out
W	Games won
L	Games Lost
PCT	Percentage

OTHER POSITIONS:

G	Games played.
AB	Times at bat.
R	Runs scored.
H	Hits.
2B	Two-base hits.
3B	Three-base hits.
HR	Home runs.
RBI	Runs batted in.
PCT	Batting average, or percentage.
POS	Position(s) played.
PO	Putouts.
A	Assists.
E	Errors committed.
PCT	Fielding percentage or average when used in section devoted to fielding statistics.

JOSEPH (JOE) BLACK, Brooklyn Dodgers

Born in Plainfield, New Jersey, February 8, 1924

Bats and throws right handed

Height: 6' 2" Weight: 220

Marital Status: Married (Mrs. Doris Black); father of a son, Joe, Jr.

Winter home: Plainfield, New Jersey

Negro League Club: Baltimore Elite Giants, Negro National League (now defunct)

Chronology: Was purchased from Elite Giants and assigned to Montreal for 1951 season, subsequently being sent to St. Paul (Minnesota) Saints farm, where he finished season with an unimpressive 7 won, 9 lost record. Played Latin ball the following winter and was promoted to the Dodgers in 1952, where he remained to become pitching ace.

MAJOR LEAGUE RECORD:

Year and Club	G	IP	R	HO	BB	SO	W	L	PCT	ERA
1952 Brooklyn	56	142	40	102	41	85	15	4	.789	2.15

WORLD SERIES RECORD

1952 Brooklyn	3	21½	6	15	8	9	1	2	.333	2.53

ROY CAMPANELLA, Brooklyn Dodgers

Born in Philadelphia, Pennsylvania, November 19, 1921
Bats and throws right handed
Height: 5' 9½" Weight: 200
Marital Status: Married (Mrs. Ruthe Campanella); father of Roy, Jr., Tony, David, Joyce and Betty
Winter home: St. Albans, Long Island, New York
Hobby: Fishing and Electric Trains
Negro League Club: Baltimore Elite Giants
Chronology: Campanella signed with Brooklyn organization in spring of 1946 and was assigned to Nashua, New Hampshire, of the New England League. In 1947, he was promoted to Montreal. The next year, he performed briefly at St. Paul, Minnesota, before being promoted to the parent club.

MAJOR LEAGUE RECORD

											FIELDING		
Year and Club	G	AB	R	H	2B	3B	HR	RBI	PCT	POS	PO	A	E	PCT
1948 Brooklyn	83	279	32	72	11	3	9	45	.258	C	413	45	9	.981
1949 Brooklyn	130	436	65	125	22	2	22	82	.287	C	684	55	1 1	.985
1950 Brooklyn	126	437	70	123	19	3	31	89	.281	C	683	54	1 1	.985
1951 Brooklyn	143	505	90	164	33	1	33	108	.325	C	722	72	1 1	.986
1952 Brooklyn	128	468	73	126	18	1	22	97	.269	C	662	55	4	.994

WORLD SERIES RECORD

1949 Brooklyn	5	15	2	4	1	0	1	2	.267	C	32	2	0	1.00
1952 Brooklyn	7	28	0	6	0	0	0	1	.214	C	39	5	0	1.00

LARRY EUGENE DOBY, Cleveland Indians

Born in Camden, South Carolina, December 13, 1924

Bats left and throws right handed

Height: 6' 1" Weight: 185

Marital Status: Married (Mrs. Helyn Doby); father of daughter, Christina Lynn, age 4

Winter home: Paterson, New Jersey

Hobbies: Movies, auto rides, Shakespeare

Negro League Club: Newark Eagles (now defunct), Negro National League (now defunct)

Chronology: Sold to Cleveland by Newark Eagles in July, 1947. Never played in minor leagues.

MAJOR LEAGUE RECORD:

Year and Club	G	AB	R	H	2B	3B	HR	RBI	PCT	POS	PO	A	E	PCT
1947 Cleveland	29	32	3	5	1	0	0	2	.156	INF	11	4	0	1.00
1948 Cleveland	121	439	83	132	23	9	14	66	.301	OF	287	12	14	.955
1949 Cleveland	147	547	106	153	25	3	24	85	.280	OF	355	7	9	.976
1950 Cleveland	142	503	110	164	25	5	25	102	.326	OF	367	2	5	.987
1951 Cleveland	134	447	84	132	27	5	20	69	.295	OF	321	12	8	.977
1952 Cleveland	140	519	104	143	26	8	32	104	.276	*OF	399	12	6	.986

WORLD SERIES RECORD

1948 Cleveland	6	22	1	7	1	0	1	2	.318	OF	11	0	1	.917

*Played 136 games in outfield.

LUSCIOUS (LUKE) EASTER, Cleveland Indians

Born in St. Louis, Missouri, August 4, 1921

Bats left and throws right handed

Height: 6' 4½" Weight: 235

Marital Status: Married (Mrs. Virgil Easter); father of two sons, Terry Lee, and Luke, Jr.

Winter home: Cleveland, Ohio

Hobby: Big cars.

Negro League Club: Homestead Grays (one of the all-time-great Negro clubs, now defunct), Negro National League, and independently operated

Chronology: Easter was purchased following the 1948 season while he played in Puerto Rico. In 1949, he was farmed to San Diego of the Pacific Coast League, where he became an immediate sensation, hitting 25 homers, driving in 92 runs, and batting .363 before he was sidelined after 80 games by an old knee injury. Following an operation at Cleveland, he joined the Indians.

MAJOR LEAGUE RECORD:

Year and Club	G	AB	R	H	2B	3B	HR	RBI	PCT	POS	FIELDING PO	A	E	PCT
1949 Cleveland	21	45	6	10	3	0	0	2	.222	OF	9	0	0	1.00
1950 Cleveland	141	540	96	151	20	4	28	107	.280	1B-OF	1114	82	11	.991
1951 Cleveland	128	486	65	131	12	5	27	103	.270	1B	1043	68	14	.988
1952 Cleveland	*127	437	63	115	9	3	31	96	.263	1B	942	91	17	.984

*Played 118 games at first base, nine as pinch hitter.

MONFORD MERRILL (MONTY OR MONTE) IRVIN,

New York Giants
Born in Columbia, Alabama, February 25, 1919
Bats and throws right handed
Height: 6' 1" Weight: 195
Marital Status: Married (Mrs. Dorinda Irvin); father of two daughters, Patricia and Pamela
Winter home: Orange, New Jersey
Hobbies: Hunting and fishing
Negro League Club: Newark Eagles (now defunct), Negro National League (now defunct)
Chronology: Irvin was purchased from Eagles by New York Giants after being signed by the Dodgers in a deal that was voided. The deal was made after he had performed in Latin league ball during the off-season. Joined Jersey City farm club in 1949, playing briefly at New York the same year. Played with both clubs in 1950, but stuck with Giants throughout 1951, becoming its "big man" offensively.

MAJOR LEAGUE RECORD:

											FIELDING			
Year and Club	G	AB	R	H	2B	3B	HR	RBI	PCT	POS	PO	A	E	PCT
1949 N.Y. Giants	36	76	7	17	3	3	0	7	.224	OF-INF	56	17	1	.986
1950 N.Y. Giants	110	374	61	112	19	19	15	66	.300	OF-1B-3B	569	51	12	.981
1951 N.Y. Giants	151	558	94	174	19	19	11	121	.312	OF-1B	585	60	9	.986
1952 N.Y. Giants	46	126	10	39	2	2	1	21	.310	OF	44	3	0	1.00

WORLD SERIES RECORD

1951 N.Y. Giants	6	24	3	11	0	1	0	2	.458	OF	17	0	1	.944

SAMUEL (SAM) JETHROE, Boston Braves
Born in East St. Louis, Illinois, January 20, 1922
Throws right and bats left and right handed
Height: 6' 1" Weight: 178
Marital Status: Married (Mrs. Elsie Jethroe); father of a daughter
Hobby: Billiards
Winter home: Erie, Pennsylvania
Negro League Club: Cleveland Buckeyes (now defunct), Negro American League
Chronology: Purchased from Cleveland Buckeyes by Brooklyn organization during
1948 season and farmed out to Montreal, where he remained through 1949. In the
latter year, he stole 89 bases to set an International League record. He was sold to
Boston by Brooklyn, joining the former club in spring training, 1950.

MAJOR LEAGUE RECORD:

Year and Club	G	AB	R	H	2B	3B	HR	RBI	PCT	POS	PO	A	E	PCT
1950 Boston Braves	141	582	100	159	28	8	18	58	.273	OF	355	17	12	.969
1951 Boston Braves	148	572	101	160	29	10	18	65	.280	OF	356	18	10	.974
1952 Boston Braves	151	608	79	141	23	7	13	58	.232	OF	413	10	13	.970

WILLIE HOWARD MAYS, JR., New York Giants
Born in Fairfield, Alabama, May 6, 1931
Bats and throws right handed
Height: 5' 10½" Weight: 175
Marital Status: Single
Winter home: Fairfield, Alabama
Negro League Club: Birmingham Black Barons, Negro American League
Chronology: Was purchased from Barons by the Giants and sent to the Trenton'
New Jersey, farm club for a portion of 1950 season, Where he hit .353 in 81 games.
Was promoted to Minneapolis in 1951 and again promoted to the Giants after 35
games in which he batted .477. After 34 games in 1952, he was drafted, and shipped
to Fort Eustis, Virginia, for army duty.

MAJOR LEAGUE RECORD:

Year and Club	G	AB	R	H	2B	3B	HR	RBI	PCT	POS	FIELDING PO	A	E	PCT
1951 N.Y. Giants	121	464	59	127	22	5	20	68	.274	OF	353	12	9	.976
1952 N.Y. Giants	34	127	17	30	2	4	4	23	.236	OF	109	6	1	.991

WORLD SERIES RECORD

1951 N.Y. Giants	6	22	1	4	0	0	0	1	.182	OF	16	1	0	1.00

ORESTES SATURNINO ARRIETA ARMAS (MINNIE) MINOSO,
Chicago White Sox

Born in Perico, Matanzas, Cuba, November 29, 1922

Throws and bats right handed

Height: 5' 11" Weight: 175

Marital status: single

Winter home: Havana, Cuba

Hobbies: Movies, clothes, gadgets for cars

Negro League Club: New York Cubans (now defunct), Negro National League (now defunct)

Chronology: Sold to Cleveland Indians by Cubans in 1948; joined Dayton, Ohio, farm club, where he hit .525 in 11 games. Played both 1949 and 1950 at San Diego in the Pacific Coast League. Traded, 1951, by Cleveland to Chicago White Sox, where he became first Negro player.

MAJOR LEAGUE RECORD:

Year and Club	G	AB	R	H	2B	3B	HR	RBI	PCT	POS	FIELDING PO	A	E	PCT
1949 Cleveland	9	16	2	3	0	0	1	1	.188	OF	11	0	0	1.00
1951 *Cleveland-Chicago	146	530	112	173	34	14	10	76	.326	OF-INF	264	130	22	.947
1952 Chicago	147	569	96	160	24	9	13	61	.281	**OF-INF	313	11	7	.979

*Played 8 games at Cleveland.

**Played 144 games in outfield.

DONALD (NEWK) NEWCOMBE, Brooklyn Dodgers

Born in Madison, New Jersey, June 14, 1926
Bats and throws right handed
Height: 6' 4" Weight: 220
Marital Status: Married (Mrs. Freddie Newcombe)
Winter home: Colonia, New Jersey
Hobby: Golf
Negro League Club: Newark Eagles (now defunct), Negro National League (now defunct
Chronology: Was signed by Brooklyn organization in October, 1945 (an agreement to sign with a club to be designated by Branch Rickey). Began career at Nashua, New Hampshire, of the New England League in 1946, winning 14 games and losing 4. The next season, with same club, he won 19 and lost 6. Promoted to Montreal in 1948, he won 17 and lost 6. He split four games in 1949 prior to joining the Dodgers. Entire 1952 season was spent in the army. Station: Camp Pickett, Virginia.

MAJOR LEAGUE RECORD:

Year and Club	G	IP	R	HO	BB	SO	W	L	PCT	ERA
1949 Brooklyn	38	244	89	223	76	149	17	8	.680	3.17
1950 Brooklyn	40	267	120	258	75	130	19	11	.633	3.71
1951 Brooklyn	40	272	115	235	91	164	20	9	.690	3.285

WORLD SERIES RECORD:

1949 Brooklyn	2	11 $^{2}/_{3}$	4	10	3	11	0	2	.00	3.09

LEROY ROBERT (SATCHEL OR SATCHELL) PAIGE, St. Louis Browns

Born in Mobile, Alabama, September 22, 1908 (or on one of any number of other dates

Throws and bats right handed

Height: 6' 4" Weight: 185

Marital Status: Married (Mrs. LaHoma Paige); father of four children

Winter home: Kansas City, Missouri

Hobbies: Antiques, old guns and pistols, hunting, music (playing and singing), photography, telling tall tales, motor vehicles

Negro League Club: Kansas City Monarchs, Negro American League, and many others (see Chapter 6)

Chronology: Paige was playing with his All-Star team on the Northwest Coast in the summer of 1948 when Abe Saperstein, representing Bill Veeck, contacted him relative to his joining the Indians. Paige subsequently signed. He remained there through the 1949 season, whereupon he was released. In 1950 and a portion of 1951, he was out of organized ball, at one time being a part-owner-of-record of the Chicago American Giants, a club operated by Saperstein. Shortly after Veeck began operation of the Browns, he made his second appearance in the majors.

MAJOR LEAGUE RECORD:

Year and Club	G	IP	R	HO	BB	SO	W	L	PCT	ERA
1948 Cleveland	21	73	21	61	25	45	6	1	.857	2.47
1949 Cleveland	31	83	29	70	33	54	4	7	.364	3.04
1951 St. Louis	23	62	39	67	29	48	3	4	.429	4.79
1952 St. Louis	46	138	51	116	57	91	12	10	.545	3.07

WORLD SERIES RECORD:

Year and Club	G	IP	R	HO	BB	SO	W	L	PCT	ERA
1948 Cleveland	1	$^2/_3$	0	0	0	0	0	0	.000	0.00

JACK ROOSEVELT (JACKIE) ROBINSON, Brooklyn Dodgers

Born in Cairo, Georgia, January 31, 1919

Bats and throws right handed

Height: 5' 11½" Weight: 195

Marital Status: Married (Mrs. Rachel Robinson); father of three children, Jackie, Jr., Sharon, and David

Winter home: St. Albans, Long Island, New York

Hobby: Sports.

Negro League Club: Kansas City Monarchs, Negro American League

Chronology: Was signed by Brooklyn organization on October 23, 1945, the first Negro in modern times to enter organized baseball. Played with Montreal in 1946. Was promoted to Dodgers the next spring.

MAJOR LEAGUE RECORD:

											FIELDING			
Year and Club	G	AB	R	H	2B	3B	HR	RBI	PCT	POS	PO	A	E	PCT
1947 Brooklyn	151	590	125	175	31	5	12	48	.297	1B	1323	92	16	.989
1948 Brooklyn	147	574	108	170	38	8	12	85	.296	2-1-3B	514	342	15	.983
1949 Brooklyn	156	593	122	206	38	12	16	124	.342	2B	395	421	16	.981
1950 Brooklyn	144	518	99	170	39	4	14	81	.328	2B	359	390	11	.986
1951 Brooklyn	153	548	106	185	33	7	19	88	.338	2B	390	435	7	.992
1952 Brooklyn	149	510	104	157	17	3	19	75	.308	2B	353	400	20	.974

WORLD SERIES RECORD

1947 Brooklyn	7	27	3	7	2	0	0	3	.259	1B	49	6	0	1.00
1949 Brooklyn	5	16	2	3	1	0	0	2	.188	2B	12	6	1	.955
1952 Brooklyn	7	23	4	4	0	0	1	2	.174	2B	10	20	0	1.00

HARRY LEON (SUITCASE) SIMPSON, Cleveland Indians

Born in Atlanta, Georgia, December 3, 1925

Bats left and throws right handed

Height: 6' 1½ " Weight: 175

Marital status: Married (Mrs. Johnnie Simpson); father of three children: Gwendolyn, 5; Harry, Jr., 4; and Michael Lynn, 2

Winter home: Dalton, Georgia

Negro League Club: Philadelphia Stars, Negro National (now Negro American) League

Chronology: Purchased from Philadelphia Stars by Indians and farmed to Wilkes-Barre club of the Eastern League for 1949 season. Promoted to San Diego of the Pacific Coast League in 1950, where, despite season-long injury, he batted .323, hit 33 homers, and drove in 156 runs. Was promoted to Cleveland in 1951.

MAJOR LEAGUE RECORD:

Year and Club	G	AB	R	H	2B	3B	HR	RBI	PCT	POS	FIELDING PO	A	E	PCT
1951 Cleveland	122	332	51	76	7	0	7	24	.229	OF-1B	458	20	8	.984
1952 Cleveland	*155	545	66	145	21	10	10	63	.266	OF-1B	226	11	3	.988

*127 games played in outfield; others at first base.

HENRY (HANK) THOMPSON, New York Giants

Born in Los Angeles, California, December 8, 1925
Throws and bats right handed
Height: 5' 9" Weight: 171
Marital Status: Married (Mrs. Mary Thompson)
Winter home: New York City
Negro League Club: Kansas City Monarchs, Negro American League
Chronology: Sold on option to the St. Louis Browns by Monarchs in 1947. Released after play in 27 games. Returned to Monarchs for 1948 season. Purchased by the Giants, he was farmed out to Jersey City for 1949, but joined the parent club later the same season. In 1950, he played exclusively for the Giants. In 1951, however, he played with the Giants and the Minneapolis Millers, a farm club, finishing the season at New York. In 1952, he played exclusively for the Giants.

MAJOR LEAGUE RECORD:

Year and Club	G	AB	R	H	2B	3B	HR	RBI	PCT	POS	FIELDING PO	A	E	PCT
1947 St. Louis Browns	27	78	10	20	1	0	0	5	.256	2B	55	55	5	.957
1949 N.Y. Giants	75	275	51	77	10	4	9	34	.280	2B-3B	198	180	15	.962
1950 N.Y. Giants	148	512	82	148	17	6	20	91	.289	3B-OF	154	305	26	.946
1951 N.Y. Giants	87	264	37	62	8	4	8	33	.235	3B	64	120	15	.925
1952 N.Y. Giants	128	423	67	110	13	9	17	67	.260	*OF	182	5	4	.979
										**3B	47	96	11	.929
										***2B	7	7	1	.932

WORLD SERIES RECORD

1951 N.Y. Giants	5	14	3	2	0	0	0	0	.143	OF	6	0	2	.750

*72 games in outfield.
**46 games at third.
***4 games at second.

Printed in the USA
CPSIA information can be obtained
at www.ICGtesting.com
LVHW020855191024
794262LV00025B/588